FABLES OF
RESPONSIBILITY

MERIDIAN

Crossing Aesthetics

Werner Hamacher

& David E. Wellbery

Editors

*Stanford
University
Press*

———————

*Stanford
California
1997*

FABLES OF RESPONSIBILITY

*Aberrations and Predicaments
in Ethics and Politics*

Thomas Keenan

Stanford University Press
Stanford, California
© 1997 by the Board of Trustees of the
Leland Stanford Junior University

Printed in the United States of America

CIP data appear at the end of the book

For my parents

Acknowledgments

I am very grateful to all those who have read, commented on, sponsored, and criticized various parts of this book over the years. I owe special thanks to my teachers Paul de Man and Jacques Derrida; to my dissertation directors, J. Hillis Miller and Andrzej Warminski, who oversaw its first incarnation; and to my collaborators on the project which came between that version and this one, Werner Hamacher and Neil Hertz. I have learned much about what is written here from Emily Apter, Ian Balfour, Eduardo Cadava, Cathy Caruth, Cynthia Chase, William Connolly, Karin Cope, Jonathan Culler, Rosalyn Deutsche, Deborah Esch, Shoshana Felman, Diana Fuss, Alexander García Düttmann, Alexander Gelley, Denis Hollier, Bonnie Honig, Barbara Johnson, Alan Keenan, Thomas Levin, Elissa Marder, Claire Nouvet, Jeff Nunokawa, Andrew Parker, William Pietz, Bruce Robbins, Andrew Ross, Diane Rubenstein, John Santos, Dominique Séglard, Gayatri Chakravorty Spivak, Michael Sprinker, Kendall Thomas, and Lynne Tillman. I am also grateful to my imaginative research assistants, Ria Davidis, Ginger Strand, Wendy Chun, and Bruce Simon, and to my patient editor, Helen Tartar. My greatest thanks are reserved for Laura Kurgan, who made this book possible.

Research for this book was supported by grants and leave from Princeton University, and by a fellowship at the Center for the Critical Analysis of Contemporary Culture at Rutgers University.

Earlier versions of parts of Chapter 1 appeared in *Cardozo Law Review* 11, nos. 5–6 (July–August 1990), and in Marie-Louise Mallet, ed., *Le passage des frontières* (Paris: Galilée, 1994); part of Chapter 2 appeared first in Alexander Gelley, ed., *Unruly Examples* (Stanford: Stanford Univ. Press, 1995); part of Chapter 3 appeared first in Claire Nouvet, ed., *Literature and the Ethical Question, Yale French Studies* 79 (1991); part of Chapter 4 appeared first in Emily Apter and William Pietz, eds., *Fetishism as Cultural Discourse* (Ithaca: Cornell Univ. Press, 1993); and part of Chapter 5 appeared first in *Political Theory* 15, no. 1 (February 1987). Thanks to the original copyright holders (*Cardozo Law Review*, Yale University Press, Cornell University Press, and Sage Publications) for permission to reprint.

New York
September 1995

Contents

FABLES OF
RESPONSIBILITY

Introduction:
Literature and Democracy

Allegories are always ethical.

—Paul de Man, *Allegories of Reading*

"No democracy without literature; no literature without democracy"—thus writes Jacques Derrida, in a recent text called "Passions."[1] To investigate some of the consequences, at a theoretical level, of this chiasmus is the task of this book.

My argument is situated, somewhat tenuously, between literature and politics. Here, literature is not simply a matter of novels and poems, not a given body of work, but a question of reading, its strategies, difficulties, and conditions. By "reading" I mean our exposure to the singularity of a text, something that cannot be organized in advance, whose complexities cannot be settled or decided by "theories" or the application of more or less mechanical programs. Reading, in this sense, is what happens when we cannot apply the rules. This means that reading is an experience of responsibility, but that responsibility is not a moment of security or of cognitive certainty. Quite the contrary: the only responsibility worthy of the name comes with the removal of grounds, the withdrawal of the rules or the knowledge on which we might rely to make our decisions for us. No grounds means no alibis, no elsewhere to which we might refer the instance of our decision. If responsibility has always been thought in the Western ethical, political, and literary traditions as a matter of articulating what is known with what is done, we propose resituating it as an asymmetry or an interruption between the orders of cognition and action.

It is when we do not know exactly what we should do, when the effects and conditions of our actions can no longer be calculated, and when we have nowhere else to turn, not even back onto our "self," that we encounter something like responsibility. In the "fable"—in the sense both of the Aesopian narrative and moral, and more generally of any exemplary allegory of decision—we read the most rigorous paradoxes or enigmas of this ethico-political tradition.[2] Devoted again and again to installing or restoring subjectivity as the sine qua non of responsible action and the claim to rights, the fable, which wants to offer lessons, only opens the most abyssal aporias instead. To teach singularity it offers comparison, to underline independence it resorts to necessity. What this fragility of the genre means is not that it is incoherent or somehow "simple," but rather that it opens the possibility of another kind of reading, less the search for a lesson or a rule to be applied than our exposure to something that breaks with the regimes of meaning and sense it purports to offer, to something irreducible to ourselves and what we already know how to do. This experience of intolerable complexity, linked with the ongoing inevitability of a decision (we cannot simply stop reading, even when we put down the book), is what we call here, in a variety of registers, an openness to the other, impossibility, or simply difficulty. For a politics of difficulty.

This implies a thorough rearticulation of a set of associated concepts and values in the Western tradition, chief among them freedom, equality, and rights, in order to demonstrate how what is at stake in the break with the humanist or subjectivist paradigm is not the abandonment of these questions but the chance to reinvigorate them, to sketch some possibilities for what Derrida has called a "democracy to come." In this regard, *Fables of Responsibility* locates itself within what has been called "post-structuralism" or "deconstruction," but in a way that seeks to resist the easy division between the so-called "literary" and "political" wings of the work named with these slogans. It began as a dissertation at Yale University in the 1980's, and it remains firmly committed to the protocols of rhetorical reading advanced by Paul de Man and others, in particular the insistence on the experience of undecidability and unreadability. It subscribes equally to the claim advanced by such political theorists as Ernesto Laclau and Chantal Mouffe (in the manifesto of their Phronesis series) that "the critique of essentialism . . . is the necessary condition for understanding the widening of the field of social struggles characteristic of the present stage of democratic politics."

Ethics and politics—as well as literature—are evaded when we fall back on the conceptual priority of the subject, agency, or identity as the grounds of our action. The experience of literature, ethics, and politics, such as it is (and it cannot be the experience of a subject), emerges only in the withdrawal of these foundations. This means that we are not interested simply in undermining or "deconstructing" foundational or essentialist ethico-political discourses, but in demonstrating that what we call ethics and politics only come into being or have any force and meaning thanks to this very ungroundedness. We have politics because we have no grounds, no reliable standpoints—in other words, responsibility and rights, the answers and the claims we make as foundations disintegrate, are constitutive of politics. So "deconstruction" is not offered here as an antiauthoritarian discourse, an attack on grounds, but as an attempt to think about this removal as the condition of any political action or (in a slightly different register) as the condition of democracy. Democracy, in theory and in practice, is the most rigorous effort we know to take into account the difficulties that condition, or de-condition, our action. What Claude Lefort has called "the dissolution of the markers of certainty," our exposure to others without the security of any pregiven social order (natural or supernatural), structures all ethico-political decision, and democracy tries to come to terms with it.[3]

Who speaks, writes, and reads, then? Not simply humans—in spite of all the tired protests against deconstructive antihumanism or even inhumanity.[4] Just as there is no extra-political ground to which we might turn for help, likewise there is no meta-language. This is the democratic invention, as Lefort has argued: "The idea of human nature, which was so vigorously proclaimed at the end of the eighteenth century, could never capture the meaning of the undertaking inaugurated by the great American and French declarations. By reducing the source of right to the human utterance of right, they made an enigma of both humanity and right."[5] One name for that enigma within humanity is inhumanity, and it emerges in language, in the terrible way language dispropriates us, precedes and exceeds us, without in its turn offering or constituting itself as a reliable ground. In this book, I have tried to return again and again, in situations that share only the fact that they put at stake something non-negotiable about the ethico-political, to the moment when a text removes this ground, exposes us to the difficulty of language, and leaves us to our own responsibilities—but without anything we could call our "own" anymore. Jean-François Lyotard calls what remains a "no-man's land": "If we do not preserve this inhuman region where we can encounter this or that something, that which completely escapes the exercise of rights, we do not deserve the rights granted to us. What use is the right to freedom of expression if we have nothing to say but what has already been said? And how can we have any chance of finding a way to say what we don't know how to say if we don't pay attention to the silence of the other inside us?"[6]

When Derrida suggests that there is "no literature without democracy" and vice versa, he returns to the Sadean formulation that the democratic revolutions were marked by a "right to say everything," usually understood as "a certain non-censure." "This authorization to say everything (which goes together with democracy, as the apparent hyper-responsibility of a 'subject') acknowledges a right to absolute non-response, just where there can be no question of responding, of being able to or having to respond." The non-response, the right not to respond, runs counter to the general determination of the subject as calculable, accountable, and to the notions of democracy which depend on this thought of the subject. In this no man's land, Derrida finds the exemplary secret of literature: it happens "when there is no longer even any sense in making decisions about some secret behind the surface of a textual manifestation . . . , when it is the call of this secret, however, which points back to the other or to something else."[7]

But only at the cost of constant, recurrent exposure to risk. Literature, like politics and ethics, is understood here as the experience of risk, chance, the undecidable. Not the decisionist celebration of the pathos of pure resolution, of having to decide once and for all, without reason but with firmness and conviction. It is just this proud, last man, the subject of the decision, that is in question here—and without its being in question, just as any "external" or objective ground is lacking, there would be no politics and no literature. Language is the time and space of this risk, and we understand reading here as the experience of language in this sense, language when its power to make sense or to perform can no longer be taken for granted. Which is not to say that we should not be interested in its meanings or its powers—quite the contrary. But thinking about what happens in language can only begin to take the measure of its enigmatic character if we suspend our cheerful confidence in the fact that it does or has to make sense and perform. Literature tells us that letters can always not reach their destination, as Derrida said to Lacan, and this originary dispersal is the condition or the chance of anything (new) happening at all.

§ 1 Left to Our Own Devices: On the Impossibility of Justice

> Even if time and prudence, the patience of knowledge and
> the mastery of conditions were hypothetically unlimited, the
> decision would be structurally finite, however late it came, a
> decision of urgency and precipitation, acting in the night of
> non-knowledge and non-rule. Not of the absence of rules and
> knowledge but of a reinstitution of rules which by definition
> is not preceded by any knowledge or by any guarantee as
> such.
>
> —Jacques Derrida, *Force of Law*

At the Front

The curtain rises, to reveal nothing.[1] Nothing but speaking—in
the dark, at a frontier, two sentinels. One stands guard, the other
comes to take his place. In the dark, a movement, followed by a
question.

Who's there?

Everything begins with a question at the front, it seems, but a
question that itself responds to a noise or a movement. A question
asked of a sentinel, by a sentinel—not the classically interrogative
demand for identification or for the password, but the question of
the one who *approaches* the frontier, the one who asks where the
frontier is, and who's at the post. In the dark, the one who comes
asks who it is who is already there, announces his coming with a
question about the identity and place of the other. If he betrays his
arrival, he betrays only that, the arrival—he does not (yet) identify
himself. Everything begins with a question about the identity of
the one who is already there, the one who has, without speaking,
provoked the question. In the dark, a question addresses its call to
the other who precedes it. And the other, the still mute and still

invisible sentry, marks the place of the border, guards without challenging and without even appearing. Is the sentry more or less vigilant in this silence?

The frontier is, as it were, itself interpellated in this originary question. And its silence does not last—but the answer takes the form of a demand, a negation, an imperative and a (delayed) challenge.

Nay, answer me. Stand and unfold yourself.

In the dark, the sentry responds by rejecting the address, by refusing to utter the *yes* that would make him the intruder or the supplicant. He continues to conceal himself, to dissimulate his position, to withhold or withdraw from the identification requested by the other. The sentry's duty, his mission and his responsibility, is to question. His *nay* identifies himself (*me*) only as the one who questions, as the only one who questions, the one who receives rather than gives the answers. His address seeks to halt the one who has asked first, aims to freeze in a standstill the movement of the unseen arrival, to stabilize the other's position before the law and the border. But his *nay* ineluctably responds, answers the question, and thus says yes before it says no. Every demand— including the first *Who's there?*—is preceded by something like this affirmation, this nonsignifying response that opens the possibility of speaking, even of questioning. But, in the dark, the sentry answers without answering, responds to the question *Who's there?* only insofar as it implicitly determines that *who* as the I who receives, rather than gives, the answers. I, I answer, am answered to. I have the right to challenge. You, the other, must stop moving, stop questioning, and answer. The sentry, listening and only now speaking, seeks to make the other appear, present himself. And the other has up to this point concealed himself, has arrived in the dark as an apparition, a moving question, closed in upon himself . . . wrapped in the night, hiding himself in the folds of the dark and of the question, in the pleats and creases constituted by his very movement, by the almost diplomatic stealth of his arrival and by the veritable implication of his question. The sentinel asks for an opening, for the other to unfurl and to unfold *as self.* The double imperative—to stop and to unfold—is virtually tautologous: to stand is to unfold, to appear as unitary subject. The address interpellates, in the rigorous sense: it brings the other into the field of the law, constitutes him as subject in addressing him, opens him out of the question into the upright stability of the self.

And at the frontier, in the dark, the other who has come responds, openly, with a password.

Long live the King!

His response exclaims—it is marked with an exclamation point—sends a cry into the night: at once a code, a citation or a formula, and a wish, even an ironic omen. The formula is a password, but not necessarily *the* password—moments later, at the same border, the other-become-sentinel accepts two entirely different passwords. But what matters is less what he says than that he says, and the way that he says: so says the exclamation point. The meaning of the four words, borne in invisible quotation marks, allows itself to be carried away, transported far from any reference or constatation, eviscerated or even harrowed to the barest remainder of the signifying form—it is as a noise, as an *énonciation* and not as an *énoncé*, that the exclamation functions. The king lives on, lives long—as repetition itself, as the afterlife of a citation. The password is a performative utterance in the strict sense: it is to be judged not by its truthfulness but sheerly by its efficacy. It aims to accomplish, to act, to raise the barrier of the question, to open or bring into the open the allegiance, the appartenance, of the one who comes. But if the citation is a performative, its residue of reference—to the king, his life and its length, the state—makes its action somewhat more complicated, folds it in on itself. The utterance does not simply do something, it does what it says it does: in it, the king lives on—not just as a quotation, but as a king, as the institution which by definition outlives any and all of its merely empirical occupants, which constitutes itself in this very *survivance*. No wonder, no accident rather, if this king will come again, if this thing (*this dreaded sight twice seen of us*) will soon appear again tonight.

But the password gives rise to recognition, or rather to interpellation, to the name in question.

Barnardo?

The name is proper, just the right name, but it is still a question. The play of the question, the ceaseless maneuvers (back and forth) for the right to question, will not stop even for the name. The response to the password, which affirms it as successful and countersigns it, refuses to echo it, offers nothing in exchange, returns no assent. The sentry erases his auto-affirmation in the ongoing pursuit of the other's response, here going so far as to propose even the expected response to the respondent, in the form of a question. It takes the name, gives it to the other only interrogatively, asks the other to assume it, to respond to and with it, and in doing so, interpellates—names without naming. The question asks the other to answer to and for his name, to take the place of the name—not to bear it passively or merely receive it, but to take it on as his own.

Barnardo responds, elliptically, no longer as other, but not quite as I. He says, (in) the third person:

He.

Not me but he. Finally, no one passes across this frontier. Something happens, but it is only ever a question of two sentinels, two watchful and questioning soldiers, and of their responsibilities. Words pass between them: Who has the right to ask? It is dark, the hour is late, preparations for war are underway, and something is rotten in the state. The sentinels, and others, maintain their vigilant watch. Later, a ghost—*in the same figure like the King that's dead, the majesty of buried Denmark*—appears, reappears. *'Tis here, 'tis here, 'tis gone.*[2]

Who's There?

We begin with a response, a question that answers to a noise, and we do it in the dark—doing without exactly knowing, making do with speaking. Who's there, or here, and who's gone? It's us, here and gone, abandoned at the border, left to our own devices—most of them, let us say, words—and our responsibilities . . . but without knowing who we are, who is there, and where is there. Our responsibilities, somehow in excess of our knowledge if not simply opposed to it, are to the other, to the undetermined other, and our vigilance consists in the care with which we attend to the noise that precedes our question, the mark or trace to which we respond at the beginning. Abandoned, errant, we happen on ourselves and others, at the frontier, but without basis, foundation, proper place or direction, coming and going, turning around the edge, arriving, waiting, speaking. And the border is no guide: in this night, night of non-knowledge and non-rule, it too moves like a ghost, limitless and unnatural.

But if this experience of a frontier without front seems to put in question the most canonical and well-established definition of the political, the distinctions between friend and enemy on the battlefield or the border, we could also venture to say that it reopens the question of politics as that of responsibility itself, the space and time of differences and thus of guards and rights, the right to question and to pass. It is difficult, but the frontier as such, with its questions and answers, is not simply something bad or to be avoided: it is a chance for politics, the chance of the political. It is the idiom and the possibility of the other, of the one who arrives. But it is also something terrifying, since perhaps we are—indeed, we cannot not be—the sentinels.

The other comes first, asking for an answer. But the one who arrives has already been preceded by something else, something unavailable and indecipherable, which provokes the question. In this scene, the questions at the front ask about the things that matter today, and tonight . . . about the aporias of interpellation and crossing, the name and the password, knowledge and power, the shifting time and space of the political, the life of the king and the democratic invention, the imminence of the ghost and the surprising arrival of the other. But they happen, for us, at night—and they expose the politics and ethics of our responsibilities as, first and last, a matter of risk.

In the dark, we guard, we cross, we decide, we reach out to the other. The aporias of so much of contemporary politics—war and humanitarian intervention, immigration and the financialization of the globe, nationalism and transnationalism, the emergence of the North-South divide out of the collapse of the East-West opposition, the glare of publicity and the hypercathexis of privacy, civil wars and human rights, the divisions of race and class and gender and sexuality—and their deconstruction occur *at* this darkened frontier. One can, and must, oppose as militantly as possible all the new obscurantisms, fight for the extension and radicalization of all enlightenments (*Aufklärung, glasnost,* and *Öffentlichkeit*), and still insist: no matter how bright the light, the crossing occurs at night. Any political responsibility is itself nothing other than an experience of a certain encounter at the border, of a crossing and its irreducible difficulty, of the aporia and the *no pasarán* which mark all frontiers as structurally undecidable. Something other than knowledge comes into play at the frontier, something that exceeds or cannot be reduced to cognition and the application of a rule—otherwise the decision at the border would make no difference. Undecidable, which is not to say uncertain: it is not a matter of knowing or not knowing where to draw the line correctly, nor of some ultimate disappearance or erasure of the border in a fog of confusion. There is aporia only because there are frontiers, because we must pass from one side to another, to the other. And there would be no passage, in any rigorous sense of the word, without the experience of the impasse, without the darkness of a certain undecidability.

To act responsibly: whatever is left of the subject is faced somehow at once with an inalterable necessity and a free choice. Would responsibility have any meaning, or even any force, were it not to be the object of a free assumption, the voluntary taking on of a charge? Or does this voluntarism strip responsibility of its force, equivocate with the utterly unequivocal call that makes of the response something that has no choice but to happen, no matter what it turns out to be? What becomes of these philosophemes, free will and determination and the subject held to bear them, when responsibility is thought as a question of questions and responses, of language? And what happens when it is put into play in a literary text that allegorizes, without thematizing, that simply reinscribes, the barest outline of the encounter with others? Nothing happens automatically—that much is for sure. Recasting the subject as a linguistic entity does not, in itself, displace it from a metaphysical context. "There is no concept that is metaphysical in itself. There is a labor—metaphysical or not—performed on conceptual systems," as Derrida remarked.[3] That the questions posed at the border, of exemplary ethical and political value, are irreducibly questions of language or textuality—not in the sense that seeks to remove them from what we so blithely call "the world" but, on the contrary, in the sense that seeks to reintroduce the complexity and the difficulty of the rhetorical into the theory and practice of politics—is the singular conceptual recognition of the disparate set of operations crudely labelled "post-structuralism." With the help of some examples—drawn primarily from law, politics, and philosophy—I will try to articulate some of the challenges faced by any "theory of justice" or of responsibility which responds to the irreducible relation between the categories "individual" or "subject" and "textuality" or "rhetoric." If we are left to our own devices, they are neither simply devices, in the instrumental sense, nor altogether our own. The difficulties and aporias that structure the encounter with the other arise in the movement that separates the subject from "itself," that renders self-presence opaque (darker or brighter), because the passage by way of the trace or the mark is irreducible. *Who's there?* is, first of all, a question of language. The noises at the border set in motion a multiple and abyssal experience of responsibilities—difficult to measure and impossible to balance—because they are not limited to exchanging significations but asymmetrically redistribute forces in the surprise of the event. "Acting in the night of non-knowledge and non-rule"[4] . . . in the dark.

Rhetoric of Persuasion

Preparations for war were well under way. Early in that decade of our discontent, the 1980's, a CIA agent code-named "Tayacan," advising the American-supplied *contras* in Nicaragua, drafted and distributed to those fighters a handbook on strategies of war called *Psychological Operations in Guerrilla Warfare*.[5] Worried about the public-relations effects of the extensive violence against civilians that seemed to characterize too many *contra* operations, the CIA undertook to educate its proxy troops in how to win, through an appropriate mix of persuasion and terror, the allegiance of the people on whose behalf they professed to fight. In all the flatness of its bureaucratic English translation, the theoretical preamble to the manual will serve us as an honest introduction to the study of the rhetoric of justice:

> Guerrilla warfare is essentially a political war. Therefore, its area of operations exceeds the territorial limits of conventional warfare, to penetrate the political entity itself: the "political animal" that Aristotle defined.
>
> In effect, the human being should be considered the priority objective in a political war. And conceived as the military target of guerrilla war, the human being has his most critical point in his mind. Once his mind has been reached, the "political animal" has been defeated, without necessarily receiving bullets. (33)

One can only dream of Aristotle's response to the work of this CIA agent—not just the Aristotle of the *Politics* but also the author of the *Rhetoric*, given that this "manual for the training of guerrillas in psychological operations" (34) offers a theory of "armed propaganda" (35) that takes as its reiterated aim "the creation of an identification of the people with the weapons and the guerrillas who carry them" (36, 51). How can one accomplish this identification? "The guerrillas should be persuasive through the word and not dictatorial with weapons" (48). To that end, the manual proposes a section called "Techniques of Persuasion in Talks or Speeches" (63–64) and a complementary Appendix (90–98), designed "to improve the ability to organize and express thoughts for those who wish to perfect their oratorical abilities" (90).[6] The political war is a rhetorical war, which of course means not that it is a matter of discourse or representation rather than reality, but that its politics—guns and all—are not simply to be imposed but demand the consent or at least the acquiescence of "the people," and thus pass essentially through the indirections and asymmetries of persuasion. When armed propagandists aim to create an identification between their weapons and the people at whom they are aimed, the identity is strictly figural, and the line between gun and word is at best rather questionable ("as the military target of guerrilla war, the human being has his most critical point in his mind"). The manual at once insists on the difference between guns and words and bases itself on the founding convergence between these different weapons.

The cover of the Spanish edition of the manual, as Joanne Omang notes in her introduction, features the words of the title "alternating between rows of people's heads. The heads had large holes in the centers, implying either bullet holes or—in the most optimistic view—an intellectual vacuum ready to be filled" (28). Exceeding the limits of conventional warfare, which is to say, erasing the conventional limits between civilian and military, between physical and psychological, seems to require, as the manual's detailed recommendations on armaments and their use in "neutralizing" opponents later underline (57), no relinquishing of the conventional weapons of war. And if it follows what we could call a Schmittian logic in defining war as the extreme possibility of the political, in theorizing "political war," it does so at the cost of the decisive definition of the political that Carl Schmitt offered: the distinction between friend and enemy.[7] The irony is as rich as the allegory here: the manual names as a "principle of psychology that we humans have the tendency to form personal associations from 'we' and 'the others,' or 'we' and 'they,' 'friends' and 'enemies' " (62), even as the practice of armed propaganda it addresses to "the people" plays essentially with the uncertainty of that apostrophe in the mode of "implicit terror" (36). As the front lines shift and blur along with the combatants in the guerrilla war, so too the relation between warrior and citizen-target (friend? enemy?) grows obscure.[8] It forces us to ask, when the mind as target is defeated without "necessarily" receiving bullets, just what is the figure for what, in this psycho-military operation. The economy of the trade-off between weapons of persuasion and of assault is left elegantly unspoken, and for this gesture of ambivalence I think we must indeed reserve the name of "terror." But the name cannot simply function as a condemnation, for terror would also be the most powerful example of the superimposition of responsibility and publicity that defines our exposure to alterity.

At Gunpoint

"Rhetoric is another word for force," writes Stanley Fish in an essay called "Force."[9] Near the end of his consideration of "the quest for a way of quarantining the process of law from force," the site of this hygienic struggle—doomed by definition to failure, of course, but an interesting failure nevertheless—is named "the mind" (519). This mind turns out to be another name for what the theorists Fish is criticizing might call "a psychological core," some settled center of rationality in the human subject that offers us the chance to guard against rhetoric, ideology, bias and prejudice, persuasion, coercion, and the like—by opening a fault or a gap within ourselves, the breach that constitutes the possibility of what is so often and so easily called "critical distance." The mind is what we lose in the face of force, or what we use to save ourselves from the appeal of force. Fish finds this notion shared by thinkers as disparate as H. L. A. Hart and Terry Eagleton—and not only the notion but the very figure that carries it.

Hart argued, against Austin, that a law organized not as rules but as "orders backed by threats" would be like a gunman who "orders his victim to hand over his purse, and threatens to shoot him if he refuses" and that "in most legal systems, to exercise such short term coercive power as the gunman has would constitute a criminal offense" (quoted in Fish, 503). This gunman, who deprives us not simply of our money but of the rationality that makes us human— the freedom and the responsibility to make our own decisions, which is to say, freedom and responsibility themselves—returns in an essay by Eagleton, who, Fish reports, "equates being 'forced mindlessly' into an action by an 'ideological obsession' with the pressure of somebody 'holding a gun to my head'" (518). Here the pressure of the gun figures the compulsory weight of the obsession, the ideological misrecognition that empties the mind by filling it with what belongs outside. The ideological error is that of metonymic reversal: what should be outside, too close for comfort but nevertheless still alien, changes places, comes to hollow out what it threatened and substitute itself for its victim. Hart's gunman is now, as Fish puts it, "in our heads," but the story remains the same.

Fish argues, of course, that the metaphor of inside/outside (what Paul de Man once memorably called "a binary polarity of classical banality in the history of metaphysics"),[10] which lends itself so well to these reversals, is itself aberrant: there is no difference between the mind, the psychological core of rationality, and all those dangerous prejudices and coercions that apparently threaten it—without them, you're nothing. These obsessions, whether we call them beliefs or fashions or biases or interests, are the very condition in and on which we "calculate, determine, and decide": a mind without them, "a mind divested of all direction, . . . could not recognize any reason for going in one direction rather than another or, for that matter, for going in any direction at all" (518). To "free your mind" of its obsessions would then amount to freeing your mind of itself, to rendering yourself mindless. "A mind so cleansed would have nothing inside it. . . . The mind, insofar as it is anything, is a structure of pressures, of purposes, urgencies, interests already in place" (519).

Without pressure or force, nothing, mindlessness—but with them everything, back with a vengeance. Fish's argument risks the temptation to replace the deconstructed polarity of inside/outside, gun up against head, with an almost-admitted monism: if the critical distance offered by the binary model is untenable and resistance to the call of the other (heteronomy) impossible—if "this is precisely what one cannot possibly do and still remain a 'one,' a being with a capacity for action"—then you can never get away from yourself, from your one self, "from the pressure exerted by a partial, non-neutral, nonauthoritative, ungrounded point of view" (519) that makes you the you that you are. Without authority or ground, folded and riven by singular coercions and imperatives, we live as we dream, alone, even if in parts—that is the conclusion of the theorist of interpretive communities. In other words, the gun is the one . . . or better, the gun makes me one (here is Fish's snowballing conclusion):

> the force of the law is always and already indistinguishable from the forces it would oppose. Or to put the matter another way: *there is always a gun at your head.* Sometimes the gun is, in literal fact, a gun; sometimes it is a reason, an assertion whose weight is inseparable from some already assumed purpose; sometimes it is a desire, the urging of a state of affairs to which you are already predisposed; sometimes it is a need you already feel; sometimes it is a name—country, justice, honor, love, God—whose power you have already internalized. Whatever it is, it will always be a form of coercion, of an imperative whose source is an interest which speaks to the interest in you. And this leads me to a second aphorism: not only is there always a gun at your head; *the gun at your head is your head*: the interests that seek to compel you are appealing and therefore pressuring only to the extent they already live within you, and indeed *are* you. In the end we are always self-compelled, coerced by forces—beliefs, convictions, reasons, desires—from which we cannot move one inch away. (520)

Fish is quick to assert that this inability to move does not signify paralysis or indecision, but rather conflict, persuasion, debate, "unpredictable and theoretically interminable," without guarantees, since "the imperatives to which he responds cannot be held at arm's length . . . because they are constitutive of the actor's every gesture" (521). Indeed, as interesting as this irreducible bias is, the emphasis on stasis seems to preserve the classical condition of decisive action, the subject's upright stance before the object, the subject of *Vorstellung* as "a 'one,' a being with a capacity for action." The radical abolition of distance, the insistence on irrevocable implication, threatens to take the immobility and fixity of the so-called self's interiority for granted. In the last sentences I have quoted, Fish's emphasis turns briskly away from the motif of compulsion and force to the definition of the subject: in the phrase "we are always self-compelled," the weight is not on "compelled" but on the breathless return of the "self," smoothly restored to its position of prominence by the identification (mechanism unex-plained) of exterior and interior: "the interests that seek to compel you . . . *are* you," "*already*." In other words, the gun disappears, or rather, the other disappears, the other whose pressure was figured by the gun will have been "always and already" absorbed into the self. Nothing interferes with the integrative power of this compul-sive self, alert to the call of the other only insofar as it recognizes itself, already, in the call: "sometimes it is a name—country, justice, honor, love, God—whose power you have already internalized," he says, so that the name is already mine. "The interests that seek to compel you are appealing and therefore pressuring only to the extent they already live within you, and indeed *are* you."

But this identification doesn't just happen: there must be a gun. I become "one" not simply in identifying (in hearing my name, in responding to what already lives in me), but in identifying with the gun, in becoming the gun; without the pressure and urgency exercised by the gun, I would not identify. The gun figures not simply force, the distorting effects of what is not properly mine, but necessity, the stark and non-negotiable demand to submit, which can only be exercised by the other. Not the other human, not someone or something (name, power, interest, appeal) I recognize and in some way internalize because it is already me, but something altogether different. The gun, and not my already-existing self, says to me "freeze." Not out of some interest, and certainly not out of some desire that I could recognize as my own, already, but because it comes from something else, something other, a gun. It, unlike the gunman, seeks nothing tangible from me, neither my purse or my money, nor my agreement or consent, but rather simply to immobilize me . . . and thus begins to define an experience of responsibility.

Hostage

It is this scenario, and not the presumed (or assumed) identifica-tion and return to self of Fish's drama, that Levinas formalized in *Autrement qu'être ou au-delà de l'essence* (*Otherwise than Being or*

Beyond Essence) in terms of the "hostage,"[11] and Blanchot radi-
calized in *L'écriture du désastre* (*The Writing of the Disaster*).[12] Fish
turns the gun back into the self and, despite his striking insights,
allows a rather conventional scene of recognition to unfold: "the
creation of an identification of the people with the weapons."
Levinas and Blanchot insist instead on the dis-propriating effect of
the address, the appeal, or the pressure to which I am subjected,
and on the contradictory burdens it puts on the one who must
respond. ("Rhetoric is another word for force.") Levinas emphasizes the odd substitutability and irreplaceability of the addressee—
"self, hostage, already substituted for the others" (118/151)—and
thus the force of the trauma inflicted by the other and the distor-
tions constitutive of this responsible self. "Responsibility for *the
other*, for what has not begun in me, is responsibility in the innocence of being a hostage" (125/161). Others address me (such as I
am) with an appeal that takes me over, and the boundaries that
would be those of identity, ego, subject are shattered in this experience: in responsibility, the hostage is first of all not "I" but "*me*, that
is to say, *here I am for the others* [moi, *c'est-à-dire* me voici pour les
autres]."[13] This "me," in the accusative case, marks first of all the
place of the addressee, of the accused, and not of an originary
agency, free or determined, or of any prior commitment:

> Responsibility for another is not an accident that happens to a subject,
> but precedes essence in it, has not awaited freedom in which an
> engagement to another would have been made. I have not done
> anything and I have always been under accusation: persecuted. The
> ipseity . . . is a hostage. The word *I* means *here I am*, answering for
> everything and everyone. Responsibility for the others has not been a
> return to oneself, but an exasperated contracting, which the limits of
> identity cannot retain. . . . The responsibility for another, an unlimited
> responsibility which the strict accounting of the free and non-free does
> not measure, requires subjectivity as an irreplaceable hostage. . . . In
> the accusative, which is not the modification of any nominative—in
> which I approach the neighbor for whom, without having wished it, I
> have to answer, the irreplaceable one is brought out [*s'accuse*]. (114,
> 124/145, 159)

There is nothing special about me, no preordained election which nominates me for responsibility—no matter how irreplaceable, I could be (I am) anyone. "But it is I—I and not another—who am a hostage for the others; in substitution my being that belongs to me and not to another is undone, and it is through this substitution that I am not 'another,' but me" (126–27/163). And yet this "substitution" does not result in a generality, a symmetry of reversal based on something held in common. "The self in a being is exactly the 'not-being-able-to-slip-out-of' an assignation that does not aim at any generality. There is no ipseity common to me and the others; me is the exclusion from this possibility of comparison, as soon as comparison is set up" (127/163).

I am in the accusative, overtaken and made to answer, because I am exposed to others . . . from the start, such as it is. Others do not befall me, like a terrible accident that disfigures an integral self. And I do not respond or find myself obligated because some self precedes mine and addresses me, but because I am always already involved and entangled with others, always caught up in answering, from the start: we begin by responding. "This self is out of phase with itself, by itself [*Soi déphasé par soi*]," originarily ruptured and exposed "by the force of an alterity in me" (114–15/146–47). Just when a conventional theory of responsible decision making would exempt the agent held at gunpoint from any obligations, with freedom suspended in the grasp of extenuating circumstances, Levinas sees the possibility of a renewed experience of responsibility. "To be oneself, the state of being a hostage, is always to have one degree of responsibility more, the responsibility for the responsibility of the other" (117/150), because others, he says, call, for help, action, response.

But do they call to *me*? What is left of the nominative in this accusative?[14] Here Blanchot radicalizes what remains hesitant in Levinas: *assignation irrécusable*, yes, singular address, but not exactly to "me" or to my subjected self.[15]

It is the other who exposes me to "unity," making me believe in an irreplaceable singularity, as if I must not fail him, all the while with-

> drawing me from what would make me unique: I am not indispensable, in me anyone at all is called by the other, anyone at all as the one who owes him aid—the un-unique, always the substituted. . . . The responsibility with which I am charged is not mine, and makes me no longer myself. (13/28)

Neither irreplaceable nor unique, and yet in receipt of an appeal, addressed with a demand (exigency, imperative, order) and held to answer, "I am only temporarily singular and a simulacrum of unity" (21/39). Who answers here? The hostage, precisely: anyone at all, who happens to be me. We are all taken hostage in this way, every day and night. Without guaranteeing any response and without justifying any action, appeals are sent—forceful ones.

> In the patience of passivity, I am he whom anyone at all can replace, the non-indispensable by definition, but one for whom nonetheless there is no dispensation: he must answer to and for what he is not. His is a borrowed, happenstance singularity—that, in fact, of the *hostage* (as Levinas says). The hostage is the nonconsenting, the unchosen guarantee of a promise he hasn't made, the irreplaceable one who is not in his own place. It is through the other that I am the same, the other who has always withdrawn me from myself. If the Other has recourse to me, it is as to someone who is not me: the first come or the last of men; by no means the unique being I would like to be. It is thus that he assigns me to passivity, addressing himself in me to dying itself. (The responsibility with which I am charged is not mine and makes me not be myself.) (18/35)[16]

The rigorous test of responsibility—what Blanchot later calls "a banal word"—comes in the quotidian and utterly ordinary experience of being held hostage: not because I'm me, not for what I've done, but because I happened to be there, because I am precisely anyone, and thus figure of anyone (airplane pilot, industrialist, pedestrian). It happens every day—on the street, on television, from passersby, friends and relatives, world leaders—and it singles us out in a peculiar way. There is a cry for help, addressed not to me in particular, not to anyone in particular, but to me as anyone—anyone can help—and my anonymity in the situation, far from offering an excuse to ignore the plea, implicates me directly. Not because I know anything or because of my "already"-existing interests and desires, but because I happen to be there. My failure to identify or to acknowledge the interpellation in no way disqualifies me or indemnifies me—the cry, the gun (or the lights and camera), insures that I remain in place, even if it is not "my" place—but becomes the condition of my response.[17]

Alone, and replaceable; alone because replaceable, a substitute for anyone and the one for whom anyone can substitute. Others do not address me because I am who I am, they do not "speak to me" because of "interest in me," as Fish would have it, but simply because I happen to be there. The call, or the gun, exposes me, as anyone, to an unincorporable alterity that has no interest in me as anything other than a placeholder, as a singular substitute. Fish is right that the gun is at my head, even in some sense that the gun is my head, but it (the gun and the head) is no longer, never, simply mine. The gun ("the imperative to which I respond") constitutes my responsibility, by withdrawing from me the ground on which I might answer, whether by reference to rule or to any interest, desire, compulsion, ideology, or even name that would already be mine. To respond, then, in the light of the gun and the camera, finally will be to speak or to act in what Derrida called "the night of non-knowledge and non-rule," without returning to or relying on anything "in me," answering for a promise which I (as someone present, intending, willing) haven't made. Would there be any other answer for which I could, or should, take responsibility?

Yo! ("Hé vous là-bas!")

This night of the address and the response is often brightly lit, it should be added . . . and the border passes not simply between territories but across our most ordinary landscapes.[18] The light can be that of the idea, of ideology itself (the ideology of the rhetorico-political war, or of Fish's "name—country, justice, honor, love, God—whose power you have already internalized," for example). For the scene, the non-recognition scene, sketched by Levinas and

Blanchot resembles nothing more than the exemplary "theoretical scene" of ideological interpellation drawn by Louis Althusser in the essay "Ideology and Ideological State Apparatuses."[19] The aporias of responsibility we are beginning to articulate here are equally those of ideology (and, as we will attempt to demonstrate shortly, of justice as well). It is very difficult to draw an unequivocal line between the regions of ethics and politics in this regard, certainly if one tries to do so by reference to some understanding of the individual, the subject, or the self.

We are constituted as subjects in ideology and not in nature, Althusser argued, and subjects are first of all subjects of recognition: "To take a highly concrete example, we all have friends who, when they knock on our door and we ask, through the door, the question 'who's there? [*qui est la?*],' answer (since 'it's obvious') 'it's me!' And indeed we recognize that 'it's her' or 'it's him.' We open the door" (172/112). This fundamentally specular recognition scene—Althusser later insists that ideology is both "centered" and built on a "*redoublement spéculaire*" (180/119)—does not depend on the framing device of the door and its sentry, however. Althusser famously relocates the scene in the street, imagining the mechanism of the constitution as an ordinary everyday interpellation: "*Hé vous là-bas!*, hey you there . . . [and] in the street, the interpellated individual turns around. By this simple 180 degree physical conversion, he becomes a subject" (174/113). The "Yo!," a cry for help or a demand to stop, produces a silently symmetrical response, and the lesson is that such appeals always reach their destinations: "experience shows that the practical telecommunication of interpellations is such that they practically never miss their man: verbal call or whistle, the one interpellated always recognizes that it is really him who is being interpellated" (174/114). Rather than being repressed or filled with false ideological consciousness, the individual is recruited as or transformed into the subject—"concrete, individual, distinguishable, and (naturally) irreplaceable" (173/112)—that he always already is by the address, which gives him a place from which to respond, a position in which to say "I" and to take responsibility.

But how stable is this "I"? Recently the security and symmetry of the Althusserian model have been challenged from a number of directions, most interestingly for our purposes by thinkers of tele-communications and of postcoloniality. In "Shahbano," Zakia Pathak and Rajeswari Sunder Rajan have called attention to the spectacular mobility, ideological and discursive, which can affect the interpellated subject.[20] They analyze a famous case in Indian politics of the mid-1980's, in which an elderly Muslim woman, having been unilaterally divorced by her husband, sought redress from civil rather than religious courts and in so doing provoked a constitutional crisis around the rights of religious minorities and the upsurge of Islamic fundamentalism. Tracing "the route traveled by the plea for maintenance initiated by Shahbano" (261), they demonstrate that the position of the central subject, the litigant named "Shahbano," is anything but stable, and is indeed regularly *displaced* across a range of ideological interpellations, "as Muslim (a minority religious community), lower class (the daughter of a police constable), and woman" (266).

Having fought in the courts for a decade and finally won a Supreme Court decision that granted her alimony—which is to say, having successfully challenged patriarchal Islamic religious author-ity by recourse to secular state institutions—Shahbano heeded the call of minority Muslim politicians and renounced the decision, "being a muslim," returning to the protection of her tradition. Pathak and Sunder Rajan insist that the complications of the case cannot be grasped, indeed that its politics simply cannot be under-stood, by taking the position of "Shahbano" for granted or by appealing to some core of identity (whether given or ideologically constituted) around which the subject reliably orbits. "Where, in all of these discursive displacements, is Shahbano the woman?" (262). Shahbano is all of these addressees and respondents (Mus-lim, poor, woman), precisely to the extent that they interfere with one another, interfere incommensurably and radically, and do not add up to one thing. There are effects of ideology and of respon-sibility, of legal and ethico-political agency, only thanks to these asymmetrical addresses and untotalizable responses: "multiple intersections of power, discursive displacements, discontinuous identities refusing subjectification, the split legal subject: to read this multiple plot is to recognize that the space of the other has no permanent occupant" (271).

Richard Dienst makes explicit, in an altogether different register, this implicit critique of Althusser's confidence in the 180-degree symmetry and the unerring delivery of the ideological address.[21] Taking seriously Althusser's word "telecommunication" ("practical telecommunication of interpellations") and exposing it to a version of Derrida's critique of Lacan, Dienst asks what happens if an ideological hailing, the kind that never misses the mark, goes astray.

> What if, in practice, an ideological sending does not arrive? What if the target turns out to have been someone else? And what if a message reaches, "practically" and not by design, the wrong man, the wrong woman? . . . Althusser's concept can only be made rigorous by Derrida's postulate of misdirection, which operates at a different level from the Lacan/Althusserian postulate of misrecognition. At this level, ideology must be conceived as a mass of sendings or a flow of representations whose force consists precisely in the fact that they are not perfectly destined, just as they are not centrally disseminated. Far from always connecting, ideology never does: subjects look in on messages as if eavesdropping, as if peeking at someone else's mail. (141)

For Althussser, the address hits home because it is simply returning home, routed temporarily through the other: we are born into ideology, into a name and "therefore an identity, and will be irreplaceable." The interpellation addresses us by the names—not simply the proper name—we already have, gives back to us what is ours by speaking directly to us, and turns us around into a response. "As ideology is eternal, . . . individuals are always-already interpellated by ideology into or as subjects" (175–76/115). The work of ideology certainly passes by way of subjectification, but the call—and hence the other—is necessary, and if the sending is irreducible then the message it transmits can never be sure to get through. The receivability of the call depends on the possibility that the lines can become crossed or that the message might stray:

to be a message it must be repeatable, iterable, and hence (as Derrida wrote in "Signature Event Context") "it can break with every given context, engendering an infinity of new contexts in a manner which is absolutely unsaturable." Once underway, the ideological message is destined to drift, and this errancy figures the irreducible interference of others as the necessary condition of the event. Interpellation and receipt, even *redoublement*, but without conversion, connection, or symmetry: "What would a mark be that could not be cited? Or one whose origins would not get lost along the way?" (12/36).

In this displacement and interference, this effective alterity, is the working of ideology and responsibility. The point here is not that ideology is somehow flawed or error-prone, and hence ineffective, but rather that its functioning is dependent on this inevitable errancy: if it is indeed a matter of telecommunication, in whatever sense, then the messages, their rhetoric or their "force consists precisely in the fact that they are not perfectly destined, just as they are not centrally disseminated." The appeal is aired or broadcast, without the certainty of connecting . . . we "look in on messages as if eavesdropping, as if peeking at someone else's mail."

Yes, Yes

Whether we call it force, rhetoric, guns, or ideology, the other is already there, and calling.[22] And there is always more than one other, which is to say, there are always letters astray, "discursive displacements," intrusive appeals, and hostages. Our entanglement with these others cannot be avoided, because they come before us and provoke a response. Like it or not, we say "yes" to others:

> *Yes* marks that there is some address to the other. This address is not necessarily a dialogue or an interlocution, since it assumes neither voice nor symmetry, but the precipitation, in advance, of a response that is already asking. For if there is some other, if there is some *yes*, then the other no longer lets itself be produced by the same or by the ego.[23]

This asymmetry structures the experience of responsibility—the gun or the hostage are premised on the failure of the "subject" to constitute itself fully, to pass through the other and return to itself. The address is not a cognitive or constative utterance, not a demand for something in particular, not the relay between two constituted subjects or consciousness who encounter each other across a language that they share. Who's there? As Werner Hamacher argues,

> if each call which issues is destined to make demands on the one who is called (but this is also questionable), is it already settled that I will hear, that I will hear this call and hear it as one destined for me? Is it not rather the case that the minimal condition to be able to hear something as something lies in my comprehending it neither as destined for me nor as somehow oriented toward someone else? Because I would not need to hear it in the first place if the source and destination of the call were already certain, and the call would be already determined as call.[24]

The call remains irreducibly different, alien, addressed to us . . . but like "someone else's mail."[25]

On the Impossibility of Justice

Did someone say justice was possible?

> "Justice," she said. "I've heard that word. It's a cold word. I tried it out," she said, still speaking in a low voice. "I wrote it down. I wrote it down several times and always it looked like a damn cold lie to me. There is no justice."[26]

This must remain an open question, if we are to give justice its due—especially when thinking about deconstruction. The point has been debated—there was even a conference, and later a book, called *Deconstruction and the Possibility of Justice*—and the phrase "possibility of justice" has been tried out, written down, even several times, but the question remains.[27] The appeal of the phrase is in what it leaves hesitantly unspoken: would thinkers or activists, even radical or critical ones, seriously consider putting the *possibility* of justice into question? Certainly some questions about its existence, its realization, have been raised—especially in the contemporary United States, where every day and every night more and more women, people of color, gays and lesbians, prisoners, people without housing, and poor people are singled out for discrimination and death, in a continuing wave of violent economic, psychic, social, political, medical, and juridical assaults. But these critical questions have, at least to my knowledge, generally operated well within the horizon of justice's possibility. Indeed, it is on the basis of the presumed possibility of justice that the critiques would have their meaning and pertinence: because justice is possible, but not actual, action is called for to bring it out of the taunting ideality of the potential and into reality. But this phrase, without abandoning any of the critical force associated recently with the more daring wings of literary and political and legal studies, hints at a more unsettling thought: the possibility that justice might simply not be possible. What might deconstruction (not that it's any more possible than justice, by the way) have to contribute to the question of the impossibility of justice?

The claim that deconstruction could contribute something to the question of justice, possible or impossible, comes these days as either self-evident or an outrage (and hence, in both cases, as unthought). More than a quarter century after *De la grammatologie* (*Of Grammatology*) and a decade and a half after *Allegories of Reading*, academic and journalistic commonplaces remain unaccountably but desperately impoverished in their encounters with the question. Deconstruction's ethico-political pertinence is either (1) taken for granted (presumed often but by no means always to be "progressive"), with an appeal to its thematic or referential considerations of issues (democracy, torture, feminism, the university and teaching, apartheid) or to its formal homologies with political interventions (deconstruction of authority as emancipatory or ideology-critique), or (2) condemned (as anti-political or paralyzing) because it appears to ruin the categories on which political discourse has tried to found itself for as long as it can remember:

subjectivity and agency, and the reliable knowledge (meaning—whether positively, theologically, or hermeneutically determined) that seems to ground its action.

By now, there is little point in enumerating examples of these paired positions: the choice itself—either familiar or foreign—needs to be obliterated. It guarantees that whatever ethico-political force deconstructive discourses might have will be evaded, or casually recognized, by reference to the reassuring certainties of well-known themes and categories. Most dangerously, the "community of complacent deconstructionists, reassured and reconciled with the world in ethical certainty, good conscience, satisfaction of service rendered, and the consciousness of duty accomplished"[28] join with those who worry loudly over "post-structuralism's anti-humanist abandonment of individual agency and responsibility"[29] in reaffirming the most bankrupt understandings of the time and space of the political or the ethical itself. The opposed poles unite themselves symmetrically around the axiom that ethics and politics are, in the first or last instance, matters of choice: determinations and acts of a subject with an identity (man, agent, consciousness, state or nation, or people) held to be—in some sense, strong or weak—free. To be free means to be capable of understanding and integrating that knowledge with a response to the demand to act. "Subject" names the time and place, always some sort of present, within which knowledge can be articulated with, and provide the basis for, action. The subject—of rights and responsibilities—grounds this passage from knowing to doing.

Much of the discussion concerning this articulation (the condition of the possibility of justice, it seems) has turned around those most vexed of deconstructive topoi, undecidability and unreadability. Even with those for whom deconstruction provides recognizably useful ethico-political benefits, the politics in question is that of reading. Building on de Man's notion of "ethicity" and Derrida's reading of Kant's Second *Critique*, for instance, J. Hillis Miller went so far as to call an entire book *The Ethics of Reading*, taking reading as the ethical act par excellence.[30] What is "the ethical moment in the act of reading"? What happens—even when "what calls to me, makes demands on me, is something else, something I would call 'other' "[31]—happens in *me*: "it is a response to something. . . . I *must* do this. I cannot do otherwise,"[32] and I do it freely, on purpose. For Miller, this experience reaches its most charged moment in the face of what he calls the impossibility of reading, where reading nevertheless takes place. In this ethical moment, "there is a response to the text that is both necessitated, in the sense that it is a response to an irresistible demand, and free, in the sense that I must take responsibility for my response and for the further effects, institutional, social, political, or historical, of my act of reading" (43). At once free and determined, the "experience of an 'I must' " (127) defines the ethical as responsibility for Miller. Bound, if not quite in the "condition or uncondition" of Levinas's hostage, between autonomy and submission to an imperative, this subject thrives on its own scission. As Miller puts it elsewhere, "though the I, the ego, is a function of language, generated, produced by language, it doesn't necessarily follow from this either that the 'I' doesn't exist, or that sentences that take the form of 'I must do so and so,' or 'I choose so and so,' or 'I accept a responsibility for so and so,' don't make sense."[33] Because I must read, which is to say, pursue "the impossible task of reading" and endure innumerable "lessons in the pain of the impossibility of reading,"[34] I experience myself as ethical subject and prepare for an entrance on the stage of society, politics, and history. Face to face with the undecidable, Miller's "I" keeps on, heroically, deciding.[35]

Yet reading also forms the political paradigm for those who fear that questioning its possibility means plunging ethics and politics, justice, into an abyss of uncertainty—incapacity and paralysis—and thus the "abandonment of individual agency and responsibility." Simon Critchley, while affirming his general sympathy with Miller's project, has worried that reading ethically, in his sense, "implies genuflecting before unreadability as the universal law of language."[36] If deconstruction, as he puts it, has supplied "a compelling account of responsibility as an affirmation of alterity" (189), it fails to make the necessary move from ethics to politics, from responsibility to questioning, because politics demands decisions:

"decisions have to be taken," so that "an adequate account of the decision is essential to the possibility of politics, and . . . it is precisely this that deconstruction does not provide" (199–200). More combatively, protesting against what he sees as a free-fall into indecision, Paul Smith voices the widespread claim that "this epistemological groundlessness can easily be understood as pointing toward an impossibility of social and political action, or to what used to be called quietism."[37] There is a felt need here, oddly shared with Miller, to discern a subject, "to provide an analysis of a 'subject' capable of resistance," as another critic puts it.[38] The choice is stark—either a subject and a ground, or no decisions and no action. The subject, with or without scare quotes, names this "resistance" to the undecidable and hence the possibility of action, justice, and the political itself. At the heart of the discourse of social practice and resistance, then, is a certain idealism, or even a theoreticism. The subject articulates questions of epistemology with those of action, and loudly asserts its capability. No doing without (first) knowing, it seems. The capacity of resistance—the certainty of a knowledge or a meaning which grants a reason to action, and to which action can appeal for guidance—is the possibility of reading as determined interpretation. The subject who reads is the subject who chooses, who decides, and justice is its right and responsibility: its possibility alone. But surely justice, like reading, involves some exposure to language and its difficulties, and hence can only exceed the horizon of the human subject, its understandings and guarantees.

"An Other like Others"

Drucilla Cornell raised this specter of justice's impossibility at the end of a text which marked one of the first intrusions into critical legal studies of a pointedly political deconstruction.[39] If her essay "Post-Structuralism, the Ethical Relation, and the Law" hesitates in its concluding call for ethico-political vigilance and responsibility, withdrawing just that sharp differential edge (the repeated insistence on the "remaining of the other") which had earlier allowed its most politically provocative operations, it is the doubly bound structure of the hesitation that is of most interest.

Cornell quotes Levinas on this question of the possible conditions for rendering justice: "Justice is impossible without the one that renders it finding himself in proximity. His function is not limited to . . . the subsuming of particular cases under a general rule. The judge is not outside the conflict, but is in the midst of proximity. . . . This means that nothing is outside of the control of the responsibility of one for the other" (1627–28). The emphasis is of course on the "without," and the constant and irrevocable impact of the other on the one who judges or responds, the interference or the disappearance of exteriority (not being "outside the conflict" is here called "proximity"), provides the paradoxical condition of the possibility of justice. Because we (who judge, as we do all the time) are implicated, are in the midst of conflict, justice is possible. Because we are all implicated, because the absence of any exterior has plunged us all into the proximity of one another ("nothing is outside"), there can be justice and responsibility. Justice cannot simply be the application of general rules to particular cases, because any exteriority from which the general might govern its particulars is lacking. We are involved, which is why we have to judge.

This requires that the decisions or judgments made not be of the order of the constative or cognitive, of the actually present and interpretable ("we can no longer read off what the ideal is as if it were *there*, present in the actual" [1628]). To this new responsibility belongs the future-oriented temporality of the performative or positing (an active, ungrounded, initiatory call to some ideal not yet available), of what Cornell's redemptive, Benjaminian strategy allows her to call "hope," as a promise and a call from within the confusion and the blurred boundaries of conflict:

> When we interpret, we posit the very ideal we purportedly find "there" in the legal text, and as we posit the ideal or the ethical we promise to remain true to it. Our promise of fidelity to the ethical or to the ideal is precisely what breathes life into the dead letter of the law and provides

a barrier against the violence of the word. . . . To heed the call to responsibility within the law is both to remind our students of the disjuncture between law and the ideal and to affirm our responsibility to make the promise to the ideal, to aspire to counter the violence of our world in the name of universal justice. (1628)

This promise would not be thinkable outside our contaminated implication in the conflict, which disqualifies the definition of justice as the impartial application of universal laws to particular cases (justice as fairness), just as it erodes any pretense to interpret something with the status of an object for a subject, some fact outside of our investments. There's no there there, because all theres are too unavoidably here, others fracturing our present, proximately interfering with the self-sameness and self-certainty of our interpretations. Of course, objectivity has not been replaced with the whimsical arbitrariness of subjectivity, because the thought of our implication in the other has to imply the other's intervention into our "present," that effect of a "here and now" constructed only thanks to the trace of the other's having already traversed and disrupted it. (This irreducible condition is what Laclau and Mouffe call, not negativity or contradiction, but *antagonism*: "the presence of the Other prevents me from being totally myself; . . . insofar as there is antagonism, I cannot be a full presence for myself.")[40] The "positing" is not that of a subject but a response to the call of something else, radically immune to any intention or cognitive mastery . . . we could call it, not an experience of proximate intimacy, but rather (with Lacan) of "extimacy," of an auto-opacity that disrupts the articulation of cognition with action.[41] Who are we to know what we do when we respond? As Cornell suggests, "better to do it even if one thinks one cannot say what one does" (1621), even or particularly if that doing is saying.[42]

If Cornell describes as "a double gesture" (1628) this blind and self-blinding "aspiration" to nothing short of universal justice, this in-spiriting of the dead letter with the breath of life, its doubleness nevertheless does appear to lack the asymmetrical negativity, the respect for impossibility, often associated with such gestures in

Levinas and Derrida.[43] To breathe life into the dead letter, to mark the disjunction between actual and possible (as ideal), and hence to offer against particular violences the protection of the universally just, all suggest a certain resurfacing of the phono- or logo-centrism which has dominated (and crippled) critical political discourse and to which deconstruction has formulated the most startling challenges. Cornell remains more or less true in this to the dialectical negativity of Levinas's claim (which she cites) that "justice can be established only if I, . . . always in non-reciprocatable relationship with the other, always for the other, can become an other *like* others" (1625; my emphasis). Because we all are, or can be(come), others for the others, we have something in common—this is the transcendental condition of possibility for what is called justice. This "establishment" of justice, and of some universal justice at that, has to be predicated on the aberrant and utterly unreliable (tropological) substitution of myself for the other, the dialectical identification of the two of "us" as equally or at least comparably (and a little comparison goes a long way) nonreciprocally related to "each" other. The possibility of justice is the possibility that "I . . . can become an other like others." This is likewise the temporal structure of the "promise" directed toward the "ideal," which depends on the interpretation of the futurity of that future as simply an accidentally not-yet-present present. The possibility of (the establishment of) justice means that the "disjuncture" between now and then, me and the other, the actual state of injustice and the ideal future of universal justice, can in principle, however negatively, be reduced. These promises are also promises to the ideal, to an ideal of comprehension or understandability, of universality, an ideal universality which the very performative structure of the promise has to disregard and indeed to disfigure.[44]

Doesn't the appeal to a universal justice of the future with which to counter the evident violence of today and tonight risk precisely this erasure of the alterity of the future (i.e., its futurity), which the thought and practice of the promise first opens? If elsewhere Cornell's deconstructive gestures push at the very limits of, and threaten to shake, our most oppressively familiar and powerful political theories, these last pages of her essay seem to begin, in their hope- or wish-fulness, a retreat from its otherwise militant and activist demand that "we mark the ethical relationship as the limit of the possible, and therefore, as the Saying, rather than as the said. The possibility of the ethical lies in its impossibility; otherwise, the ethical would be reduced to the actual, to the totality of what is" (1616). Cornell associates this reductive maneuver with a certain politics, denouncing "a right-wing Hegelian's complacency that reduces the ethical to the actual and therefore . . . to the perpetuation of order" (1616). Refusing to take the possibility of ethics or justice for granted, marking instead "the limits of the possible" breached in the ethical relation (to the other in its utter and incomprehensible difference, the futurity of a saying without predetermined or predictable content), resists this totalizing affirmation of the permanence of the present (order) and its unlimited extension into (and thus erasure of) the future. If this resistance is not as optimistic or wishful as Cornell's final phrases, they should not be understood as pessimistic, either. "By the impossible we should not understand an absolute barrier, for to erect such a barrier would be again mistakenly to attempt closure. Nor should the impossible simply be understood as the not-possible, a formulation that would also reduce the ethical to the mere Other of the same. As Derrida reminds us, the impossible occurs at every moment" (1616).

Nor should the fact of this occurrence be taken to mean that the impossible is simply possible at every moment, or even actual, especially when we're speaking of justice or responsibility. Impossibility means that ethics, and justice, can find no privileged ground for their articulation, no unquestionable epistemological standpoint somehow removed from the strife, investments, and contamination regularly associated with them. Justice and responsibility are only possible, if they have a chance of happening at all, starting from their exposure to a strict and unpredictably recurring impossibility.[45] Because that privilege is impossible, we have what we call ethics and politics, and responsibility is an ineluctable necessity. The "we" here can be a community only in the strangest sense, a community without ground in any common "like"-ness and without a universal law, without the present in which any subject might articulate itself, but only a terrifying proximity.

> A community of decision, of initiative, of absolute initiality, but also a threatened community, in which the question has not yet found the language it has decided to seek, is not yet sure of its own possibility within the community. A community of the question about the possibility of the question. This is very little—almost nothing—but within it, today, is sheltered and encapsulated an unbreachable dignity and a duty of decision. An unbreachable responsibility. Why unbreachable [*inentamable*]? Because the impossible has already occurred.[46]

If the impossible calls for a response which exceeds its own possibility, what gives it that right?

Claiming Rights

There is a strange persistence in the rhetoric of rights and responsibilities, beyond and thanks to their deconstruction, and this survival enacts something irreducible and unforgiving about politics: that it is a game with the highest of stakes and without the security of predictability or of uncontaminated instruments, without even the comfort of reliable standpoints or positions, without guarantees—that it is just this "experience" of the failure of guarantees. And far from being a contingent or neutral piece in this game, a discourse which might just as easily be replaced with another one, the rhetoric of "rights" and "responsibilities" has a certain unavoidability to it, an inevitability which is continuous with that of the political itself.

Michel Foucault has often been understood to advocate simply abandoning this discourse because it has been surpassed by political techniques ("discipline") irreducible to it. In the last pages of *La volonté de savoir* (*The History of Sexuality, Volume I*), though, Foucault underlines the odd way the vocabulary of right has of outliving itself, of living beyond its uselessness, and of extending itself into a realm where it does not belong. "It is life much more than right which has come to be at stake in [recent] political struggles, even if these [struggles] are formulated on the basis of affirmations of rights. . . . This 'right,' so incomprehensible for the classical juridical system, has been the political reply to all these new procedures of power which did not derive, either, from the traditional right of sovereignty."[47]

How are we to understand this "even if"? Perhaps the theory is in error, and the break between life and right, between the power of the disciplinary apparatus to say "yes" to bodies and the power of the king to say "no" to his subjects, isn't so radical after all? Or perhaps the practice is simply outdated, and the struggles woefully undertheorized? Or perhaps these are new rights, new kinds of rights, long hidden within the discourse of "human rights," rights to different kinds of events and experiences which never could have been reduced to rights of sovereignty but which have now become available to us? Or perhaps right in general, the claim to rights, is another name for the complex strategic situation in which political demands are made because epistemologically justified grounds are not available, not in the nature or the essence of humanity, not in the experience of a subject or a group, not even in this very reality of the body, not anywhere. If claims to rights persist as the rhetorical structure of our political responses, whatever their content, then we need to raise the possibility that this is not just a matter of "rights-talk" but that, as Claude Lefort insists, rights and politics are coextensive.[48]

What does it mean to claim a right, or what is it to do such a thing, since to assume that it is meaningful in advance is to presume too much? Who claims, and on what basis, if any? The most obvious, if not the best, answer is simply: *I* claim, I claim something that belongs to me as my property, as what is proper and essential to me in virtue of what I am or what I have or what I do (and I am, for starters, human, but I am all sorts of other things too, various identities, understood here as given or, better, as taken, taken for granted). Right is my (own) right, not even right of or on behalf of others (no representation is possible here), what is owed to me as me and no one else—the claim to a right is justified here precisely on the grounds that the site of the claim and of the right are identical. In short, I am right, and claiming rights is really nothing other than reclaiming or rescuing them, since they are essentially mine and their loss can only be accidental or contingent.

But what of this claim? Why *claim* what is one's own? Why even open up the relation to the other that the linguistic act of claiming implies, when my relation to my rights is essentially a relation to myself without mediation through, or openness to, an other? This claim could only be a statement, the constative declaration of a fact which had fallen into temporary oblivion. Is this act of claiming necessary? For if rights must be claimed, then (1) the relation to other, and the supposed "loss" of rights in the other, cannot be merely contingent, and (2) the rights claimed cannot simply pre-exist the claim that is made for them. In other words, if there is an irreducibility to the act of claiming rights, then they cannot simply be given, and the "I" that claims them for itself cannot be given either but must occur only in relation with an other, an other that implies the possibility of the dispropriation of oneself and one's "rights" and "property," an other whose inevitability is this experience of dispropriation, that is, of language as something other than a system of signs or representations.

Lefort has argued something like this in an important series of essays on the question of rights and democracy.[49] He articulates exactingly this structuring paradox, fundamental to what he calls the "democratic invention": without a king or any transcendental authority, rights have no foundation, and so they come to depend on the very declaration which would seem to refer them to that missing elsewhere:

> the rights of man are declared [*énoncés*]; they are declared as rights that belong to man; but, simultaneously, man appears through his representatives as the being whose essence it is to declare his rights. Impossible to detach the statement [*l'énoncé*] from the utterance [*l'énonciation*] as soon as no one is able to occupy the place, at a distance from all others, from which he would have the authority to grant or ratify rights. Thus rights are not simply the object of a declaration, it is their essence to be declared.[50]

Whether of rights or independence, this ungrounded—or somehow auto-ungrounding—declaration aims at producing the condition it requires as its condition (freedom or right). Here, who has
the right to claim a right? Without exteriority, the declaration
cannot appeal to any elsewhere for its authority. The word "human" at best marks or holds the place of an aporia, or what Lefort
calls an enigma: who could decide whether something like humanity exists before it claims its rights?

> By referring the source of right to the human utterance of right, [the
> French and American declarations of human rights] made an enigma
> of both humanity and right. . . . [It was] an extraordinary event, a
> declaration that was an auto-declaration, that is, a declaration by
> which human beings, speaking through their representatives, revealed
> themselves to be both subjects and objects of the utterance in which,
> all at once, they named the human in one another, "spoke to" one
> another, appeared before one another, and, in so doing, erected them-
> selves into their own witnesses, their own judges.[51]

The declaration is the declaration of the right to declare, the claim
of what Hannah Arendt called "a right to have rights."[52]

This difficult situation parallels the one Paul de Man analyzes in
his reading of the so-called "blessed babe" passage in Book 2 of
Wordsworth's *Prelude*.[53] This babe's "soul claims manifest kindred
with an earthly soul," namely that of his mother. De Man argues
that this event of claiming is nothing like the stereotyped scenarios
we have come to expect of the *droits de l'homme*: "this encounter is
not a recognition, a shared awareness of a common humanity. It
occurs as an active verbal deed, a claim of 'manifest kindred' which
is not given in the nature of things" (91). De Man here exploits the
difference that opens up between the verb "claim" and its object
"manifest kindred." If the relationship, the shared identity or the
commonality, the community, to be exact, is manifest—not latent,
not hidden, but as evident as the hand that reaches out to touch—
then why the necessity to claim it? What is strange here, as in
Lefort's paradox, is that the claim ought to be a constative utterance, a statement of the facts, the fact of a relation or a state of

things. Why is the noise, the clamor, of the speech act required, if it happens only in order to make what's already so manifest manifest? It seems as though this right, the right to the mother and to the natural intimacy of the relation to the mother, is not so much being taken for granted here as it is being thrown into some doubt. Why is this baby screaming? Because, manifestly, the attachment to the mother is somewhat questionable, because the apparently natural legitimacy of the relation is not guaranteed by anything other than the most fragile of conventions. The baby has to claim what is so obvious because it threatens to disappear, because the legitimacy or the foundation of the relation is lacking: when the guarantee is missing, when there is no certainty, then we claim. In this sense, the baby's claim is a performative speech act in the strongest Austinian sense (an active verbal deed, like a promise), which does what it says and makes something happen: a claim claims, and in its wake—and only then—we can say that something has been claimed. But this is no ordinary performative, because in fact it does claim a fact, the fact of a relation, of a state of things: I am related to you. It superimposes a performative and a constative in a way which renders the difference very difficult to make out. It claims in a way that is in principle discontinuous with and irreducible to any declaration of the facts of the case and with the performance of any already-constituted subject: it is thanks to the absence of this cognitive foundation, in the default of any grounded guarantee, that the baby claims—and claims precisely this unfounded foundation.[54]

"We" are that child. Unlike one another, related only in our asymmetry, we should not hesitate to call our predicament a literary one. Not in order to aestheticize it, nor to appropriate the ethico-political for the discipline of literary criticism, but to insist on the linguistic character of this irreducible conflation and disarticulation of constative and performative, cognition and position, without which no politics would be necessary or possible. Or we could call it a social one, instead, a function of what is often so carelessly assumed to be "our" community, intersubjectivity, social bond, provided we accept Laclau's postulate on "the impossibility of society" . . . "there is politics because there is subversion and dislocation of the social."[55]

Without cognition, without recognition, and without any sharing, least of all of a common humanity.[56] Not because we are monadic and singular subjects, but because language—as it opens (breaches) us to others—removes the foundations to which we might refer together. If we claim a right, a right to justice—if, hearing the word, the cold word of justice, we try it out, write it down, several times, and it nevertheless continues to taunt or haunt us, to deny itself: "there is no justice"—then its difficulty and its persistence stem from its terrifying, challenging, removal of guarantees. We can take nothing for granted, least of all the *we* of any right—or of any justice. But without that unreadably cold word, in all its confusion and errance, we would have no politics. This impossible claim is what politics is like for us, we who are not alike and are only barely human; what we call justice is the undergoing of this impossibility. Without a we, we have politics, the politics of claiming our right to it, still speaking in a low voice.

Who's there?

PART ONE

Fables

§ 2 Examples of Responsibility: Aesop, with Philosophy

2600 years ago Aesop said: It is not always safe to imitate a bad example.

—*Aesop's Film Fables*

Bad Examples

What would we humans do without bad examples—without the example of the bad example, and without our regular innoculation by and against it? Responsibility begins in the bad example: one could even say that the only good example, the only one worthy of the imitation, interiorization, and identification that the example calls for, is the bad example. The classical subject is installed in its stance of responsibility and the safety of identity after the passage through the bad example, after the security failure that teaches the fragility of identity and the defense against the other. And yet there could be no experience of difference, no change, and no relation to the other without the adventure of the comparison and its failure . . . precisely because it is not always safe.

These aporias of exemplarity and identification are at the heart of any theory of responsibility, and we turn now to the literary genre, if it is one, of the fable to analyze these difficulties. What is at stake in the fable is, more than anything else, the interpretation and practice of responsibility—our exposure to calls, others, and the names with which we are constituted and which put us in question. Contemporary scholarship, whether of semiotic, new historicist, or deconstructive bent, concurs in seeing the fable as an exemplary ethico-political mode—not simply for its themes but for its strategies and modes of operation—and as a model of the practical effectivity of literature.[1] Annabel Patterson, for instance, charts the politics of what she calls "the fabulist grammar," noting the "bizarre" historical fact that for three and a half centuries Western "political and social analysis was frequently conducted . . . in a symbolic vocabulary that could . . . be called Aesopian."[2] For Patterson, this grammar extends to include the obviously rhetorical character of the fable, and it has a very determined function: "in the fable, the role of metaphor is to mediate between human consciousness and human survival, [and here] the mind recognizes rock bottom, the irreducibly material, by rejoining the animals, one of whom is the human body" (15–16). The fable exemplifies and accomplishes this speculative *Aufhebung*, the metaphor uniting consciousness and matter in a dialectic of recognition, like La Fontaine's soul and body, joined or rather "rejoined" in the text itself.

But the fable, as Louis Marin pointed out, is an "uncertain model of praxis."[3] In a word, the Aesopian fable—from Socrates' dream in the *Phaedo* through all those innumerable translations and collections to Zora Neale Hurston's mules and men and Francis Ponge's "Fable"—has at once offered responsibility as its central teaching and put it at risk. The uncertainty of this model, which in no way reduces its ethico-political force, constitutes a structuring difficulty that goes some way in accounting for the equally peculiar persistence of the fable, even in the texts that have most rigorously questioned traditional theories of responsibility.

The fable is offered for example, but for the kind of example that asks to happen in an act of something like imitation or identification, in the rhetorical event of a comparison. The fable aims to articulate "narrative examples and moral meanings," in Alexander Gelley's phrase.[4] In its repeated coordination of the rhetorical (example) with the narrative, and hence of trope with temporality, and in its destination in the ethical and semantic values generated by such textual complications, the phrase suggests a certain hesitation in or over the text—its figures and their deployment—which might at least delay the final establishment of those values. The promise of the "and," which guides us through text to value, whether ethical or semantic, is also a threat: the threat of example's excess, its iteration rather than its graceful self-effacement.[5]

When the examples are fables of responsibility, aimed at producing and securing the morality of, precisely, meanings and of the subject who means, can they finally be submitted to the logic of an evaluative destination with such thoroughness that they will efface themselves in the accomplishment of their mission? Or might the example, the fable, remain, and if it does—which cannot be taken for granted, any more than the converse—what remains of moral meaning, of responsibility, for example, along with it? When the very rhetorical mechanism of the fable, the rule of comparison and a certain identification, is in its turn named and put into question by the example that depends on it for its operation and its coherence, what exactly is being exemplified?

Wolves of Undecidability

This question cannot be evaded when, toward the end of the section lettered "r" in *Limited Inc,* Jacques Derrida raises the possibility of an inability to assume the place of the other, to know what the other calls for, a structural inability that he associates with the ambivalence marking everything given in response to a desire and even perhaps every response as such.[6] The names he offers for this inability include "undecidability" and "the unconscious," and *Limited Inc* is, among other things, an analysis of the necessity of taking the unconscious and the other into account in any consideration of the ethics and politics of responsibility. But even before the frequently quoted concluding passage, which proposes "something like a relation [*comme un rapport*]" between "the notion of responsibility manipulated by the psychiatric expert (representing the law and politico-linguistic conventions, in the service of the state and its police) and the exclusion of parasitism" in speech act theory (106/196), Derrida suggests that a certain policing of the subject and its identity is already required by conventional theories of responsibility, and that the unconscious and undecidability name possible disruptions of this control. The theoretical maneuver is important, and almost twenty years later remains largely unassimilated by contemporary political and literary theory. Of even greater interest here, however, is the mode of its enunciation and the literary vehicle entrusted with its exemplification.

Derrida asks, "What is the unity or identity of the speaker? Is he responsible for speech acts dictated by his unconscious?" and offers a number of hypotheses about his "own" unconscious. He concludes with a fable:

> All that simply to suggest, briefly, that it is sufficient to introduce, into the fold of speech acts, a few wolves of the type "undecidability" . . . or of the type "unconscious" . . . for the shepherd to lose track of his sheep [*il suffit d'introduire dans le bergerie des* speech acts *quelque loups du type 'indécidabilité' . . . pour que le pasteur ne puisse plus compter ses moutons*]: one is no longer certain where to find the identity of the "speaker" or the "hearer," . . . where to find the identity of an intention. (75/143)

The fable of the shepherd, his sheepfold, and the wolves named "unconscious" and "undecidability" draws, of course, on the Aesopian story of the wolf in sheep's clothing, the predator that dissimulates itself by simulating its prey and that provides the permanent example of the ruses of infiltration and tactical deception, of stealth and parasitism.

As the nineteenth-century scholar Joseph Jacobs "retells" the fable from William Caxton's *Aesop*:

> A wolf found great difficulty in getting at the sheep owing to the vigilance of the shepherd and the dogs. But one day it found the skin of a sheep that had been flayed and thrown aside, so it put it on over its own pelt and strolled down among the sheep. The Lamb that belonged to the sheep, whose skin the Wolf was wearing, began to follow the Wolf in Sheep's clothing; so, leading the Lamb a little apart, he soon made a meal of her, and for some time he succeeded in deceiving the sheep, and enjoying hearty meals.
>
> *Appearances are deceptive.*[7]

Responsibility in the Aesopian fable begins with this: self-evidence, self-consciousness, the identity of the speaker, and the free binary choice (wolf or sheep, appearance or reality).[8] In Aesop the fable names the simulation—the borrowing, comparison, or simile (wolf as sheep)—*as* the very definition and signature of the predator. La Fontaine's version ("Le loup devenu berger"), which has the wolf imitating the shepherd instead of the sheep and finally giving itself away when unable to counterfeit his voice, makes this principle of identity as the unmasking of appearance explicit. "Toujours par quelque endroit fourbes se laissent prendre. Quiconque est loup agisse en loup: c'est le plus certain de beaucoup" (in Marianne Moore's translation: "A counterfeit's sure to be exposed to the light. A wolf is a wolf in every pulse; no use pretending something else").[9] Both versions teach eternal vigilance, the exclusion of the parasite, and the law of the closing of the gate and the identification of subjects as the task of responsibility. The fable of the threat of the wolf as deep-black sheep installs a certain regime of responsibility—border controls, identity checks, and the transparency of essence to appearance—as the space of ethics and politics, the regulation of the play of forces through the control of self-presentation. The classical and Aesopian theory of the responsible subject is constructed against the threat of this predator, designed to produce the conditions for the counting and accounting of agents. It is the sheep who demand that the wolves expose themselves as wolves, as such and not as sheep.

Derrida's fable adds at least one more turn to the sequence of simulations by reinscribing this most traditional story of responsibility as the fable of its own undoing. In its insistence on the effects of a "structural unconscious" at odds with "the ethical and teleological discourse of consciousness," what is at stake is an effort "to make appear (and to leap) the security barrier which, *at the interior of the system,* . . . condemns the unconscious as one condemns or bars access to a forbidden place" (73/139–40). But this opening is not simply stated as a theorem that intervenes from some outside to protest the systematic exclusion of "appearance," "deceit," or the unconscious. The fable of responsibility is not exposed as a theoretical error to be rectified by a higher-order discourse. Rather, the breaching of the barrier happens in the very place which was to have been secured, from some other "interior of the system." "It is sufficient to introduce, into the fold of speech acts, a few wolves of the type 'undecidability' . . . or of the type 'unconscious' . . . for the shepherd to lose track of his sheep." The wolf of undecidability imitates, that is, not only the sheep but also the earlier wolves, and so the fable itself plays the part of the wolf in fable's clothing. With the introduction of this wolf, in this sentence itself, the first fable (appearance is deception, identities must be verified, sheep must be accounted for, a wolf is a wolf) is infiltrated by the very thing it sought to exclude, and in precisely the mode against which it had warned. The measured and accountable space of the first fable, the oriented sheepfold, is replicated by another fable that actively disorients it, that redeploys the same elements so as to lose track or count of them. A fable, yes, but a counterfeit, even a simulacrum of a fable: the unconscious of the fable. The parasite here simulates the host designed to resist it. The fable of losing count, that is to say, produces within the body of the fable the very situation it describes—it states just the threat, the loss of control and the difficult decision, that it practices.

And it performs what it describes. As Derrida has said of another text, Francis Ponge's "Fable," its inventiveness "results from the single act of enunciation that performs *and* describes, operates *and* states. Here the conjunction 'and' does not link two different activities. The constative statement is the performative itself since it points out nothing that is prior or foreign to itself. Its performance consists in the constation of the constative—and nothing else."[10] Derrida argues that Ponge's fable thus exemplifies Paul de Man's characterization of undecidability as an infinite and intolerable acceleration: the oscillation is that defined by the unstable circulation between the mode of the fable and its undoing in its "own" terms. The fable here is at once ironic and allegorical, in the fullest sense which he gave to these terms, linked as they are in "their discovery of a truly temporal predicament" (329/28). The experience of that predicament defines another responsibility, and the moral of the story undergoes a sharp mutation. *Fabula docet*: "This is only another reason why, at the 'origin' of every speech act, there are only societies which are (more or less) anonymous, with limited responsibility or liability—Sarl—a multitude of instances, if not of 'subjects,' of meanings highly vulnerable to parasitism—all phenomena that the 'conscious ego' of the speaker or the hearer . . . is incapable of incorporating as such."[11]

The fable is doubly difficult: not only does it practice the very tactics of stealth and simulation excluded by the ethical and teleological discourse of consciousness (the dominant theory of responsibility), which is to say of fable, in order to reinscribe the form of the fable against itself, but the theory of responsibility it articulates anew begins from the very impossibility of that exclusion. After all, what could responsibility mean without the risk of exposure to chance, without vulnerability to parasitism, without the opening of the conscious ego by what it cannot contain . . . without the indiscernible wolf. Without them, there would be nothing of responsibility but the choice between yes and no, this or that, nothing but the application of a rule of decision and a program. No responsibility without undecidability, without the unconscious and its parasites, and no fable, no example, without the risk of a certain simulation. In real life, as in fable: "as if . . . the simulation of real life were not part of real life!"[12]

Without Poetry or Philosophy

From the putative origins of the fable on, there has always been a vexed relation between literature and philosophy, sheep and wolf, slave and master, and this uncertainty has come to be concentrated most powerfully in the question of how responsibly the fable, as it were, behaves. Hegel, for one, found the relation rather artificially articulated, the fable a little too exemplary. He claims in the *Aesthetics* that "Aesop himself is said to have been a misshapen humpbacked slave; . . . his notions are only witty [*witzig*], without any energy of spirit or depth of insight and substantive vision, without poetry and philosophy. His views and doctrines prove indeed to be ingenious and clever, but there remains only, as it were, a subtle investigation of trifles."[13] Like the first wolf in sheep's clothing, hidden in order to be discovered as an example, lost track of in order to be recounted at a higher level, the fable, according to Hegel, simply mines its material for its exemplarity. "Instead of creating free shapes out of a free spirit, this investigation only sees some other applicable side in purely given and available materials, the specific instincts and impulses of animals, petty daily events; this is because Aesop does not dare to recite his doctrines openly, but can only make them understood hidden, as it were, in a riddle which at the same time is always being solved. In the slave, prose begins, and so this entire genre is prosaic."[14]

But what Hegel marks as prose or wit, "without" either poetry or philosophy, can be rewritten as the intervention of a rhetorical dimension of language between literature and philosophy. At least that is the strategy in the earliest known *Life of Aesop*, probably written by a Greek-speaking Egyptian in the first century A.D. but apparently dating in the main to at least the fourth or fifth century B.C., where the story of the fable is again told, if this time somewhat more irreverently, as that of literature's (ir)responsibility to philosophy.[15] The central narrative of the *Life* begins when Xanthus the philosopher decides to buy a slave, goes with his students to the slave market, and encounters the disfigured Phrygian Aesop (recently granted the power of speech after assisting a priestess of Isis and hence become too difficult for his previous master to handle). Their first exchange is exemplary, as the philosopher interrogates the slave in order to determine whether "he knows anything," receives equivocal replies, and finishes by asking, "Do you want me to buy you?" Aesop responds by specifying the rhetorical situation of the question and its implied reversal of the relation of instruction and example, thus outlining the conditions of the philosopher's responsibility: "What do you mean? Do you think that you already own me as an adviser so that you can get advice from me about myself? If you want to buy me, buy me. If you don't, move on. I don't care what you do. . . . No one is putting you under bond to buy me. You're entirely free to make your own choice. If you want to take me, pay the price" (43). Xanthus completes the transaction and pays the price, and the story that follows narrates the difficulty of knowing in advance what the price will turn out to be. Over its course the relation of master to slave, philosophy to literature, is reversed and undone, rearticulated as the predicament (and its exploitation) of responding in a language not one's own, in language both literal and figurative.

Aesop, at once *witzig* and responsible, does what he is told—which can always mean more than one thing. "Aesop said: '. . . I wasn't supposed to do anything more than I was told. If I slipped up on my instructions, I was going to be answerable at the cost of a beating'" (51). The free choice of the free man, the philosopher as master, is shown to depend on a language that always passes through the other, making "What do you mean?" a question often asked and just as often answered, usually more than once. Its inevitable appearance in language renders the unity and intention of the philosopher permanently questionable. If the philosopher gives orders and lessons, Aesop, enslaved and obligated to respond, determines to "give the philosopher a lesson in how to give orders." The general form of Aesop's response is to exploit the difference that always opens between the presumed literality of an order or an intention and the inevitably figural appearance it assumes. Every encounter thus becomes a philosophical lesson for the philosopher, in the form of a fable:

> Aesop said: "You shouldn't have laid down the law for me so literally, and I would have served you properly. But don't feel sorry about it, master. The way you stated the rule for me will turn out to your advantage, for it will teach you not to make mistakes in the classroom. Statements that go too far in either inclusion or exclusion are no small errors."(53)

Of course, one can only do more—or less—than one is told. The general lesson of all these bad examples (and the philosopher is his own best bad example) is that statements, precisely because they are statements, dictated by nothing reducible to the unity of an intention or the identity of a conscious ego, can only go too far. Language, language as the rhetoric of instruction and persuasion, only takes to the extent that it mistakes, especially when it gives and takes for example. But there is no slave revolt in morality here:

what the *Life of Aesop* undoes most compellingly is any stability that might ground the hierarchical subordination of literature to philosophy as master to slave . . . and vice versa.

"If the relation that unites and divides philosophy and literature is a relation of *master to slave* (and one of them has indeed feared for its life), what discourse can be undertaken about philosophy which would not already be that of philosophy itself, the one that always precludes in advance . . . the possibility of asking in relation to it a different type of question about it?" With this question, Philippe Lacoue-Labarthe (in a 1969 essay called "La fable") proposed "the fable" as a name for the mutual implication and asymmetrical interference of literature with philosophy.[16] If in the years since then this interrogation has been much maligned, misunderstood, and abused, it is clear that for Lacoue-Labarthe the term "fable" required precisely the effort that today remains largely untried: the suspension of the self-evidence of the categories "literature" and "philosophy" in order to use each to put the identity of the other into question. The governing opposition of any consideration of this relation must be the one we have already encountered in the fable: appearance and reality. Reading the extraordinary sixth moment of Nietzsche's "How the 'True World' Finally Became a Fable (History of an Error)"—"with [the abolition of] the true world we have also abolished the world of appearances!"—Lacoue-Labarthe follows Nietzsche's midday thought of a kind of fiction (*incipit Zarathustra*) that would not simply oppose (the deceit of) appearance to (the truth of) reality, since in this sixth step "appearance is nothing other than the product of reality. To think fiction is precisely to think without recourse to this opposition, *outside* this opposition: to think the world as fable. Is it possible?" (5/16)

To reach this exterior, the moment of the shortest shadow and the end of the longest error, requires thinking fable as language. *Fabula* (narration or account), derived as it is from the Latin root *fari* (to speak) and linked to the Greek *phanai* (to speak or to say), finally implies nothing other than language as such. Littré defines *fable* simply as "ce que l'on dit, ce que l'on raconte." *Fabula* thus translates at once *logos*, true discourse, and *mythos*, fictive or fabricated discourse, not by subsuming them under some abstract generality of language but by referring them both to a more originary difference.

> The identity [between appearance and truth] that Nietzsche suspects does not in fact hide a deeply dialectical identification, where *logos* is the truth of *mythos* (as true speech), but where *mythos* authenticates the ontological originarity of *logos*, its purity prior to their separation and opposition. *Mythos* and *logos* are exactly the same thing, but the one is not more true (or more false, deceptive, fictive, etc.) than the other; they are neither true nor false; both are the *same* fable. The world has actually become fable. So, therefore, has what is said of it (*fabula, fari*), as well as what is thought of it. (7/19)

Fable—"a saying [*dire*] pure and simple" (8/20)—thus renders secondary, impertinent, and irrelevant the division of language into true and false, *mythos* and *logos*. In erasing the difference between the deception of appearances and the truth of reality, in undoing the opposition as an error, Nietzsche's fable retraces the error of "the occultation of [another] difference, but one which is not the *originary* difference between the truth and its other. . . . History of an error: history of a language, history of language insofar as it has desired and willed itself as a literal language, at the very moment when it proceeded essentially and necessarily by figure(s)" (8–9/20–21). This desire, the philosopher's desire as well as that of the traditional fable, is here frustrated by the fable itself, which tells the story of the desire as the history of an error. An error *of* language: "the fable is the language with respect to which (and in which) these differences, which are not differences, no longer obtain: literal and figurative, transparence and transference, reality and simulacrum, presence and representation, *mythos* and *logos*, logic and poetry, philosophy and literature, etc." (9/21–22). This means that fable is not exterior to philosophy, nor contained by it; it reinscribes the division between philosophy and literature as the language on which they both rely but which opens them up, from "within," to an other over which they finally have little control. Each plays the wolf of undecidability to the sheep of the other, at once allegory and irony of the other in a superimposition and an oscillation that break the mirror of reflection and open it to the alterity of an ungoverned figuration.[17]

Reading

According to the entry under "fable" in the *Dictionnaire Le Grand Robert*, there is a psychological examination called the "test des fables," defined as a "projective test or trial consisting of ten fables in which the hero is placed in a situation that requires a choice. In order to interpret the *test des fables*, the hypothesis is made that the child identifies itself with the hero of the fable." This test is the test posed by the fable as such, the adventure of an identification that can only occur in the comparison that a fable demands. The governing rule of the fable as an exemplary tale, as a certain experience or a trial, has always been Horace's dictum in the *Satires*, "mutato nomine de te fabula narratur" ("with a change of names, the fable is told about you").[18] The fable is an address or a call to the other, a direct address to a second person singular (*te*), even if it proceeds by the indirection of a change of names and the detour of a thematization. In doing so, it opens a difficult responsibility: it superimposes the relation of an address to the other in its singularity and in its anonymity (responsibility for the other) onto the traditional predicament of an articulation between the order of knowledge or cognition and that of action, ethico-political or otherwise, between what La Fontaine called the body and soul of the fable, the narrative and its moral (responsibility for oneself). The fable does not bear this burden simply on those occasions when the story told exemplifies the savoir-faire, the self-consciousness of knowing what or how (not) to do, by which the Western philosophical tradition has come to define responsibility. Rather, it carries it in its very structure, in the peculiar mode of enunciation, an address to an other, which makes it a fable and which immediately reinterprets the category of responsibility.

The motto "mutato nomine de te fabula narratur" functions as a kind of moral for the fable as such, a densely layered summary of its difficulty. Before anything else, the fable is simply something told

or recounted, "that which is said" (*fabula narratur*), but in the
mode of a strangely insistent passivity and anonymity, even an
automatism. Subjectless, it appeals, issues the call of a narration
from an undetermined location: something like a saying pure and
simple, it appeals to the other, aimless and heedless of its origin.

If in telling the fable issues a call or an appeal, that address
is structured as an appellation, even an interpellation, but with
a twist: the apostrophe calls the other by a different name. We
are addressed in the fable under what can only be a pseudonym, in
the intimate (and properly ethical) singularity of the *tu-toi*, but
stripped of a proper name. The rhetorical strategy of reading the
fable consists in undoing that mutation and in the experience of
having it come undone for "you." The Horatian mechanism, again
impersonal, of the *mutato nomine* suggests a trans-subjective movement in which names are changed, exchanged, substituted, and
simulated: a tropological system, but not exactly one of metaphor
or metonymy, in which the exchanges are governed by a logic
of resemblance or contiguity. The motion is somewhat more
disorderly—call it, with a nod to the sheep and to the other,
mutonymy.

And the other is, among others, "you." The fable, before and
after all else, poses the questions of address, of apostrophe, and of
reading. The fable at once thematizes and calls, is addressed to
(about *and* for, subject matter *and* destination) the second person
singular—in general. The rhetoric of fables does not limit itself to
tropes as such, to nouns exchanged symmetrically for one another,
but opens or posits, without substitution or exchange, its reader
(you) and the difficulty of its reading.

It is here that the question of responsibility can be posed with the
greatest rigor. The address to the other—to the other as at once the
you who reads and who might be lured into an identification, into
the risk or the experience of an imitation or a comparison, a
mutation—must be somehow as open as it is focused, a public
address with a strangely singular destination, impossible to antici-
pate. In this structure it exemplifies, as it were, the experience of
responsibility that we have earlier encountered in Levinas and
Blanchot, the "disastrous" asymmetrical substitution of first and

second person. In the fable, the other appeals to me, as Blanchot argues: "It is the other who exposes me to 'unity,' . . . all the while withdrawing me from what would make me unique: I am not indispensable; in me anyone at all [*n'importe qui*] is called by the other. . . . The responsibility with which I am charged is not mine, and makes me no longer myself."[19] We are, strictly speaking, the "hostage" of the fable; at once directly addressed and nameless, except as "you." As Levinas says: "self, hostage, already substituted for the others. 'I am an other'—but without the alienation of Rimbaud, outside of any place," displaced in the address of the other.[20] Nonindispensable and without dispensation, for Blanchot, "the irreplaceable one who is not in his own place," "the nonconsenting, unchosen guarantor of a promise that he hasn't made."[21]

There is no rule for behavior in this situation; the call or appeal of the other, the cry for help, withdraws from me any self-consciousness, any transparency, with which I might have been able to govern my actions. Which is to say, it renders me responsible. As Derrida has argued in *L'autre cap* (*The Other Heading*):

> morality, politics, responsibility, *if there are any*, will only ever have begun with the experience of the aporia. When the path is given, when a knowledge opens up the way in advance, the decision is already made, it might as well be said that there is none to make: irresponsibility, good conscience, one applies a program. Perhaps, and this would be the objection, one never escapes the program. In that case, one must acknowledge this and stop talking with authority about moral or political responsibility. The condition of possibility of this thing, responsibility, is a certain *experience of the possibility of the impossible*: *the trial of the aporia* from which one may invent the only *possible invention, the impossible invention.*[22]

Responsibility, like the fable that teaches it, must be an invention or it is nothing at all.

Raven and Eagle, via Sheep

We need an example. The second section of Nietzsche's *Zur Genealogie der Moral* (*On the Genealogy of Morals*) opens with an etymological consideration of the moral concept "responsibility," *Verantwortlichkeit.* "To breed an animal which can promise—is this not the paradoxical task that nature has set itself in the case of man? . . . To be able to stand security for *his own future* [*für sich* als Zukunft *gutsagen*: to make good his word as future, for himself] is what a promisor does. . . . This is precisely the long story of how *responsibility* came to be."[23] Responsibility names the capacity to respond, to answer—which is to say, to be able to give and give back, to keep, one's word, or to promise and to promise to answer. For Nietzsche, the ability to make and keep one's promises means being (able to be) held accountable not simply by another but, already in advance, by and for oneself: to act in anticipation of the call to answer to the other for one's actions, in other words, to answer to oneself in the place of the other. The responsible animal can account for the way in which it keeps, or fails to keep, its promises—and it must do this to and for *itself.* On Nietzsche's reading, this animal comes from a fable.

> That lambs dislike great birds of prey does not seem strange: only it provides no ground for reproaching these birds of prey for bearing off little lambs. And if the lambs say among themselves: "these birds of prey are evil; and whoever is as little as possible like a bird of prey, but rather its opposite, a lamb—would he not be good?" ["*diese Raubvögel sind böse; und wer so wenig als möglich ein Raubvogel ist, vielmehr deren Gegenstück, ein Lamm—sollte der nicht gut sein?*"] . . . the birds of prey might view it a little ironically [*spöttisch*] and perhaps say: "*we* don't dislike them at all, these good little lambs; we even love them: nothing is more tasty than a tender lamb." (44–45/278–79)

If the fable does not seem strange to begin with, it has a strange moral: the lambs triumph in gaining the ability, and then the right, to hold the birds of prey responsible for doing what they do, for being what they are. In fact, the fable enacts the victory, does the trick. Nietzsche explains the moral—morality itself—as resulting from the exploitation of a purely linguistic resource and approaches the story as *at once* a fabulous narrative about language and how it gets turned—with animals playing its roles—into an ethical and epistemological system, *and* the medium of the exploitation, the putting to use or the abuse of a linguistic possibility. Thus the fable not only enacts but also reveals the invention of responsibility, does and undoes the trick. Nietzsche analyzes it as follows: "only thanks to the seduction of language, . . . which understands and misunderstands all effects as conditioned by something that causes effects, by a 'subject,' " do the birds first appear to have had a choice in their action, to have made a decision about the lambs. The interpretation or institution of the birds as *subjects*, as choosing, willing agents, depends on a fiction, a fable: " 'the doer' is merely a fiction added to [*hinzugedichtet*] the deed." Language makes action without a subject impossible, allowing what Nietzsche calls "popular morality" to "separate strength from expressions of strength, as if there were a neutral substratum behind the strong man, which was *free* to express strength or not to do so." This linguistic necessity, a grammatical position and nothing else, is "exploited" into the claim that "*the strong man is free* to be weak, the bird of prey free to be a lamb—thus is gained the right to make the bird of prey *accountable* for being a bird of prey [*dem Raubvogel es* zuzurechnen, *Raubvogel zu sein*]" (45/279, 280).

The rest of Nietzsche's analysis, which pursues the genealogy of responsibility through the promise, memory and forgetting, debt, and writing, need not be followed any farther here, so long as the moral of his fable of the birds and the lambs is underlined.[24] First, it is a fable, and the promising animal is a creature of fable. Second, the fable narrates a story about language—about the grammatical subject, promising (*versprechen*), keeping one's word (*gutsagen*), and answering—and about the peculiar way language makes responsibility possible: responsibility is an exploitation of a verbal possibility, nothing more, but nothing less. Third, the fable does not simply tell *about* language: it *is* the language which prosaically turns the merely grammatical subject into the fiction of the acting, responsible, human subject, thanks to a tropological operation we might call not anthropomorphism but zoomorphism. But the fable puts the reliability of that rhetorical expansion into question to the extent that it performs it. The operation is as suspect as it is inevitable.

However difficult, this version of the fable remains relatively simple. It bears comparison with the fable of the eagle and the raven, an Aesopian standard that opens the sixth part of William Caxton's *Aesop*: *Life and Fables*, or the *Book of the subtyl histories and fables of Esope* (1484).

> The fyrst fable is of the Egle and of the rauen
>
> No One ought to take on hym self to doo a thynge / whiche is peryllous withoute he fele hym self strong ynough to doo hit / As reherceth this Fable / Of an Egle / whiche fleynge took a lambe / wherof the Rauen hadde grete enuye wherfor upon another tyme as the sayd rauen sawe a grete herd of sheep / by his grete enuy & pryde & by his grete oultrage descended on them / and by suche fachon and manere smote a wether that his clowes abode to the fleece of hit / In soo moche that he coude not flee away / The sheepherd thenne came and brake and toke his wynges from hym / And after bare hym to his children to playe them with / And demaunded of hym / what byrd he was / And the Rauen ansuerd to hym / I supposed to haue ben an Egle / And by my ouerwenynge I wende to haue take a lambe / as the egle dyd / But now I knowe wel that I am a Rauen / wherfor the feble ought in no wyse to compare hym self to the stronge / For somtyme when he supposeth to doo more than he may / he falleth in to grete dishonour / as hit appiereth by this present Fable / Of a Rauen / whiche supposed to haue ben as stronge as the egle.[25]

Paraphrased, the fable tells the story of the raven that, having once watched with envy as an eagle snatched a lamb from the flock and carried it off, later attempts a similar feat. But a raven is not an eagle, and his claws get stuck in the fleece of a wether (not a lamb): his prey becomes his trap. He is captured by the shepherd, his wings are broken and taken from him, and he is given to the shepherd's children as a plaything. An interrogation, or rather, an identity check, follows. The shepherd demands "of hym / what byrd he was," and the raven answers by retelling the fable itself as a narrative of a false supposition and its correction: "I supposed to haue ben an Egle / And by my ouerwenynge I wende to haue take a lamb / as the egle dyd / But now I knowe wel that I am a Rauen." Thus the moral warns against mistaken comparisons or self-confusions, in strikingly Nietzschean terms: "the feble ought in no wyse to compare hym self to the stronge."

While this fable is not simply one among others, given its later appearance in the *Genealogy*, it exemplifies a general pattern or determined configuration in fables: the triple coincidence of a choice, a confusion of identities or names, and a response (the wolf in sheep's clothing exposed).[26] Here, the fable weaves this configuration into a thought of responsibility, or responsibilities. Its destination, reading backwards from its conclusion, is the establishment of the raven as an (ir)responsible agent, one that—because it *is*, is an "I," has a name and a choice about its action, because it could have done otherwise—can be called to respond for itself (to render itself and the reason for its action) and can be shown its error and its fault. Its errancy consists precisely in wandering away from its name—or more radically, in not knowing or not even having its own name—and thus mis-taking itself for another (name). The lesson of responsibility can thus be formulated: act in accord with the fate prescribed for you by your name, "in no wyse to compare." As Caxton puts it elsewhere: "none ought to fayne hym self other than suche as he is" (105).

So, if the raven *was* confused a first time, we trust that "now," in the fable's word, with its error corrected it can act responsibly. If it forgot its name, forgot who it was, once, that is all in the past, *now*. Now it knows it is the responsible agent it always has already been but didn't know until just now. The fable narrates the raven's narration of the temporalized passage from being to knowledge, the making explicit or the speaking of being as knowledge, from an unspoken *I am* to the cognitive utterance "now I knowe wel that I am a Rauen." The raven's is the history of an error—corrected. In this case, the raven errs in comparing itself with, and then taking itself to be, an eagle. It takes the other's name, takes it seriously. The comparison or simile—"as the egle dyd"—operates as the hinge of the error, the rhetorical mechanism of feigning or dissimulation that the fable aims to ward off by exposing. And here the process, the trial or the test of the fable, works to undo the aberrant name, to restore the proper name to the proper bird, to allow the raven to say "I" and with that self-assertion reconnect the name and the thing—or perhaps to connect them for the first time. The establishment of the responsible agent, the raven as subject, thus coincides with the rectification of the tropological error against which the conclusion warns. Don't change your name, in other words. Or, know your name, and what it means, you can do. The fable narrates the passage from error to knowledge and installs—as its moral, as moral—the subject that can link its "I" with its name in a cognitive proposition. And with the ability to say "I am . . . ," which always hides behind it an "I promise (that I can)," enters the active or ethical order. The aberrant tropological substitution ("I supposed to haue ben an Egle") and its undoing ("now I knowe wel that I am a Rauen") together secure the institution of responsibility with a powerful dialectical negativity: the subject, the linkage of the I with the name, is found on the far side of its loss, tested so as to be guaranteed. This critical system (error, correction, I = name) thus fixes the link between the order of cognition (whether false supposition or true knowledge) and that of action ("take a lambe / as the egle dyd / But")—because I know what I am, I know what I can, and cannot, do, and will act accordingly in the future. I, *raven*, promise: to be a raven.

The fable of responsibility can be read, then, as a story about language and its dangers, a demystification of its pretended powers. A raven may be *like* an eagle, but it *is not* an eagle. It would have us understand that only the names, the words "raven" and "eagle," not the creatures themselves, can be transposed or substituted. The raven's response ("the sheepherd . . . demaunded of hym / what byrd he was / And the Rauen ansuerd to hym") corrects its prior linguistic mistake and re-establishes the proper proper name with the proper "I." It is thanks to that link between I and name, and on the basis of the error's earlier erasure, that cognition and action, knowing and doing, articulate themselves: know your name, and do what it says. Responsibility is nothing other than the response to the name by which one is called: "now I knowe wel that I am a Rauen."

Earlier we encountered the question of whether we are to read the raven's summary self-assertion ("I am a Rauen") as a restoration of a lost or confused proper name to its proper owner, as a recognition in the strict sense of a second or recovered cognition, as a reconnection of an only momentarily unhinged articulation, as the result over time of an I coming into its own name "now" out of a momentary misnaming "then," . . . *or*, rather differently, we are to read this auto-appellation and its now as a more irruptive explosion of a singular, new, unprecedented, strictly literal or starkly verbal, "I"—and of a now without then. This suggestion forces itself on a reader mindful of an excess, a certain rhetorical slippage or overhang, in the responsive narrative the bird gives the shepherd. "I supposed to haue ben an Egle / And by my ouerwenynge"—excess of comparison, envy—"I wende to haue take a lambe / as the egle dyd / But now I knowe wel that I am a Rauen." The questionable aspect, simply put, of this passage from supposition to knowledge is whether supposing and knowing belong to one and the same homogeneous system, such that the latter can erase the former without leftover or excess. If supposition means dissimulation as disguise or false knowledge, or even as guess or surmise or premise, then new knowledge known well will surely unmask error's true face and make possible its reconfiguration. But if in "supposition" we read the more ungovernable and unrecoverable force of positing, of position or imposition, then we may find a more active operation of disruption at work. The first narrative—the recovery of the knowledge of the proper name on the basis of its (temporary) ignorance—is only possible thanks to a different, and strangely prior, forgetting, this time of the arbitrary initial donation of the name, the saying by which what the fable calls "the sayd rauen" gets its name. If the fable is to be read as the story of an undoing, then the second substitution of proper ("raven") for improper ("eagle") names ought to reverse, symmetrically, an initial aberrant substitution of improper for proper. But the fable raises the possibility that the second turn, rather than erasing the initial error, only adds another one, because the bird began without a name, by losing a name it didn't yet have.

This other fable narrates the invention or the institution of the name, the response that precedes and posits, after the fact, its call. The bird begins the fable without (knowing) its name, covers the gap by comparing "itself" to another by borrowing the other's name (a supposed eagle), learns the hard way of its figural error and pays the penalty in its disfiguration (a wingless not-eagle). Then it attempts to recover from this loss by taking—or better, assuming— a name it never had ("now I knowe wel that I am a Rauen") but is left with nothing other than this name, as it is "no longer" a raven but merely a child's plaything, is no longer the raven it never was. Which means that the first figure ("eagle" for "raven") was no substitution but an arbitrary imposition, a sup-position, as there was no name ("eagle" for "   "), only a covering over of the blank that marks an initial deferral of the name. So the chiasmus that ought to reverse, symmetrically, the substitution of eagle for raven founders on an initial excess of comparison, or lack of name. Too much eagle and not enough raven, never enough raven. The raven is only ever "the sayd rauen," and that is the whole difficulty of the thing. Still, difficulty or no, the imposition is as necessary as it is groundless. How could one not confuse oneself with a name? But the fable tells the story, this time, of a non-symmetrical move-ment from nameless bird to birdless name, the generation of the pure name that is the precondition for the invention of the "I." This I is just as disfigured as the so-called raven, a plaything for children, just as empty and robbed of its properties, and this doubled blank provides the equivalence that makes the utterance "I am a raven" possible. With difficulty, and at the price of its intelligibility.

This asymmetry on the level of tropes and their narration opens onto a second-order asymmetry of reading and puts our under-standing of the fable into question—which is to say, it opens the question of a responsibility, ours, which would not take its own possibility for granted: a difficult, even abyssal, responsibility, all the more demanding for its difficulty. To put it simply, you are responsible for reading the fable, but the fable refuses to be read. The moral—be responsible, which is to say, don't compare yourself with what you're not, heed the call of your own name and resist the seduction of a false supposition, a mistaken comparison—requires, in order that it be understood and taken seriously, that it be ignored. You, reader, are asked to compare yourself with the raven, to assume its name and follow its example, in order to learn not to compare yourself with what you're not. The apostrophe of reading (which is the signature of the fable as a genre, the moral as address to the reader) is just as aberrant as the simile of the fable. You are not a raven, not even like a raven, and don't think you are. But to learn not to make this figural error, you must compare yourself to the raven, with its disfigured self-knowledge. *Mutato nomine de te fabula narratur.* You must (not) compare, by changing your name. And a change in names is what got the raven into the trap in the first place. In no way compare: no one ought to feign himself as other than he is. The fable is a trap, for you: its address cannot be avoided. The fable is structured as a double bind: to heed its call you must ignore its call, you must make the mistake the fable denounces. In order to read, you must not read, and you cannot choose not to read. But what is reading if not a response in this impossibility?

Accidents Will Happen

To come to terms with responsibility, then, requires breaking with the horizon of subjectivity, or at least referring the experience of subjectivity—decision, choice, agency—to a constitutive alterity that precedes it and that it cannot comprehend. We can call this "elsewhere" language—rhetoric, text, literature, or fable—not to distinguish it from some would-be empirical reality or history but to underline that others and their traces are always working within us already, in a space and time that cannot be reduced to that of consciousness or self-presence. There is no coming face-to-face with language, and this asymmetry constitutes the experience of the undecidable or the unreadable that marks off responsibility from the simple application of a program. Only when the subject is not taken for granted, when the profound linguistic or rhetorical complexity of the call and response, the figure and the mistake,

reading and writing, are admitted, do we stand a chance of thinking this experience . . . this history, ethics, and politics.

The raven speaks, and finally says, "I am," starting from a feint, a
fiction, a borrowed figure. Or rather, it answers—answers not to its
name but to the question of the name: what bird it was. In
feigning, it becomes . . . not "becomes what it is," as in the
Nietzschean formula, but simply becomes, takes place, occurs. In
"Mundus est fabula," Jean-Luc Nancy has formalized the Cartesian
fable of subjectivity to locate the interruptive force of language in
the deepest folds of the *cogito*: "the subject takes place in that it says
I feign, in that it says *I fabulate*—or *I am, fabulating*—and that it
says it at such a distance that it is carried to the fable's origin, in
other words, that it transports fable itself, withdrawn from fiction
as well as from truth, to the illumination of its own etymology: *fari*,
to speak, to say."[27] Nancy sees in this the pure or extreme form of
the performative utterance, where "the event is nothing other than
the performation itself, or the *being* coextensive with this performation: *I am*. Such a being *is* only . . . in and by the time of its
pronounciation" (123). The bird talks—"now . . . I am a raven"—
and invents itself as it tells the story of its error, its feint and its fall:
" 'I am' is *true* only when I say 'I am.' But 'I am' says only that 'I am
feigning,' and 'I am feigning' finally means, or begins to mean,
always (instantaneously): *for*, I say."[28]

But feigning takes time: the fable deploys across a narrative the
dehiscence "within" the bird, its exposure to others. The bird does
not just start talking—it *responds*. Everything starts with others:
with the eagle, the wether, and the shepherd, which is to say, with
the question "Who's there?" And there, where there was nothing
more than a comparison or the slippage of a simile, a name and an I
(or at least an utterance) come to pass. The bird's is just what
Blanchot called "a borrowed, happenstance singularity,"[29] which
arrives in the trap that responding is. Recall Levinas: "It is an
assignation to answer without evasions which assigns the self as
self. . . . The oneself is exposed as a hypostasis, of which the being it
is as an entity is but a mask. It bears its name as a borrowed name,
as pseudonym, as pro-noun."[30]

The borrowing does not stop here, though, as I've tried to demonstrate. This raven, or whatever it is, takes itself, such as it is, as an example. A rhetorical example, masquerading as a grammatical one,[31] and a bad one at that: one that depends on the very slippage that it pretends to condemn. In tracing the aporias of self-(de)constitution in Heidegger and elsewhere, Philippe Lacoue-Labarthe has demonstrated that identification, "the self-becoming of the Self," has always been thought as a matter of examples and their appropriation, in accord with this "ever-paradoxical imperative of propriation: imitate me in order to be what you are."[32] But, as he shows, this "you" cannot pre-exist the event of imitation, or the identification would have no chance of taking hold:

> The subject of the imitation (subjective genitive) or, in other words, the imitant, has to be nothing in and of itself or must, in Diderot's words, have "nothing characteristic of itself." It must not therefore already be a subject. This supposes an inherent impropriety, an "aptitude for all roles"—provided, however, that this im-propriety or aptitude should not in turn be considered as subject or support. . . . The "subject of the imitation" must therefore be a "being" . . . originally *open to* or "outside itself"—ek-static. . . . [And] this ecstatic (de)constitution has itself to be thought as lack [*défaut*]or insufficiency, . . . an inherent infirmity, without which no relation (either to oneself or to others) could be established and there would be neither consciousness nor sociality. (82–83/126–27)

Already there, not yet a subject. Hence, as he writes elsewhere, the classical problem of mimesis and of exemplarity, the philosophical double bind of the fable: what threatens there is "exactly that kind of pluralization and fragmentation of 'the subject' provoked from the outset by its linguistic or symbolic (de)constitution: an effect of discourses, the 'self'-styled 'subject' always threatens to 'consist' of nothing more than a series of heterogeneous and dissociated roles and to fraction itself endlessly in this multiplied borrowing."[33]

In a word, Lacoue-Labarthe summarizes, "let us say that the 'subject' *de-sists*" (129/260). In "Desistance," his introduction to *Typography*, Derrida underlines the fact that this thought of desistance is one of the most demanding thoughts of *responsibility*. The fact that the traditional categories of responsibility no longer suffice places irresponsibility *rather* on the side of these categories. How can one assume a responsibility in desistance, the responsibility *of* desistance itself? One can vary or deconstruct all the predicates of responsibility in general, yet one cannot completely reduce the *delay*: an event, a law, a call, an other are *already* there; others are there—for whom and before whom one must answer. However "free" it is supposed to be, the *response* inaugurates nothing if it does not come *after*.[34]

Better late, we might say, than never. Like us, caught in the structural delay or the crippling lag of reading, the raven "is" this *morcellement du 'sujet,'* passing without return across the trope or the pseudonym—the error—that marks its only possibility: there are borrowed names, or no names at all.

In the classic version of the fable of the wolf in sheep's clothing, translated in Handford's Penguin *Aesop* as "A Case of Mistaken Identity," the wolf of undecidability finally falls victim to another sort of error, a mistake of chance that reinstalls the identity of the responsible subject in its demise. The moral defines the seriousness of the subject, over against a certain "play," as a matter of life and death: "Assuming a character that does not belong to one can involve one in serious trouble. Such playacting has cost many a man his life." Another bad example, that is to say, and another change of names to be undone. But the fable of the wolf in sheep's clothing tells the story of an accident: "A wolf thought that by disguising himself he could get plenty to eat. Putting on a sheep-skin to trick the shepherd, he joined the flock at grass without being discovered. At nightfall the shepherd shut him with the sheep in the fold and made fast all round by blocking the entrance. Then, feeling hungry, he picked up his knife and slaughtered an animal for his supper. It happened to be the wolf."[35] The moral of La Fontaine's "Corbeau voulant imiter l'aigle" says it another way: *L'exemple est un dangereux leurre.*

§ 3 Freedom, the Law of Another Fable: Sade's Insurrection

> According to the text of the 1791 Declaration, "the free communication of thoughts and opinions is one of the most precious rights of man: every citizen may therefore speak, write and print freely, but must answer for the abuse of that liberty in particular cases determined by the law." As each one acquires the possibility of addressing others and of listening to them, a symbolic space is instituted, without definite frontiers, and no authority can claim to control it and to decide what can and cannot be thought, what can and cannot be said. Speech as such, thought as such, prove to exist independently of any given individual, and belong to no one.
>
> —Claude Lefort, "Human Rights and the Welfare State"

Freedom, Without Guarantees

If fable has always been the name of the literary thing that aimed to teach responsibility, to institute it as the self-understanding of the free subject, what becomes of it when, responding, we are exposed to something in language that troubles the possibility of that understanding? Caxton's fable of responsibility teaches this more difficult lesson: that there is no experience of freedom and responsibility except on the basis of the encounter with the undecidable or the unreadable. And it teaches this in a way that ruins the categories by which a "literary criticism" might seek to comprehend it. Neither theme nor form, the fable of the raven and the others offers an allegory—of unreading, of reading without limits and without guarantees, which is to say, of another freedom.

I am interested here in marking out the provisional terms of a project to retheorize responsibility on the basis of the persistence, even the intensification, of the ethico-political question in the deconstructions of its governing concepts—subject, agency, will, choice, freedom, rights—and in the passage through something literary or linguistic. Rather than responding to that question by reaffirming those categories in a defensive maneuver of good conscience, these deconstructions have exploded the limitation of ethico-political responsibilities to the regulated articulation of knowledge with action, cognitive with performative, in the stable presence of the subject that decides what it does on the basis of what it knows. When reading's possibility remains in question, when the ethico-political event is exposed to its implication in a contaminated linguistic field that no subject could ever hope to master, it becomes necessary to reopen the question of responsibility, which is to say, the question of freedom.

As Geoffrey Bennington has argued, these deconstructions have meant that: "the free community of rational beings can no longer simply be invoked, even regulatively, to orient our ethical and political judgment, nor can its various surrogates. . . . The paradox of traditional political thinking of all colours would be that by taking its model from conceptual thinking, it projects freedom as a state at the end of a progress ideally oriented by calculable and programmable laws. Freedom is ejected from now except in the negative form of unforeseen obstacles."[1] Responsibility names the predicament in which coincide the necessity, the inevitability, of action and the failure of laws with which to calculate and program it. Thus freedom cannot be limited either to the negativity of freedom from obstacles or the positivity of self-understanding and self-legislating autonomy.[2]

Freedom, not the determination of any subject, names the risk of exposure to others in language, the chance of the alterity of a future and the impossibility of protection against it. Derrida calls it the "provocation to thought" of a watchful sentinel, which "brings together in the *same* instant the desire for memory and exposure to the future, the fidelity of a guardian faithful enough to want to keep even the chance of a future, in other words the singular responsibility of what he does not have and of what is not yet."[3] At the least this requires an effort: to ask the questions of freedom and responsibility without taking the subject for granted, starting instead from its interruption (not its transcendence) in language—the relation to others as another kind of inter-subjectivity—as what opens it to the necessity of reading, to the political. With this exposure arrives the guardian's singular responsibility—as Bennington says, "the point being that the ethical is radically 'particular' . . . and therefore bound to an always particular context" (45–46). There is no outside, then, to ethics or politics, but only because the inside is opened onto the inevitable encounter with alterity (others, language, futurity) and thus provides no present in which to calculate or ground or guarantee a response. Possibility implies calculability and hence the erasure of the ethico-political. If ethics and politics name the urgency and necessity of a response, freedom and responsibility name the impossibility of doing it with any guarantees.[4] As we noted earlier, Drucilla Cornell has cogently argued that: "the possibility of the ethical lies in its impossibility; otherwise, the ethical would be reduced to the actual, to the totality of what is. . . . By the impossible we should not understand an absolute barrier, for to erect such a barrier would be again to mistakenly attempt closure. Nor should the impossible simply be understood as not-possible, a formulation that would also reduce the ethical to the mere other of the same. As Derrida reminds us, the impossible occurs at every moment."[5] These "moments" do not belong to the spatio-temporal continuity of a subject, though. The temporality of such ordinary impossibility can only be that of what we will call the effort of reading, *encore un effort.*

Reading Sade?

What happens (to us)—if anything, which cannot of course be taken for granted before the fact—when we read? If reading is not simply possible, are we free to do it? Since we only ever read something, no matter how ill-defined or trembling its status as an object for a subject might be when reading is the verb, our response calls for an example. Over the last thirty years, the texts, and especially the "political" ones, of the Marquis de Sade have given rise to a remarkable series of readings which share a double fascination: with Sade's professed interest in "saying everything"—"Have we not acquired the right to say everything?" asks the revolutionary tract "Français, encore un effort si vous voulez être républicains" ("Yet Another Effort, Frenchmen, If You Would Become Republicans") inscribed (and read aloud) within *La philosophie dans le boudoir* (*Philosophy in the Bedroom*)—and with our inability to read what he says.[6] Michel Foucault, for example, has lyrically drawn these questions together: "The precise object of 'sadism' is not the other, nor its body, nor its sovereignty: it is all that could be said [*c'est tout ce qui a pu être dit*]. Even farther and still in retreat, it is the mute circle where language deploys itself: to this whole world of captive readers, Sade, the captive, withdraws the possibility of reading."[7] Are we—captive, captivated, obsessive, everyday and everynight readers that we unavoidably are—free to read? The deconstructive predictability of the question should not allow us to hide from its enormous interest for a theory of freedom and responsibility, nor from its value as a *fil conducteur* through the work of this most difficult and radical thinker. Of what are we captives if not the very language in which those texts are written and which they take as their object—is there, even, some necessity at work here? With the possibility of reading withdrawn from those who can still nevertheless be called (and be called readers), does the opposition of freedom and necessity retain any pertinence? In this impossibility, who responds? More exactly, who is addressed? After all, as Foucault rightly continues, this possibility of reading has been withdrawn so effectively, "so well, that to the question of knowing to whom the work of Sade was addressed (and addresses itself today), there is only one answer: no one [*personne*]" (62/50).

Who reads, and how, a text addressed to no one, and what status does it have? Something happens. This text "withdraws from itself—but by confiscating it in a gesture of repetitive appropriation—the space of its language; . . . it can, and in the strict sense, must [*devrait*] continue without stopping, in a murmur that has no other ontological status than that of a . . . contestation" (62–63/50). We, and others, encounter this *murmure sans arrêt* every time we let ourselves be called by a text not destined for us, and it goes without saying that no text is ever (structurally speaking) addressed particularly to one or more of us; it could not be a text, something written or said in a language, if it were able to specify its reader. A text is an open, apostrophic structure, a call incapable of encoding in advance or predetermining the response it might receive or who might give it. Addressed, to no one. Evidently, that is reading's only chance, its terrible freedom and its exhilarating captivity.

It is this possibility—reading Sade, reading (the) everything said there—that Maurice Blanchot has put into question more rigorously than any other reader of Sade. "Whoever has read in Sade only what is readable there, has read nothing," concludes the opening paragraph of his preface to Sade's "Yet Another Effort, Frenchmen."[8] How could we read something other than what is readable, and why would reading only this readable turn out to be reading nothing at all?[9] What else is there in the text of Sade, if the activity of reading exceeds merely what can be read? In other words, if what is simply readable is nothing, as far as reading goes, then reading what can already be read is not enough, is not even reading. How? What can be read has already been read, and reading it amounts to nothing more than applying a ready-made interpretive code to a set of signs, in order to (re)interiorize their essentially accidental exteriority. What is to be read here is something else, neither something already read nor even something readable, but some excess of inscription or language that remains when the work of reassimilating or incorporating the readable is done, a textual element not susceptible of being reduced to something codable. As Derrida epigrammatically put it, "writing is read; it is not the site, 'in the last instance,' of a hermeneutic deciphering, the decoding of a meaning or truth."[10]

There is much in Sade ready to be decoded and understood—the text calls out for this rationalization: what Blanchot has called "la raison de Sade" can never be underestimated, even if, as he always adds, "it is almost not possible to read it, . . . [this] perfectly unreadable work."[11] But Sade's rationalizing interpreters pay the price of erasing just what cannot be read in his text, which is to say his text insofar as it is a text, language and not merely meaning or saying something. Granted that what Sade has to say, what is readable there, is difficult enough, but overcoming the interferences posed by his text and its language for the sake of what it has to say—no matter how enlightening, outrageous, dangerous, even evil—is not reading. Nothing could be more deluded than to expect that we could avoid that work, and simply be done once and for all with interpreting, making sense. Except perhaps thinking that it is all there is to do. Which means that: (1) we never *read* just once, and (2) what Blanchot calls reading demands the risk of a terrible insusceptibility, a resistance to affect or pathos, the radical in-difference Sade calls *apathie*, without pathos.[12] "Too bad for those whom these great ideas corrupt, too bad for those who fasten only upon the evil in philosophical opinions, susceptible of being corrupted by everything. . . . It is not to them, not at all, that I speak; I address myself only to those people capable of understanding me, and they will read me without danger" (311/506).

What Do You Call What We're Doing?

What enables—which would be also to say, what disables—reading? Blanchot's answer is difficult enough: language, and its ease. "Sade is difficult reading. He is clear, his style is easy, his language without detour."[13] Everything is called by its name(s): "He aspires to logic; he reasons,"[14] and the reason is that of the *logos*, the word that names and relates, properly. Sade's ease, the clarity and distinction in representation, by which the "great truths" he has to tell are brought into the light of day and discourse, finds its privileged example in the opening moments of *Philosophy in the Bedroom*, during which Eugénie learns the correct and proper names, *sans détour*, for a bewildering variety of organs and activities (especially the "lesson" in the third dialogue, 199–208/396–404). Among many others, take these passages for example:

> EUGENIE—. . . But a word, dear friend, a word has just escaped you again and I don't understand it. What do you mean by this expression *whore* [*putain*]? Pardon me, but you know, I'm here to learn. (208/404)

And again:

EUGENIE—Oh, dearest, what pleasures you give me! . . . What do you call what we're doing there? [*Comment appelle-t-on ce que nous faisons là?*] (204/400)

In more ways than one, "j'appelle un chat un chat" is the strategy of the Sade of the *Philosophy*, and asking—and learning—what to call what is one of the student's basic tasks.[15] But the will to clarity pushes beyond the striving for precision in descriptive vocabulary and grammatical linkages to the modality of their rhetorical deployment. If there are many questions about the articulation of names with things and activities here, and just as many answers, the emphasis is nevertheless on the naming as such, the activity of calling or giving names itself—"I love to be called that" ("j'aime qu'on me nomme ainsi"), says Saint-Ange (208/404). For Eugénie, here to learn, the learning is (in) naming, the lesson is a lesson in names, not simply about names, in general or in particular, but an event in naming. The text underlines the constitutive duplicity of naming and calling: both the inaugural gift of an insignia, the bestowal of a name, and the interpellation or identification of the bearer of a name by means of it. Reading as understanding takes this latter articulative, relational moment as its focus, determining the name as the coded, significant, meaningful marker (whether literal or figurative, it matters not, as Eugénie and her teachers demonstrate) of the thing. But the success of this effort depends on an *active* moment that cannot be incorporated into this cognitive economy—the name as affirmation, as call.

"Something," Blanchot writes, "is sought in Sade. The search, which is that of a new lucidity, is not pursued in an interrogatory mode but rather by clear, assured, and always decisive *affirmations*."[16] The search proceeds through the postulates and demonstrations of an analytic reason, but one which for Blanchot is attracted by something else it can in no way account for. Reason and its names, the sunshine of enlightenment, find themselves exceeded by themselves, propelled or interpellated, drawn out from themselves, by their very articulation, by their capacity to reason or to name, called to affirm (in the name of reason) something else, other than reason or the proper name, that remains hidden in the

nocturnal darkness of language and thus exercises a certain magne-
tism. For Blanchot, Sade is difficult not because something is left
unsaid or unreasoned in an irrational obscurantism, but because
"reason is excessive" (219/326), because of the "alliance, the mixture of a clarity and an obscurity, which troubles and complicates
our reading, renders it internally violent" (218/325). The difficulty
is that the obscurity can thus not simply be cleared up by more
reasoning or better names; it is in fact just that attraction to say or
do *more*, that *exigence d'excès*, in which naming and reading are not
halted or negated but disturbed, complicated, suspended, temporalized, repeated—which is to say, affirmed, demanded, called
for. There is no one name or thing to read here, but a mixture,
more than a name. More than any name as a coded unit(y) in a
signifying system, more than meaning(s). Reading is in trouble
because names affirm, call to others beyond anything they or any
reason can possibly account for—the force, the interruptive intervention, of this elsewhere opened by the call complicates reading
by refusing to let it stop, tears it apart by attracting it beyond itself
without going anywhere else. "This *exigence d'excès* does not affirm
simply its right to reason . . . but knows itself more reasonable than
it [reason]" (218–19/325). The affirmation of the name, more than
an answer to a question, resists understanding even as it demands it
and as it frustrates any attempt to stop, to treat it as simply
impossible (no despair or nihilism here).

> Sade, perhaps, is crazy, as we all must be in our beautiful nocturnal
> hours, but what he writes does not succumb to such a judgment. The
> sign [of this] is that we always come away from reading him less
> troubled in sensibility than belied in thought, not convinced, but
> somehow offered a way of understanding which escapes us and still
> attracts us. From there, in spite of ourselves and regardless of our desire
> for a simple logic, we take up reading again, carried away by a
> movement which will no longer stop. (218/324)

It is this movement away, on and on, this self-exceeding reading in
spite of our selves, which must be read here, in Sade and in
Blanchot. "Yet Another Effort, Frenchmen" is structured by this
repetitive movement, the movement of *encore un effort*, and it calls

on a twisted or divided temporal "logic" to teach a difficult lesson in reading its affirmations—all those names. "I'm here to learn," says Eugénie, and the lesson we learn with her is not about something else, not even about itself as some object called language. The lesson is nothing other than (the) reading, insofar as it depends on and cannot fail to encounter language or a text (in its possible unreadability), again and again, without pathos (*a-pathie*) but simply as what happens. And it is taught by example.

The Fable of Freedom

In fact, all of *Philosophy in the Bedroom* is nothing if not a pedagogical text, more precisely, a text which teaches about (the ethics and politics of) teaching, even if the famous altered letter in its epigraph suggests a kind of oscillating hesitation over the proper relation that reading might take up with regard to that teaching. Where the *Philosophy*'s first edition bore the epigraph "the mother will *pre*scribe its reading to her daughter," the next version found the mother giving contrary orders: "the mother will *pro*scribe its reading to her daughter." The text, though, argues that the most effective instruction is given not by command—whether prescription or proscription—but by example. If it teaches most effectively, as it often suggests, by "joining practice to theory" (202/398), its theory and its practice share the trait of progressing *by example*, as the preface "Aux Libertins" spells out in recommending that its addressees follow its "models" and "examples" (185/309). Recall the advice of "Yet Another Effort, Frenchmen" that to make good citizens one should "give them . . . many more examples than lessons" (305/499). The lessons given by the "instituteurs immoraux" rely again and again on the enumeration of examples, not only the *tableaux vivants* acted out or practiced by the teachers and their eager student (as well as her considerably less willing mother), but also a multitude of more abstract models from Socrates to the Romans to the Tahitians, from the animal kingdom to the world of plants and minerals.

I will borrow a word from Sade and call these examples "fables," taking seriously their tendency to draw didactic lessons from the so-called natural world in the manner of La Fontaine or the authors of *Aesop*s. As I've already argued, fables are generally deployed to provide models of ethical action, to instruct their readers in what must (prescription) or must not (proscription) be done. The classical fable teaches the one who is free how to exercise that liberty, how to enjoy it responsibly. It takes freedom (to know, to act, and to speak) as its presupposition, and teaches it as a practice. It defines freedom as self-knowledge, as knowing one's name and living up to or within it. That Sade's ethical tales conclude in immorals rather than morals in no way changes their structure, and only confirms their (perhaps disturbing) pedagogical force.

For example—but it is not just one example among others, as it concerns freedom—consider the personal and political problem posed to Eugénie by "la belle et dépravée Saint-Ange" midway through the third dialogue.[17]

> MADAME DE SAINT-ANGE—Listen to me, Eugénie. It is absurd to say that as soon as a girl is weaned from her mother's breast she must from that moment become the victim of her parents' will, and remain that way to her last breath. It is not in a century when the extent of the *droits de l'homme* has come to be widened with so much care that girls ought to continue to believe themselves their families' slaves, when it is clearly established that these families' powers over them are absolutely chimerical. (218/414)

Faced with this illusion or fiction of dependence, an example from what is called "nature" is provided in order to demystify or delegitimate the belief—this is the basic gesture of *Philosophy*, a relentless hammering away at the idols as merely fictional constructs: chimeras, fantasms, phantoms, ghosts, . . . fables. More often than not—this is the excessive movement marking this text—the anti-fable is structured as a fable. Here is what Madame de Saint-Ange says:

> Let us listen to nature on such an interesting question, and let the laws of animals, so much closer to her [nature], provide us for a moment with examples. Do paternal duties among [animals] extend beyond primary physical needs? Do not the fruits of the pleasure of male and

female possess all their freedom, all their rights? As soon as they are
able to walk and feed themselves, from that instant, do the authors of
their days recognize them? And do they [the young, in their turn]
believe that they owe something to those who gave them life? Doubtless not. (218–19/414)

Fabula docet:

> By what right thus are the children of men compelled to other
> duties? . . . Is it not prejudice alone that prolongs these chains? . . . Let
> us hope that eyes will be opened and that in assuring the freedom of
> every individual the fate of unhappy girls will not be forgotten; but, if
> they are so unfortunate as to be forgotten, then of their own accord
> rising above usage and prejudice let them boldly trample the shameful
> irons with which we presume to subjugate them. (219/414)[18]

The standard elements of the classical fable are present here: the
turn to animals for examples of human behavior (one paragraph
later Saint-Ange suggests to Eugénie that "the destiny of woman is
to be like the bitch or she-wolf [*comme la chienne, comme la
louve*]"), the claim that such examples constitute laws ("les lois des
animaux . . . nous servent un moment d'exemples"), and the
narrative structure of a movement in time from one condition
(dependence) to another (freedom) turning on a decisive moment
("dès cet instant"), here, an instant of self-recognition and self-
sufficiency ("sitôt qu'ils peuvent marcher et *se* nourrir *seuls*").
    Sade's fable warps this third element, though, in making the
instant of emancipation, the break into the condition of freedom,
itself break with the conditions of possibility for the first condition
(namely, recognition of the other). It makes a difference, because
this fable is an argument about freedom, a declaration of Eugénie's
independence—a dis-claim of manifest kindred, a radical break
which cuts off any relations of recognition and indebtedness, in
either direction, between the animal and its offspring. The narrative tells the story of the movement from a narrative (I authored
you, I come from you, I depend on you) to the oddly *a*narrative (I
owe you nothing, I do not recognize you, you?). It relates relation

and irrelation, narrates the break into something that makes narrative impossible.[19] This implies that the movement is irreversible, in the sense Paul de Man gives to that word.[20] The outcome—since it is not based on a dialectic of master and slave or of *ressentiment*—rather than reaffirming them ruins the conditions that gave rise to it. No recognition, no authority, no duty. No mirror.

Independence does not depend, here, even negatively, on that from which it has separated. The fable (*mythos*) spells trouble for the *logos*, the relation, that it seems to serve, in that freedom or emancipation is exemplified as the absolute absence of relation or tie, as doing without.[21] Hence Saint-Ange can spell out the fable's im-moral as a lesson in corporal singularity and natural autonomy, iterating and reiterating: "Your body is yours, yours, alone [*ton corps est à toi, à toi, seule*]; in all the world there is only you who has the right to enjoy it and to make it enjoy as seems good to you" (221/417). In "Sade," Blanchot recasts the *moralité* of the fable as follows: "Each of us must do as he pleases, each of us has no other law than his own pleasure. . . . This morality is based on the primary fact of absolute solitude. Sade has said it and repeated it, in every conceivable form: nature has it that we are born alone, there is no sort of relation between one person and another" (40/19). Of course, just because it's impossible doesn't mean it doesn't happen. If there is a relation to others, we owe it to nothing other than this impossibility—because no subject masters the time and space of the encounter, deprived of any ground of symmetry or reciprocity on the basis of which it might recognize itself or any other, we are instead opened by it. From the singularity of this event are derived what Sade calls freedom and rights ("all their freedom, all their rights").

This fabulous declaration of independence is structured by the logic of the *encore*: Sade insists that this fable (the animal law of liberty) takes a prior fable, precisely insofar as it is a fable, for its target. The next application of the lesson concerns the liberation from the purely fictional or conventional bonds of marriage (first the family, then marriage). "To chain them by the absurd link of a solitary marriage [*hymen*] is obviously to outrage the destiny that nature imposes on women" (219/415), holds Madame de Saint-Ange; later she urges, "Among all the bonds to be burst, those whose annihilation I'd recommend first would surely be those of marriage. . . . No, Eugénie, no, it is not for that end that we are born; those absurd laws are the work of men, and we must not submit to them" (222–23/418–19). Thanks to the example from the laws of animals, that man-made institution and its pretensions to law have already been dismantled. "We are rid of this chimera today" (224/420), she says. What a wife does is of concern to her only, and dishonor or outrage no longer matter; the only harm done is to pride, which is to say, to nothing: "this pretend wound is thus only a fable, whose existence is impossible" (224/420–21).

The fable of freedom, having recourse to a more originary order of existence, undoes the aberrant laws of human institutions with examples from the animal kingdom.[22] Blanchot: "the first and last instance is nature. In other words, no morality; the fact reigns."[23] Nature (fable) exposes human morality and ethics as fictive constructs, inventions substituted for nothing, mere phantoms entirely lacking in (any justified claim to) existence if not in effect. In a word, it reveals instituted law as fable, by telling a fable. It exposes it to its fictional origin with a story of its origination.[24]

A certain political tradition has made this exposure the very definition of freedom. Today this tradition is increasingly referred back to Kant, who famously defined Enlightenment as "man's release from his self-incurred immaturity, . . . his inability to make use of his understanding without direction from another."[25] In his landmark 1958 essay "Two Concepts of Liberty," Isaiah Berlin properly associated it as well with "Marx and his disciples," but it also describes this moment in Sade's argument quite well. Freedom is understanding that social institutions are created by humans, unmasking the "myth" that "man-made arrangements [are] independent forces. . . . Not until we have reached a stage at which the spells of these illusions could be broken, that is, until enough men reached a social stage that alone enabled them to understand that these laws and institutions were themselves the work of human minds and hands, historically needed in their day, and later mistaken for inexorable, objective powers, could the old world be destroyed."[26] Freedom or liberation is the event of this understanding: knowing and acting are articulated in the free subject, define it as free. This "understanding is appropriate action." I am free if and when I understand this negative lesson, and a positive lesson as well: that laws are necessary. I am free, then, only if I in turn impose a law on myself, "having understood [that] . . . it conforms to the necessities of things" (143–44). Berlin associates with this "positive" concept of freedom (distinguished as profoundly divergent from and irreconcilable with the "negative" liberty of simply "not being interfered with by others" [123]) "the thought and language of all the declarations of the rights of man in the eighteenth century, and of all those who look upon society as a design constructed according to the rational laws of [among other things] . . . nature" (148). The free subject of this law recites this creed: "I wish, above all, to be conscious of myself as a thinking, willing, active being, bearing responsibility for my choices and able to explain them by references to my own ideas and purposes. . . . I am free because, and in so far as, I am autonomous. I obey laws, but I have imposed them on, or found them in, my own uncoerced self" (136). The self-understanding of the transparently reasonable and readable subject depends on its definition as natural, and nature means possibility. Berlin paraphrases: "Knowledge liberates not by offering us more open possibilities amongst which we can make our choice, but by preserving us from the frustration of attempting the impossible" (144).[27]

This attempt, of course, is what Sade's text does not seek to evade, in spite of its deep investment in nature and its laws, and the effort ultimately puts the possibility of this self-understanding into question. Here, though, knowledge does liberate, as it has before—after all, this is not even the first fable to be exposed (nor is it the last). This gesture of undoing defines the movement of Sade's text, especially in "Yet Another Effort, Frenchmen." In fact, the particular critique of ethical norms (here, family and marriage) as fabulous inventions which we have just followed is itself based on a previous critique of fables. The first section of "Yet Another Effort, French-

men," having taken for granted the practical revolutionary demystification of royal authority, is devoted to religion, before morals even get into the act, and the program is unambiguous: "let us
not be content with breaking scepters, we will pulverize the idols
forever" (300/494). What we might call Sade's first critique, in this
relentlessly enlightening text ("j'aurai contribué en quelque chose
au progrès des lumières, et j'en serai content" [296/490], concludes
the tract's opening sentence), is of the particular rhetorical aberration by means of which organized human religions have claimed
the right or the ability to speak on behalf of the divine, or rather, as
Sade puts it, to make the gods speak. This ventriloquism of the
"empty god" (300/494) or, more strictly speaking, the prosopopoeia by which the absent—whether dead, never alive, or simply in
flight—are given a face and a voice and made to speak, has been for
Sade the second and perhaps the most important victim of the
revolution he now seeks to "consolidate" or render permanent
(303/497): "We sensed that this chimerical divinity, prudently
invented by the first legislators, was in their hands only a way to
chain us, and that, reserving to themselves alone the right to make
this phantom speak, they knew very well to make it say only what
would support the ridiculous laws by which they pretended to
serve us" (300/494). Hence the call to practice the critical gesture,
yet again, and behead "a phantom more illusory still [*encore*] than a
king could ever be" (303/498). Even if the priests have been dis-
patched along with the king, their human, all-too-human artifact
"that infamous and fabulous religion" (296/490) survives, living on
to haunt the already-considerable effort of demystification with the
threat of a relapse, in spite of its essential "incoherence with the
system of freedom" (301/495). Freedom is freedom from fable, and
this rhetorical survival, no matter how aberrant its animation was
and continues to be, still plays its role in fable and requires, for the
sake of freedom, "*encore un effort*; since you labor to destroy all
prejudices, do not let any of them subsist, because it only takes one
to bring them all back" (301/495).[28]

Where fable had taught—and chained—before, a resolutely human and freely chosen (that is to say, freely read) institution and its
laws will now take its place: "Let us take the greatest care to avoid

mixing any religious fable into our national education. Never lose sight of the fact that it is free men we want to shape [*former*]" (304/498). For the free, namely those "without religious fables," the responsibility that keeps them free is "to enjoy [nature] and to respect its laws, laws that are as wise as they are simple, that are written in everyone's heart; and it is only necessary to interrogate this heart to discern its impulse" (304/498–99). Because humans are natural, the freedom from fable is as simple as reading or understanding oneself. The fable and the laws of its creatures are to be replaced with an enlightened, reasoned education in human institutions as being human, a lesson in human autonomy (self-legislation) and auto-legibility. Laws do not need to be dictated from elsewhere, interpreted by others through their puppets, when they can be read freely and independently in each human (body and spirit).

Immediately, however, the status of these laws is put in question as well—which is the point at which we entered this structure some pages earlier. If gods have been displaced by humans, it does not take very long—only another effort—to remove humans from any position of privilege: we need only quote again Madame de Saint-Ange's first fable. "These absurd laws are the work of men, and we must not submit to them." Not only divine animation but also human law is "only a fable, whose existence is impossible." Where the first critique had seemed to suggest that it would suffice to "train [people] to cherish th[ose] virtues which, . . . without religious fables, make for individual happiness" (303/498), the second-order dismantling reveals those virtues to be just as aberrant as any religious belief. The rhetorical strategy that organizes this critique, and Saint-Ange's fable of freedom, becomes explicit later in "Yet Another Effort, Frenchmen" when Sade theorizes the structure of similitude or resemblance (simile or metaphor) aimed at delegitimating the aberrant religious and human laws of prosopopoeia and catachresis. Humans are born into, and hence are like, nature. Nature levels.

> The time has come for error to disappear; that blindfold must fall alongside the heads of kings. . . . Doubtless, we are going to humiliate

man's pride by lowering him to the level of nature's other productions, but the philosopher hardly flatters small human vanities. . . .

What is man, and what difference is there between him and other plants, between him and all the other animals of nature? None, certainly. Fortuitously placed, like them [*comme eux*], on this globe, he is born like them [*comme eux*]; he propagates, increases, and decreases like them [*comme eux*]; he arrives like them [*comme eux*] at old age and falls like them [*comme eux*] into nothingness after the term nature assigns each species of animal. (329–30/525–26)

Mutato nomine de te fabula narratur, as Horace said. As when Madame de Saint-Ange suggested that "the destiny of woman is to be like the bitch or she-wolf (*comme la chienne, comme la louve*"), here everything happens in the *comme*, the operator of the transition or the mutation between names. Like the real-life fantasy of capital described by Marx in the first chapter of *Capital*, where the commodity form allows everything to be substituted for everything else, including people, nature treats all its creatures as the same: "to declare that all men are equal means that no creature is worth more than any other, all are interchangeable, each has only a signification of a unit in an infinite enumeration."[29]

Everything, to the extent that it can be treated and manipulated as a mere sign, can be compared with everything else: *comme eux*. Nature is this principle of similarity, the third term that provides the axis of resemblance around which humans and "other plants" can be compared. "What becomes of the tree when you transplant it from a soil full of vigor to a dry and sandy plain? All intellectual ideas are so greatly subordinate to the physicality of nature that the comparisons furnished by agriculture will never deceive us in morals" (333/529). Figurative language raises no obstacle to interpretation here; similarity slides easily into identity at the hermeneutic level, naturally. Fable is this structure of analogy, of metaphor, comparison, the horizon of generality within which species can relate themselves as *comme eux*, like everything else (natural). Nature guarantees this resemblance or semblance; indeed, from the viewpoint of the "examining eye of the philosopher," the "rapprochements" between all the animals "are so exact that it becomes absolutely impossible . . . to perceive any dissemblance" (330/526). Thus fable is law, "law of nature" (329/525), "all individuals . . . being equal in the eyes of nature."[30] The appeal to nature made by this fable functions to remove the human from any position of privilege, in a gesture comparable to that of Nietzsche at the beginning of "Über Wahrheit und Lüge in aussermoralischen Sinne" ("On Truth and Lies in a Nonmoral Sense"). Nature is not human—it comprehends the human, as the whole to a part, without being reducible to it, is the condition of possibility which cannot be comprehended by what it enables and which thus is entitled to give laws with authority and without prejudice. Compared to nature—and how could it not be?—humanity is itself but a prejudice: "After the extinction of half the world, of its totality, if one wishes, . . . would [anything surviving] feel the slightest material alteration? No, alas! All of nature would not feel it either, and the stupid pride of man, who believes everything made for him, would be astonished, after the total destruction of the human species, were it to be seen that nothing in nature had changed" (332–33/529).

Nature is an example for us, as Saint-Ange told Eugénie, because it is so peculiarly inhuman, because it is a principle of likeness, of ineluctable comparison (*comme eux*), organizing the exchanges that articulate humanity with the plants and animals and enable their laws to address us as well. Nature displaces humanity by replacing it with anything, by inscribing it in a system of generalized exchange which denies it any privilege, by subsuming its specificity within the generality of everything. Nature exceeds humanity as (*comme*) the general rules the particular.[31]

The Law of the Law

It appears that these first two critiques have left a certain unquestionable residue called nature as the genuine state of things, the source and endpoint of our fables. This is perhaps Blanchot's strongest insight into Sade's writing:

> Nature is one of those words Sade ... wrote most willingly. It is in the
> name of nature that he waged his battle against God and against
> everything that God represents, especially morality. . . . For him, this
> nature is first of all universal life, and for hundreds of pages his whole
> philosophy consists in reiterating that immoral instincts are good,
> since they are facts of nature, and the first and last instance is nature.
> In other words, no morality: the fact reigns.[32]

And yet. Although this attraction to nature and the law, to the
principle of general resemblance and hence of generality itself,
never ceases in Sade, it is interrupted or troubled at times by a very
different impulse. Ultimately, there is no last instance, no final
appeal, least of all to the law. Whereas the rhetoric of similarity can
always perform its critical function, and does so with the ruthless
indifference of generality, it too falls victim to the still more relentless force of something that resists the substitutive and symmetrical
exchanges of the trope.

Finally, the strength of that "in the name of" and the force of
that analogy (everything can be substituted for everything else, all
individuals are equal, we are all natural) are what draws the most
furious wrath of the Sadean character. What must be questioned is
the stability of the axis of comparison, the frame that organizes the
exchanges and grounds the law: "always faced with this frame of
reference [nature], Sade's man becomes gradually annoyed, his
anger mounts, and before long his hatred for nature [becomes] . . .
unbearable . . . : 'yes, I loathe nature'" (62/40). Sade's strangest
moments turn on this extra effort of loathing, finding in the so-
called laws of nature only another fable, another rhetorical confusion dangerously seeking to relate the unrelated. Blanchot quotes
Juliette's apostrophe to nature, addressed as if to a creature of fable:
"perhaps you deceive me, as in the past I was deceived by the
infamous deific chimera to which you are, we are told, submissive;
we are no more dependent on you than you on him; perhaps the
causes are useless to the effects" (64/41). To be free means to be free
of comparison. The laws of nature, then, insofar as they attempt
the metonymic substitution of cause for effect or indeed any

substitution at all, are structured in the same confused and mistaken way as are the laws of gods or humans. The critical undoing of these errors in each case comes down to disengaging the pretended link between an abstract and a particular, between something general and something specific. This undoing is announced in the name of freedom, a freedom neither negative nor positive in that it depends on nothing (no obstacles to be overcome) and is ruled by nothing general (no law, not even one given by or read in the self). The *comme* that aimed to articulate everything within the synecdochal horizon of nature comes to be seen, with the eyes of a reader, as the enumeration of a stutter ("instead of analogy, we have enumeration, and an enumeration which never moves beyond the confines of a set of particulars").[33] There is nothing else to which to appeal, no frame or axis—nothing but the call "in the name of" . . . the name, in its singularity. One after the other, frames or names are tested—king, god, man, nature—and, as Blanchot argues, the test confers a certain value on them only in order that it may then in turn be resisted; "the experiment consists precisely in ruining them and nullifying them one after the other" (64/42). What is ruined in each case, in succession, is the claim to generalize, to exemplify, to draw (abstract) lessons from irreducibly singular events, . . . in a word, what is annihilated is the fable as the form of law.

"Yet Another Effort, Frenchmen" turns, of course, to fable to make the case, offering the lesson of the general and its particulars as the fable of the general and his soldiers:

> it will be agreed [that] to want to prescribe universal laws would be a palpable absurdity; this proceeding would be as ridiculous as that of the army general who would have all of his soldiers dressed in a uniform made to the same measure [of the same size]; it is a terrible injustice to demand that men of dissimilar [*inégaux*] characters all be ruled by the same [*egal*] law: what goes for one does not go at all for another (310/504–5)

What Sade, the philosopher or the text, revolts against, whether it assumes the figures of God, man, or even nature, is the law as such,

the law of generality, universality, uniformity, measure.[34] At stake is
the structuring difficulty of the fable and the law: the terrible
address of the law, open, to no one and to only one in particular. In
de Man's words, "no law can ever be written unless one suspends
any consideration of applicability to a particular entity," yet "no
law is a law unless it applies to particular individuals."[35] This
means that the revolt does not seek to overthrow one law in the
name of another, to replace a harsh law with a lenient one, to
humanize divine law or naturalize human law. Sade aims at the
very law of the law, the possibility of articulating the general with
the particular, the principle of relation or *rapport* that must be
presumed by any law desiring to exceed the idiosyncratic or the
private, which underlies as its condition of possibility any substitution (any example, any prosopopoeia, any metonymy, any metaphor) with a common measure or trait.[36] Sade simply removes that
commonality, that relation, and with it the foundation of the law,
the law's law, in all of its disfiguring violence. If "Sade puts himself
so completely outside generality, places himself so unconsciously
far from the possibility of laws," then the only rule in the end
(which is no rule and no end) must be: "Plus de lois, dit-il, presque
pas de lois."[37] And if the emphasis in the example of the general
and the soldiers was on a certain violence of uniformity, Sade
understands it as a disfiguration superimposed on a "prior" violence which begins by interpreting singularity as particularity in
order to inscribe it as specificity within a system of generality. First,
blinding, then a demand for visual distinctions: "Would the iniq-
uity you would commit in this not be equal to that of which you
would make yourself guilty if you wanted to force a blind man to
distinguish between colors?" (310/505).

The violence is the violence of relation, and thus we return to the
declaration of independence Saint-Ange proposed for Eugénie. Act
as the animals do, leave, with rights and without debts. You are
obligated or connected to nothing but yourself, and even that
"self-"relation is questionable since independence is self-exceeding
and self-abandonment, the erasure of the *as*. No recognition, no
debt, no relation. The fable erodes its own condition of possibility

here, irreversibly. If the violence (what Derrida calls the non-ethical opening of ethics, a violent opening)[38] cannot but be met with a certain violence, freedom requires that it occur "without the destroyed object deriving the slightest value from this operation. This principle has another advantage: it assigns man a future without imposing on him the recognition of any ideal notion."[39] Blanchot reads this principle of future alterity as a kind of negation without position, and hence without negation in the strict sense, an affirmative negation which attempts to disable the dialectical motion in which negation can be recuperated by the position it presupposes. It does so as the exercise of freedom. It is a "power which does not depend in any way on objects, which to destroy them does not even presuppose their anterior existence" (58/36). Because of this freedom, this power without object is thus not the power of a subject, and certainly not of a subject which can enter into relations with other subjects, even to negate them—"what relation can there be between exceptions? [*Mais quel peut être le rapport de l'exception avec l'exception?*]," Blanchot asks (46/25). And the structure of the *encore un effort* deploys this relation without relation (even or especially to our "self") over time: we have a future, but it has nothing to do with and thus owes no recognition to any past. If there is an other, it occurs only to the extent that we are incapable of recognizing it. This is what Sade calls *liberté*, freedom, this non-subjective openness in textual space and time, a radical singularity that allows for no stable identity but only iteration without relation. We are lacking only the freedom to consider this liberty (of absolute exceptionality without comparison, which is to say of the simple fact of difference) as anything but a matter of language.

Language, like reading, proves difficult, though, because it works by relying on and erasing the difference between singularity and generality, between the name as sign and as call, between *comme* as "comparative simile" and as "enumerative repetition," between the individual as singular and as example—by enforcing a law of exceptions.[40] That the singular claims its freedom as a law, that freedom is the "entanglement" of no difference (equality) *and* no relation (exceptionality), that one fable undoes another (without opposing it from any other privileged ground)—this permanent predicament always demands another effort.[41] Sade's strange rigor, his irony, is to entrust the task of teaching this lesson to fable: example of the singular, thus example of nothing, nothing but example.

Fable Speaks

In other words, there is no evading the fable, the appeal to an elsewhere to which the last name given is that of nature.[42] But that does not imply that this appeal could occur once and for all, that this last instance could last. The fable is the call that invents the place from which the imperative (the law) is uttered and robs it of any authority, submits it immediately to the law of its own undoing: yet another effort. The imperative, the law, finds its necessity in just this unreliability of ground: everything must be said—again, because there is no guarantee that it can be. Without justification, but not without fable.[43]

Which is why we never read just once, as Blanchot argued: "We leave off reading it, . . . we take up reading again [*Nous sortons de sa lecture, . . . nous reprenions la lecture*]."[44] Why must we leave off reading only to return to it? What is its difficulty such that it does not simply frustrate us but instead incites us, regardless of our desire for simplicity, for the simplicity we associate with our selves, necessarily to return to what is impossible for us? What would reading be if we could do it, if we could finally succeed, stop reading? This *sortie*, and its retraction, is no accident but rather the very condition of reading, in its necessity and impossibility. Hence the imperative read by Werner Hamacher in "LECTIO": "If it is still possible to read, then only in the aporia of undecidability articulated by literary texts themselves. In all writing and in all meaning is read the imperative: *Sors de la lecture. Sort*" (179).

What Sade and Blanchot allow us to think, finally, is the condition of reading, or rather, the *unconditioned* character of our exposure to language and its demands. Reading, thanks to what we are calling its impossibility or its endlessness (the persistence and recurrence of the fable), takes place only on the basis of:

1. Nothing—it has no ground, no foundation or basis, no law other than what Hamacher calls "the law of the impossibility of identifying any epistemological instance that could secure the meaning of language and even its very capacity to mean" (179). Naming makes reading possible only by withdrawing it, paying the price of the imperative.

2. Everything—"Have we not acquired the right to say everything [*le droit de tout dire*]?" asks "Yet Another Effort, Frenchmen" (329/525).

Foucault evades the rigor of Sade's formulation when he translates "the exact object of 'sadism' " as "everything that could have been said [*tout ce qui a pu être dit*]," because *possibility* does not restrict the scope of this everything—possible or not (not a question to be answered epistemologically), an imperative is in force here. Blanchot translates this necessity: "Everything must be said [*Il faut tout dire*]" (220/327). On the last page of *Juliette*, Juliette herself makes it imperative, giving the task to philosophy: "However much men may tremble, philosophy must say everything [*la philosophie doit tout dire*]."[45] Indeed, an imperative or a right is required, acquired, *because* the possibility of saying (everything) is just what cannot be taken for granted.[46] If it were simply possible, rights would be unnecessary. Whether or not it can be, everything demands to be said, and it demands its rights and its freedoms.

Blanchot insists that this *tout* transforms the classical philosophemes of totality or universality:

> The "everything" at stake in this freedom to say everything is no longer only the universality of encyclopedic knowledge . . . or even the totality of an experience in which meaning is achieved by the movement of a negation carried to term—a circular discourse which is thus the closed and completed affirmation of a mastery of everything. Sade's *tout dire* . . . goes even farther. It is no longer everything possible that is given and expressed. Nor is it . . . the whole set of values that a religion, a society, and a morality interdicts us from saying. (220/328)

It is a right or a freedom, not the already-existing property of a willing subject but something acquired, something properly political in its passage through language. The right has nothing voluntary about it. A subject cannot choose to exercise this right, to say everything, and nothing separates the right from a responsibility, an ineluctable or irrevocable call. Blanchot insists that this everything is nothing possible (not knowledge, not the experience of mastery, not even what is prohibited) but something else, which he associates in Sade with the political: "Everything must be said. The first freedom is the freedom to say everything. That is how [Sade] translated the fundamental demand [*exigence*]—in the form of a claim that for him was henceforth inseparable from a true republic" (220/327). The right and freedom to say everything is a political one *because* it is not necessarily possible; its possible impossibility makes it breach the limits of any subjectivity, opens the one who claims the right to the impossibility of making the other, the others, and thus language his own. Here to be free is to be responsible, but this fundamental equation of all ethico-political metaphysics encounters the disruption of its subjectivist (whether liberal or communitarian) prejudice in the double bind that constitutes the predicament of this responsibility: it may not be possible, separated as it is from any ground in knowledge or meaning, but that makes it necessary. Because the field of the political is by definition ungrounded, which is to say, the claim for and acquisition of rights is in principle unlimited by any given structure or social totality, undecidability or (as Ernesto Laclau has put it) "dislocation is the source of freedom." But this freedom, Laclau insists, is not "the Sartrean freedom of being a chooser who no longer has any grounds to choose" and thus falls back on the self as the only reliable defense against its own dislocation, but rather "a structural failure" in which "the ambiguity of freedom contaminates freedom itself."[47]

Sade's effort, in its recurrence, to say everything and his claim that this is not merely a possibility or an essence but a *right*, more exactly, an "acquired" right (hence something ethico-political, whose enunciation and exercise constitute an affirmation or an intervention), leaves his text and any reading of it open to a constant encounter with the condition of its possibility—language. This is a lesson in language as the open extent of saying, the freedom of all that must be said—without knowing, without pathos, which is not to say without politics. Reading, like politics, if it is still possible, must be unavoidable, allowing no opting out and requiring no commitment (in the sense of cognitive decidability and intention). Its irresistibility or necessity means that its freedom cannot simply be a matter of choice or decision, a willed relation of a subject to an exterior object, but an *effort*, and always another effort. "Yet Another Effort, Frenchmen" teaches this effort of reading in its inevitable recurrence as politics.

Politics and reading have their necessity in the withdrawal of security. These fields, because they expose us to events that cannot be calculated, programmed, "settled by experts or machines,"[48] demand responses (in another vocabulary, decisions) that cannot be referred to anywhere else, to something we know or mean. Our freedom is defined by this responsibility, not that of a subject that knows what it does, which is why politics is not finally a matter of interpretation. We read, ethically and politically, when something (others, for example) demands a response we cannot give, at least not on the basis of anything we know or have under our control, but that we cannot avoid giving. If what we did could be authorized by something we knew (nature, truth), doing it would have nothing of the political or of reading about it. Unreadability only frustrates politics to the extent that politics is understood as something a subject does when it knows. Otherwise, it offers a chance to think about a politics open to the future, to others, others "within" and without us. Indeed, the possible impossibility of reading makes politics—freedom and responsibility—ineluctable.

In politics speaks the imperative of this exposure to all language: "Everything must be said. The first freedom is the freedom to say everything." What Sade calls the "revolution" is built on this linguistic structure, which is why another effort is needed if we are to be republicans. The irony, as Blanchot insists, is that this revolution comes from nowhere else, has no privilege or guarantee of its own, but is just as fabulous as the state it would threaten. "It is not enough to live in a republic to be a republican; . . . nor is having laws enough for that constituting act, that creative power, to persevere and maintain us in a state of permanent constitution. An effort must be made, and *always* another effort—there is the invisible irony. . . . Sade calls it *insurrection, the permanent state of a republic* [315/510]. In other words, the republic knows no state, but only a movement" (222/330). No state, no state of security, no standpoint or present in which knowledge and action might be coordinated. Rather, a permanent state of emergency. Thus the "invisible" irony of the title—irony can only be read, if it can, and not seen—the irony of the unending exigency of another effort, the law of another fable. Just as fable undoes fable in a structure that cannot finally be reduced to opposition or demystification (a cognitive, recognitive critique), so revolution and the law lock themselves in a double bind whose temporal deployment is what we call history. "Sade thus calls 'a revolutionary regime' the pure time in which suspended history makes an epoch; this time of the between-time where, between the old laws and the new, there reigns the silence of the absence of laws" (226/336). As Geoffrey Bennington insists, this interruption occurs only when the law of readability or of meaning is exposed, not to another law, but to all that in language refuses simply to make sense or be read: "the *entre-temps* is not a temporal gap between two regimes of law but, *within* a system of law, the silence in the law between the sense and non-sense of the words, the movement which marks with its trace any legislative statement with a sort of internal transgression."[49] Politics aspires to this condition of revolution, and when it happens—everyday and everynight?—Blanchot writes, "it is *absolute* freedom which has become event. . . . At this moment, freedom aspires to be realized in the *immediate* form of *everything* is possible, everything can be done. A fabulous moment—and no one who has known it can completely recover from it, since he has known history as his own history and his own freedom as universal freedom. Fabulous moments, in fact: in them, fable speaks; in them, the speech of fable makes itself action."[50] Only a fable could teach this, if it could be taught.

PART TWO

Rhetoric

§ 4 The Point Is to (Ex)Change It: Reading 'Capital,' Rhetorically

> We suffer not only from the living, but also from the dead. *Le mort saisit le vif.* . . . Perseus used a magic cap as protection from monsters. We draw the magic cap down over eyes and ears, so that we can deny the existence of the monsters.
>
> —Karl Marx, Preface to the First Edition of *Capital*

General Principles, Immediate Questions

"The philosophers have only *interpreted* the world differently; the point is, to *change* it" ("Die Philosophen haben die Welt nur verschieden *interpretiert*; es kommt darauf an, sie zu *verändern*").[1] The eleventh and final thesis on Feuerbach, uninterpreted and unchanged,[2] stands in for a sometimes quiet, sometimes vociferous hope that regularly circulates in intellectual encounters with ethico-political questions. It is a call for responsibility, and its urgency is even more charged when what is encountered is a text by Marx. A reading of *Capital* carries with it, after all, a double promise of relief: not only the promise of the potential for theoretical or meta-rhetorical "progress beyond [the] local difficulties of interpretation"[3] which too often obstruct or stall the reading of literary texts, but also the even more desirable promise of some intervention in what is called economic or political reality, the last instance or brute facts of capitalism, which call out not just for interpretation and its inevitable difficulties, but for change.

It is by no means naive or "untheoretical" to put one's faith in this promise. Indeed, it is the exemplary promise of philosophy or theory itself, the attraction of a reflected conceptual apparatus purified of the local and merely immediate particularities of a text or a situation—not because those peculiar difficulties have been ignored, but because they have been bracketed and accounted for at a more fundamental level. One does not have to be a Leninist to subscribe to the dictum that without revolutionary theory there is no revolutionary practice. Philosophy has always thought responsibility as just this articulation of understanding and action, interpretation and change, where each "and" stands in for the "thus" that signifies a foundation. In that final thesis, perhaps, Marx was only recalling the philosophers to their responsibility, which they have often lacked the patience—if not the desire—to pursue to an end: interpret, so as to change. This was Heidegger's reading, at least, although he seems to have thought he was criticizing Marx when he quoted the eleventh thesis to a television interviewer and commented that "changing the world presupposes changing the *representation of the world* [Weltvorstellung], and a representation of the world can only be obtained when one has sufficiently *interpreted* the world."[4] If for Marx there was too much interpretation without change, surely for philosophy there would be no changing without interpreting. The groundedness, and hence the responsibility, of both change and the imperative to change would depend on the secure installation of that *Vorstellung*. The final thesis, then, serves not only as what Heidegger called an "unspoken demand for a philosophy" (35), for that in philosophy which aims to make a difference (*verändern*) responsibly (a change governed by a prior interpretation), but also as the exemplary demand *of* philosophy.

But can the possibility of this articulation be taken for granted? What interpretation of philosophy, and of politics, is presupposed when theory and its interpretations are required to found or ground the interventions that seek to change? These are the questions most radically posed by the eleventh thesis and by the reading of *Capital.* Paul de Man once figured what he called ironically the "highly respectable moral imperative" of a reconciliation between cognition and action by reference to Marx and "the wishful hope of having it both ways, of being, to paraphrase Marx in *The German Ideology*, a formalist critic in the morning and a communal moralist in the afternoon."[5] Neither this hope nor the investment in moral conscience could properly be attributed to the Marx of *Capital*, though. The moral imperative is moral to the precise extent that it considers the passage already secured by an extra-political authority. But if interpretation and change *must* be articulated, then the force of the imperative is to admit that this possibility is by no means guaranteed. Indeed, to say simply that "es kommt darauf an" is to make the demand without regard to its possibility. This implies that even if the confidence in the passage and the respectability of the demand are foregone, even if the moral foundations give way, the imperative is in no way undone or avoidable. In shorthand, its survival simply signals its transformation from a philosophical or moral imperative to a political one. In that sense, *Capital* is a political text.

That *Capital* should make the question of reading—the passage, however ungrounded or difficult, between interpretation and change—unavoidably a political one seems to have been the particular effort of the text's prefaces. We can start with Marx's explicit reflections on the problem of reading *Capital*, a text whose "accessibility to the working class," as he wrote in the preface to the French edition, was for him the "consideration which outweighs all others."⁶ To encourage its reading by such a public, the French publisher had proposed releasing the book as a serial, so as not to overwhelm its readers. Marx welcomed the temporizing gesture, yet remained wary: making *Capital* more accessible, he wrote, is

> the good side of your medal, but here is the reverse: the method of analysis which I have employed . . . makes the reading of the first chapters rather arduous, and it is to be feared that the French public, always impatient to conclude, eager to know the relation between general principles and the immediate questions which have aroused its passions [*avide de connaître le rapport des principes généraux avec les questions immédiates qui le passionnent*], may be disheartened because it will not have been able, right away, to move on [*parce qu'il n'aura pu pas tout d'abord passer outre*]. That is a disadvantage against which I can do nothing, except to forewarn and forearm those readers who care for truth.⁷

Like the many *Aesops* that open with the fable of the cock which finds a pearl but does not know what to do with it, *Capital* begins with a warning about failing to move from knowing directly on to doing, and about the temporal structure of the desired articulation. In reading, time will tell . . . but time to read is always also time to stop reading. Against the eagerness of a reading that wants to skip over the interpretation to get to the change, that wants to know how to relate general principles to immediate questions, Marx advises that articulation takes patience. Impatience frustrates reading, and leads to change without interpretation, passionately immediate—and thus unprincipled—answers. But the demand for patience can generate a discouraged or rejecting reader and thus no reading—and no change—at all. Arduous reading always threatens to become impossible; driven by the zeal to relate, the reading public may find itself in a bind, unable, *tout d'abord*, to get out of the difficulty of that very relation and thus unable to go on reading. If reading, from the start, promises the possibility of this inability— not just the inability to make the articulation between general principle and immediate question, but, more radically, the inability to move beyond that inability, since what is in question is reading's possibility in the first place—then reading *Capital* can be no more, and no less, than an effort and a chance . . . the chance of the preface's well-known next sentence. "There is no royal road for science, and only those who do not fear the fatiguing climb of its steep paths have a chance of reaching its luminous summits."

There is no road for reading, no path or method: simply the effort and the fatigue of the difficult chance. As chance, reading and its inability defy calculation in advance, refuse prediction. If *Capital*'s French public "will have been unable to move on," worries the preface, the text itself is nevertheless equally powerless before this incapacity. "Against this I can do nothing," Marx writes, nothing except write the preface in which the inability is thematized. Faced with the prospect of a text that is discouraging at best and disabling at worst, that rigorously threatens its own impossibility, the preface suggests itself as the possible circumscription of the threats it faces. "Against this I can do nothing, except to forewarn and forearm those readers who care for truth." Readers are thus forearmed with nothing, nothing other than this warning, nothing other than the negative knowledge that their impatience for a conclusion and eagerness to connect general with immediate may disable their reading. Armed with this would-be prophylactic knowledge about the inabilities of knowledge, the reading public is freed to take its chances. The chance is the chance of difficulty, the chance that something (unexpected) might happen, that something (new) might be learned. Reading in this sense, if it happens at all, happens only in the encounter with difficulty and without guarantees.[8]

Marx never underestimated this difficulty: "Every beginning is difficult, holds in all science. The understanding of the first chapter, especially the section that contains the analysis of commodities, will therefore make for the greatest difficulty" (89/11), begins the third paragraph of the first German preface. It continues, after a justification hinging on the "power of abstraction" (to which we will return), by not quite excusing itself from its own indictment: "With the exception of the section on the value form, therefore, this book cannot stand accused as being difficult to understand. I assume naturally a reader who wants to learn something new and thus to think for him- or herself" (90/12). Only in the exposure to this difficulty, in the exhaustion of available knowledge and ways of learning more, might something new happen. If the understanding subject has named the site in which difficulty has always been overcome, this thinking called reading (something new) might mark the troubling of the very self for which we (want to) think. One can only learn this lesson if one reads—if one can. As Marx says of *Capital* a paragraph further, *de te fabula narratur*!

Monster, Carrier: Only in Use

All beginnings are difficult. The first two sentences of *Capital* read as follows: "The wealth of those societies in which the capitalist mode of production prevails appears as [*erscheint als*; *s'annonce comme*] a 'monstrous collection of commodities [*ungeheuere Waren-*

sammlung],' the single commodity as its elemental form. Our investigation therefore begins with the analysis of the commodity" (125/49/43). Cutting off the quotation quickly, we can begin rather telegraphically. The matter at issue is the appearance or self-announcement of something *as* something else, the rhetorical structure of simile or metaphor (*als*; *comme*): semblance, shine, simulation, or dissimulation. In societies where the capitalist mode of production prevails, something (economic) shows itself by hiding itself, by announcing itself as something else or in another form.

Here, what shape or form does capitalist wealth take on in its self-presentation or self-dissimulation? Wealth appears as . . . a monster: something immense,[9] colossal, but also a thing compounded of elements from different forms, wild but not natural, certainly not domesticated, simply thrown together into a heap, grown beyond the control of its creators. The *Ungeheuer* is a *riesenhaftes, häßliches Fabeltier* (a gigantic, hideous animal of fable, says the *Wahrig Deutsches Wörterbuch*),[10] etymologically, something lacking the security of a settlement or the common comfort of a home. Something(s) assembled or collected, but in such a way that the parts do not add up to a whole: nothing but parts, unnatural and uncommon, *démesuré*. Aberrant, deviant, the monstrous is the form of the appearance of wealth, the way it signifies itself, as something(s) else. The figure of this monstrosity, living and dead (the *Wahrig* links *ungeheuer* to *unheimlich*, unhomely monstrosity to ghostly recurrence), haunts this chapter, appearing, as here, when least expected and out of all proportion.

This "monstrous collection" is also a quotation, a self-presentation from elsewhere ("Karl Marx, *Zur Kritik der Politischen Ökonomie*, Berlin 1859, S. 3," says the footnote), and if we follow the lead we find not just the two quoted words but virtually the same sentence: "The wealth of bourgeois society, at first sight, presents itself as an *ungeheuere Warensammlung*."[11] The immediate question is, Why? Why the gesture of quoting oneself, from an earlier and surpassed draft, for two words, with the apparatus of quotation marks, footnote, etc.? The quotation itself functions as a monster or a ghost, an uncanny visitor accumulated from another text. And it depends on a structural condition of words—they can be reproduced, mindlessly and mechanically reproduced—which acts as if they were nothing but commodities: to be accumulated, moved and removed to and from contexts, delayed and relayed between texts only to be grafted or inserted into some other text, transferred like (*als*) property or the mechanical limb (a forearm, let's say; after all, forewarned is forearmed) on a monster.

Of what is the monster composed? Marx names the unit or elemental form of this unruly collection the *commodity* (*Ware*). *Capital*'s investigation, its under-taking (*Untersuchen*, probing beneath the dissimulative appearance of the form) "begins with" the disarticulation of the monster and "the analysis of the commodity," the dissolution of wealth's appearance into *Elementarformen* and then their reductive decomposition. It is this "method of analysis" to which Marx attributes all the interpretive difficulty in the preface, and the first chapter relentlessly pursues its destructuring mission—both as method and as theme. The commodity as such *is* analyzed, and not merely by Marx.

The initial terms of a reading can now be gathered together as an immediate question. What links the structure by which one thing appears as another, by which something is substituted for something else or transferred to somewhere else, with (1) the advent of monstrosity or haunting, and (2) the movement of analysis or reduction?

Without answering, *Capital* begins the analytic decomposition of the commodity. First of all, prior to all other determinations, at its barest and simplest, a commodity is "an external object, a thing" (125/49). The commodity is a way of doing things with things, an interpretation of some thing—but to begin with, it is nothing less or more than a thing. This kind of thing is a thing for humans, for their use or consumption, physical or imaginary, immediate or derived. Simply, the thing is useful, which is to say, it satisfies or appeases human needs, needy humans, through its properties. Marx proposes, though, that things—when they are useful—are not simple, not just one thing: "every useful thing, such as iron, paper, etc., is to be considered under a doubled point of view"

(125/49). The analysis of *Capital* consists in this double viewpoint, in the interpretation as duplicity of a difference which inhabits every useful thing. The manner of this auto-division or -duplication of the thing is both the target and the mode of the analysis. It aims to decompose the *als*-structure (in different vocabularies: appearance, simile, simulation) that gives rise to both quotations and monsters—a certain mutation, othering, in the thing that allows it to be analyzed from (at least) two viewpoints. "Quality and quantity" (125/49) make up the two aspects of the analytic point: (1) what a thing is, its properties or elements, understood as a matter of what can be done with it, what its uses are or could be; and (2) how much of it there is, what it is when it is measured. Accounting for the articulation of quality and quantity, or the conversion of the one into the other, which is to say, accounting for how quality can be determined reliably enough to allow different ones to be compared and measured, is the task of Marx's analysis. In this sense, at least, we can say that Marx poses the "transformation problem," or that Marxism is a theory of change. But we cannot say that either transformation or change is anything reliable.

What exactly quality and property mean is not immediately evident, but taking their meaning for granted (interpreting them within a metaphysics of substance and presence) has been the rule in most readings of *Capital.* Marx begins not with the thing's essence but with its use: to the extent that a thing can be used, it can be seen (first viewpoint) as a "use-value [*Gebrauchswert*]" (126/50), something that can be inscribed in a differential system of valuation, distinguished or specified, based on the use to which it is put.[12] The term *Gebrauchswert* is not an easy word to read in *Capital,* and its difficulty troubles not only the text's interpreters but the text itself.[13] Not that its definition is complicated; indeed, Marx is matter of fact about the value of use. "The use-value is actualized or realizes itself [*verwirklicht sich*] only in use or consumption" (126/50).[14] Marx does not say that every thing, because it is itself and itself alone, is different from every other thing, but rather that a use-value is and only is the use of a thing when and as it is used (*nur im Gebrauch*). This is to say, a thing has as many use-values as it has uses, all of them different and even in principle irreducibly so. It does not imply an infinity of uses—one cannot do everything with anything—but simply a structural openness to new contexts.

Rather than limiting the thing to or determining it as an essence or a set of fixed properties, the category radically de-limits or opens up the thing for different uses. As soon as the proper (value) of the thing is said to be its use(s), making it entirely dependent on the particularities of its context(s), whatever self-identity it might pretend to have across those different uses is ruptured, emptied out into its possible iterations. "Such a thing is a whole of many properties, and can thus be useful in different ways." The sentence could just as easily be reversed: because it can be used differently, it has many properties, but nothing proper. History, says Marx, is the history of these "different ways and thus the manifold ways of using the thing" (125/49–50). This potential for radical differentiation or diversity of things as use-values not only distinguishes them one from another but fragments any particular thing "itself" into a multiplicity of uses. So it is tautological when Marx states a few paragraphs later that, "as use-values, commodities are above all different qualities" (128/52), but the unstated corollary must be: different even from "themselves." Being used differently splits the thing from itself, mani-folds it onto or out of itself, since use is all there is, "really." This reusability principle puts the wholeness of the thing or the propriety of its properties into some question, or at least limits its "unity" to the accumulated traces it leaves in its manifold contexts of use.[15] The thing's thingliness is not in doubt—it is certainly not nothing—but the fact of its realization in use exposes it to the possibility of all sorts of trouble. If its "usefulness does not hang in mid-air," but is rather "limited by the properties of the commodity-body [*Warenkörper*]" (126/50), then this used body is always threatened with the possibilities of dismemberment, of being torn limb from limb and scattered like Orpheus, or of grafting, of being combined and recombined in some monstrous accumulation of body parts.[16]

But using things is not the most interesting or pressing thing to do with them. *Capital* must confront an economic fact, the fact of economy as such: use-values, different as they are, are exchanged as well as used or consumed. Use-values "constitute the material [*stofflichen*] content of wealth" (126/50), but, no matter how material it is, how is something that comes into being only in use converted to something that can be not used but accumulated and exchanged? Immediately following the difficult sentence defining use-values as realized only in use, Marx pauses—and unleashes the only term that poses more reading difficulties than "use-value." "In the form of society to be considered by us, they [use-values] also constitute the material carriers of—exchange-value" (126/50). It seems that use-values, as material, carry—support or transport— the possibility of being deported or transferred elsewhere. The *stofflich* character of the thing as use-value seems paradoxically tied to the possibility of its materiality being evacuated in exchange, in the act that appropriates it not for use or consumption but for dispropriation, not to realize it but to transfer it elsewhere. It holds, carries, its "own" vacancy; it holds nothing but a place, the site of a possible relocation. As *soutien matériel* (44) of exchange-value, the thing's use-value has all the materiality of a marker, of the empty "body" as its "properties" are erased to allow it to bear an inscription. How this effacement happens, and what a "carrier" looks like, are the questions that obsess the remainder of Marx's first chapter.

Possibility of Exchange, Power of Abstraction

Exchange-value "first of all appears as . . . the relation [*Verhältnis*]," and of necessity a quantitative one, the "proportion" (126/50) in which use-values exchange for one another. But exchange can only take place on the basis of something common to the things (use-values) being exchanged, something shared that allows them to be compared, measured, allows the proportion or relation to be calculated. The general principle of exchange, as Marx writes it, holds that "in two different things, there exists . . . something common [*ein Gemeinsames*]. . . . The two things must therefore be like [*gleich*] a third, which in itself is neither one nor the other" (127/51). When things are exchanged as commodities,[17] they are related to each other not as use-values but as exchange-values, in terms of something else. This shared third term, the axis of similarity, enables a comparison, makes the different uses or things commensurable, relatable as quantities of the same thing rather than different uses or qualities.

Needless to say, the exchange-value of a thing could never belong to it as a property, even as a use; since exchange *is* depropriation, an "immanent exchange-value is a *contradictio in adjecto*" (126/51). But, more rigorously, is not exchange-value as such a contradiction in terms? Can the difference in use be regulated or controlled in any way that would allow exchange—the relation or proportion "in which use-values of one kind exchange with [*gegen*] use-values of another kind" (126/50)—to take place without sacrificing the determining characteristic of use-value, namely, its radical contextuality or heterogeneity? Here *Capital* meets its structuring question, the question of how exchange, as such, is possible. How can a system—and doing this defines an economic system—put radically different things (uses) into relation with each other when they have nothing in common, since they are defined, acquire a certain identity or value, only in being used or consumed? How can things that do not have the stability to define themselves as things outside of their use, that differ as much within themselves as between themselves, be submitted to the rule of a common system of measurement? How can these uses be exchanged? How is exchange possible?

The radicality of *Capital*'s analysis becomes evident with its answers. First, exchange is a matter of *substitution*, of one thing standing in for another, on the basis of something similar or equal. If exchange is to occur, this substitution is a necessity: things "must . . . , as exchange-values, be substitutable or replaceable [*ersetzbar*] for each other" (127/51). This requires that the thing be put into relation even with itself (its uses), since it can be exchanged for many different things, which therefore must be mutually substitutable; by virtue of the mediation implied by substitution, the various exchange-values of a thing "express something alike or equal [*ein Gleiches*]."[18] If a thing can be exchanged for many different other things, then its exchange-value must be only a "'form of expression'" (127/51) of something else, something like the thing-itself. The substitutability of exchange-values, organized around an axis of similarity, which must occur in exchange, is thus shown to depend on a previous and just as necessary operation, effected on the level of the useful thing, called "reduction." No substitution without reduction, without the reduction of the "manifold ways of using the thing." For the relation or equation (*Gleichnung*) to happen, the things exchanged or substituted "must therefore be like or equal to [*gleich*] a third, which in and for itself is neither the one nor the other. Each of them, insofar as it is exchange-value, must thus be reducible to this third [*muß also auf dies Dritte reduzierbar sein*]" (127/51). Where the thing was, the third must be.

The reduction—which we might as well call, echoing the first sentence, the analysis, the decomposition or destructuration of the thing into its most elementary components (if there are any)—ought to reveal, as if by distillation or purification, the common core which exchangeable things share, the likeness on the basis of which they can be put into relation, measured proportionally.[19] What we can only call a double rhetorical gesture must take place here: the substitution of something for something else, based on resemblance and thus structured like simile or metaphor, can only occur on the condition that a prior reduction has occurred, within the things exchanged, by which one "part" of the thing has been made to stand in for the "whole." We know this structure as synecdoche, and *Capital* suggests that its part-for-whole substitution is presupposed within any thing as the condition of its exchange with something other. What is this whole? Use-value? The strictly contextual, singular, pragmatic difference which defines value only in use? Can use provide the basic core of commensurability?

As use-values, things are completely different, from each other and from themselves, different with every use or context (rendering even the term "themselves" problematic). Marx repeatedly insists on the *necessity* of the reduction, but for its condition of possibility, things are a little more difficult. A hint earlier in the chapter might have seemed to suggest that the thingly properties of the thing could provide the third term: the thing's status as a use-*value* is not simply ideal or spiritual, as we read, and does not make it nothing or leave it hanging in the air, but is, rather, dependent on "the properties of the commodity-body" (126/50). Do these properties of the commodity as a body make exchange possible, provide the irreducible ground or the basic part on which economy is built? Simply, no. "This something common cannot be a geometrical, physical, chemical or other natural property of commodities. Their bodily properties come into consideration only to the extent that they make them useful, as use-values" (127/51), and have no role in exchange. Things are bodies only in use, not *a priori* or as some kind of essential base. Where exchanging is the task, the commodity-body functions as heterogeneously as its manifold uses. There is no property common to things, no use, not even being a thing (nor, as Marx will show, the labor required to bring them into the economic field). Because use-values are at least as different from one another as things are from each other, the common term could not be a property of the thing as a body. The question of the possibility of exchange takes another step backwards: if what is common cannot be a natural property or a use, then how is it produced or where does it come from? *Capital* repeats: How is exchange possible?

Marx answers—in the spirit of the necessity on which he has become accustomed to insisting—with a single word, *abstraction*, calls it "obvious," and says that it simply happens, regardless of its possibility. "It is obvious [*augenscheinlich*] that abstraction from their use-value is precisely what characterizes the exchange relation of commodities" (127/51–52). Moore and Aveling translated *Abstraktion* as "total abstraction"[20]—abusive but correct, since the operation must be totalizing if it is to be at all: the radical heterogeneity of use-values must be reduced, and that reduction or overcoming is to be accomplished only by an equally radical ("total") abstraction, which massively and systematically effaces the differentiation of every use-value, every thing. The difference between every use (property, thing) *must* be dissolved by the force of abstraction. And every exchange relation is characterized by (performs) this abstraction. In the face of difference, *augenschein-lich*, abstraction is required, even if it is not necessarily possible (which accounts, in a certain sense, for the proliferation of the word "must" over these pages: in the face of impossibility, necessity imposes itself).

Abstraction is the erasure of difference in the service of likeness or equality (*Gleichheit*): "as old Barbon says, 'there is no difference or distinction in things of equal value.' " Abstraction converts the thing from use-value to exchange-value, transforms it "within" into something exchangeable. "As exchange-values, [things] can be only different quantities, and thus contain not an atom [*kein Atom*] of use-value" (128/52). The abstraction is as radical as the differences were irreducible. If it happens, the exchange of commodities must "first" erase use-values at the subatomic level, allowing the emergence of the desired third term, but what could survive the utter eradication of the difference—difference in use, difference in quality—that defines use-values as such? What is left over if the things which are (to be) exchanged on the basis of it (something alike, *gleich*, or common) "do not contain an atom of use-value?" The thing, obviously, has been emptied out, and what it was is gone. "If we abstract from its use-value, we abstract also from the bodily constituents and forms that make it into a use-value. It is no longer table or house or yarn or even a useful thing. All of its sensible attributes are extinguished [*ausgelöscht*]" (128/52). The subatomic is use-less, thing-less, and sense-less. Nothing—at least, no thing—is left, it seems, certainly not the fact that things are products of labor. Marx simply dismisses the idea that the leftover might be some attribute of its having been worked on. "Nor is it any longer the product of joining or masonry or spinning or any determined productive labor," because, first, labor is just as particular and singular as use-value and, second, it is precisely that differentiation which is made to disappear *by* the abstraction. "The differentiated concrete forms of labor vanish [*verschwinden*], they differ from each other no longer, but are all reduced to the same [*gleiche*] human labor, abstract human labor" (128/52)—which is only to say that under the pressure of the abstraction necessitated by exchange, people and their labor become commodities too.[21] (This humanity will return).

What is required of this abstraction? If it is to make exchange possible, what does it need to accomplish, and how does it do it? To answer these questions, we need to look more carefully at its structure and attempt to distinguish it from the terms it has come to replace: similitude and reduction. One hint which may help has been lying around since *Capital*'s first sentence. Pursuing Marx's footnote to *Zur Kritik*, the sentence following the phrase quoted from that earlier text reads: "Every commodity, however, has a two-fold aspect: use-value and exchange-value." The footnote there refers the reader to Aristotle's *Politics*, and quotes: "Of everything which we possess there are two uses: . . . one is the proper, and the other the improper or secondary use of it. For example, a shoe is used for wear and is used for exchange."[22] In the same way, a word has its proper meaning(s) and its figurative or derived senses, relations in which it crosses over with other meanings. The figurative ones, it is said, consist in exchanging what is proper to one word with another word, in substituting, borrowing, trading, carrying, transporting, even stealing properties. But these exchanges depend on the presence of an axis of substitution, a common term across which the crossing is articulated. Different tropes are defined by the different axes of comparison according to which their substitutions are organized.

Marx had first seemed to propose that economic exchange was simply a matter of metaphor, of exchange based on resemblance or similitude (*Gleichheit*). But in order to produce this similarity in the absence of any stable or reliable set of properties common (similar) to all things, the analysis was obliged to backtrack and propose that a certain "reduction" occurred within the diversity that marks things as use-values, so as to bring them down to some one thing. This reduction was structured like a synecdoche, a part-for-whole substitution. Yet no common part could be determined either, and the analysis stepped further back to reveal the operation of what it called "abstraction."[23]

What is the structure of abstraction? Paul de Man has argued that, at least for Condillac, abstractions are "formed by ceasing to think of the properties by which things are distinguished in order to think only of those qualities in which they agree"; it is a structure that is "precisely that of metaphor in its classical definition (i.e. substitution based on resemblance)."[24] The rhetorician Fontanier, though, in *Les Figures du discours*, thought abstraction was a synecdoche, a substitution based not on resemblance but on "comprehension."[25] "Taking the abstract for the concrete" is a synecdochal exchange in that it "designates an object by the name of another object together with which it forms a set, a whole, . . . such that the existence or the idea of one finds itself comprised in the existence or idea of the other" (87).

Evidently, neither of these definitions will do, since abstraction has arrived on the scene in order to accomplish what resisted the efforts of, precisely, metaphor and synecdoche. For exchange to take place, some axis of commonality or channel of communication between different things and within different uses must be invented or opened or breached. Something like abstraction is supposed to do it.

Ghosts of an Analysis, or Humanity

So we can return to the guiding question: How is exchange possible? Obviously it is characterized by abstraction. Does the abstraction occur on the basis of something besides the thing or its uses and its makers? What is responsible for exchange? Marx's explanation is curious in its temporality, as it "finally" seems to presuppose that what must happen (reduction) has already happened (abstraction) in order to let it happen (likeness or equality). After the fact of the exchange, we can see what will have obviously had to happen. The answer goes as follows.

If everything sensible is extinguished, and labor vanishes, "let us look at the residue of the labor-products." The impossible abstraction occurs, does its duty, only to the extent that it leaves a remainder, a *Residuum* or a *résidu* (128/52/46). Marx undertakes to name this leftover of total abstraction. What remains after the radical reduction of difference, after the vanishing of all "atoms" of use-value or productive labor? Its name is ghost: *gespenstige Gegenständlichkeit*, spectral, haunting, surviving objectivity. "There is nothing of them left over but this very same ghostly objectivity, a mere jelly of undifferentiated human labor." This phantom makes possible the relation between (or within) things or uses, grants the common axis of similarity hitherto unavailable, precisely because it is a ghost and no longer a thing or a labor. Once abstracted, as Marx's French text put it, "each one of them completely resembles the other. They all have the same phantomatic reality [*une même réalité fantomatique*]. Metamorphosed into identical *sublimés*, samples of the same indistinct labor" (46). In the rigor of the abstraction, only ghosts survive. The point is to exchange them.[26]

The timing of these ghosts is spectacular. They return just in time to make possible the operation that produces them, that leaves them as its congealed residue. Because they resemble one another, as all ghosts do, having no phenomenal or sensible features by which to distinguish themselves, the operation of which they are the remnant can finally occur. Thanks to their resemblance, the conditions of exchange are met—the very exchange that leaves them, atomless, behind. Without ghosts, no exchange, since neither resemblance (similitude) nor comprehension (synecdoche) could be taken for granted, given the volatility of use-value: which is why Marx turned to abstraction. No common term could be found that belonged properly to the commodity as a thing or a use-value: which is why Marx turned to ghosts. Abstraction leaves the ghosts as its remainder. But the abstraction *is* the exchange ("it is obvious that abstraction from their use-value is precisely what characterizes the exchange relation of commodities"). Something happens in order to let exchange happen, but it seems to happen *in* the exchange itself.

The detour through the rhetoric of tropes now turns out to have been essential. Is this kind of substitution structured like a typical trope. Is it, like metaphor or synecdoche, a symmetrical crossing of properties? Or does the spectral remnant suggest that a certain asymmetry is built into the so-called exchange, since the prior existence of properties or an axis of commonality by which they are to be related is what is most questionable here? The balanced and closed chiasmus of the trope seems to open out of itself temporally and spatially in the abstraction: the ghost is the ineffaceable excess, the oddly material if non-sensible "jelly" of a remnant that resists incorporation, and the condition of possibility for the operation that must have already happened in order to leave it behind. The maneuver succeeds (as it does all the time) only to the extent that the commodity as ghost is a figure for the most rigorous of reductions, the radical elimination of all traces of use-value, with one exception: the residue of the abstraction itself. That enables the thing to survive, as a ghost, and not just disappear, and this residue serves as the "common something" on which exchange can be based because it marks, however negatively, *all* commodities with the trace of resemblance. What remains difficult to decide is where the ghosts come (back) from. Were they there already, or did they come into being in the exchange? The operation works to the extent that this is the difference that cannot be told. What can be told, now, in the realm of ghosts, is this: "All these things now tell us is that in their production . . . human labor is piled up" (128/52).

A specter is haunting this analysis, the specter of humanity. If exchange is possible, is it thanks to humanity? Or more precisely, to the human labor embedded in commodities as the source of their value? Certainly this view has been attributed to *Capital,* especially in the encounter with sentences like this one, a paragraph after the ghost: "a use-value or a good has value only because abstract human labor is objectified or materialized in it" (129/53). But before endorsing or condemning some labor theory of value, we need to ask about the status not so much of labor but of the abstraction, the abstraction which is humanity.

Much later in the first chapter, Marx returns to the question of the possible impossibility of exchange, long after it should have been laid to rest by the ghosts or the jelly. In accounting for the development of money, Marx has been led back to Aristotle, the first analyst of value, who in the *Nicomachean Ethics* argues that exchange, in principle, has no basis. How is exchange possible?[27] What common term could there be between different objects? If, in Aristotle's example, a house is to be exchanged for (is worth as much as) five beds, then the one must be "made qualitatively like [*gleichgesetzt*]" the other, but since they are phenomenally or "sensibly different things," the two "could not be relatable to each other as commensurable magnitudes without such an essential likeness [*Wesengleichheit*]." And that's impossible. Aristotle concludes, quotes Marx, that "'there can be no exchange without likeness [*Gleichheit*], and no likeness without commensurability. . . . It is, however, in truth impossible [*unmöglich*] for such heterogeneous things to be commensurable, that is, qualitatively alike. This making-alike [*Gleichsetzung*] can only be something foreign to the true nature of the things, and thus only a makeshift for practical purposes [*Notbehelf für das praktische Bedürfnis*]'" (151/73–74).[28] In a certain sense, Marx agrees. The analysis has shown that exchange has no secure, transcendental foundation, no condition of possibility in the strong sense, but only what is called the power of abstraction and its residue the ghosts. Yet it—abstraction, exchange—happens, even if it is foreign (*etwas Fremdes*), especially to the "true nature" and the "sensible" particularity of things. If there is a difficulty it is with use; nature and phenomenality barely get into the act, certainly not as ontological impediments. Aristotle argues that exchange is purely pragmatic, that all things are likened or measured simply by the fact that they are in demand. Demand's signifier is money, which is "why money is called *nomisma* (customary currency), because it does not exist by nature but by custom (*nomos*)."[29] But the fact of conventionality does not explain the convention. Why was Aristotle unable to determine *das Gleiche*—he says, quotes Marx, that it "cannot, in truth, exist"—and forced to abandon the investigation of value without naming it but only marking its practical place? Marx supplies the missing name: "And it is—human labor" (151/74). Aristotle, though, was "unable to read" this—strictly speaking, unable. "The secret of value-expression, the likeness and equivalence of all [kinds of] labor, because and insofar as they are human labor in general, could not be deciphered [*entziffert*] until the concept of human similarity or equality had already acquired the permanence of a popular prejudice [*Volksvorurteil*]" (152/74). This would seem to explain things simply: until everyone believes they are the same as everyone else, no one, not even Aristotle, would or could think to consider them comparable. When humanist enlightenment has arrived, a human(-labor) theory of value becomes possible to read. But Marx does not say this. The next sentence ruins the humanist assumptions at their deepest level: "But this [the popular prejudice of the concept of common humanity] is *first possible only in a society where the commodity form is the general form* of the labor-product" (152/74; emphasis added).

To summarize this extraordinary move: exchange is possible because abstraction reveals the common humanity surviving in the things exchanged. Aristotle thought it was strictly impossible and only conventional because the concept of a common humanity was not available to him. Humanity itself arrives only with the domination of the commodity form, which it makes possible.

Or rather, it remains impossible, and it happens all the time: *Notbehelf für das praktische Bedürfnis*, emergency placeholder, or more precisely, prejudice. Before there can be the judgment or the justice that balances and exchanges, there is the prejudice (*Vorurteil*) that renders the parties or things commensurable: before the law of exchange, prejudice. So if there is humanity, it is as a popular prejudice, and if exchange occurs, in spite of its impossibility, it is thanks to the popular prejudice of *menschlichen Gleichheit*—itself an effect of the abstracting, eviscerating, spectralizing exchange of commodities. Which means that another name for *gespenstig* would be *menschlich*, and vice versa. Here, all humans are ghosts. Humanity as such, empty and abstract, alike and equal (*gleich*), is indistinguishable from the commodity.

As Althusser wrote, Marxism is not a humanism, but a "theoretical anti-humanism."[30] Marxism is the critical analysis of capitalism precisely insofar as capitalism is a humanism. Humanity, the abstraction, is the ghostly residue that names the pragmatic necessity of likeness in exchange. To be alike is to be abstract, which is to say, to be a ghost—to be human, or a commodity.[31]

Marx says as much and spells out its political stakes, many pages later as the second part of *Capital* comes to a close.

> The sphere of . . . commodity exchange . . . is in fact a true Eden of innate human rights [*Menschenrechte*]. Here alone rule Freedom, Equality [*Gleichheit*], Property, and Bentham. Freedom! Because buyer and seller of a commodity, e.g., labor-power, are determined only by their own free will. They contract as free persons, who are equal before the law. . . . Equality! Because they relate to each other only as commodity-owners, and they exchange equivalent for equivalent. (280/189–90)

Thus, Gayatri Spivak has argued, "there is no *philosophical* injustice in capitalism."[32] The commodity structure is the ideal of justice as fairness, as balance, symmetry, reciprocity, between humans as well as things. "Human rights" means that, before the law of exchange, humans meet, like things, as equal (*gleich*), free, responsible . . . as abstract.

At least epistemologically. When abstractions meet, though, knowledge is not the only force involved. When capitalist meets worker—for example, on the question of the length of the working day—the symmetry of balance provides no guarantees, and the exchange is opened onto political struggle: "There is here therefore an antinomy, of right and against right, both equally bearing the seal of the law of commodity-exchange [*beide gleichmäßig durch das Gesetz des Warenaustausches besiegelt*]. Between equal rights, force [*Gewalt*] decides" (344/249).[33]

Look-alikes, or *Augenschein*

To recapitulate: *Capital* performs the analytic decomposition, the analysis or abstraction, of the system of commodity exchange into its basic unit and of that unit into the duplicity of use-value ("quality") and exchange-value ("quantity"). As use-value, the thing differs irreducibly from everything else, including other uses of the "same" thing. But the thing carries, bears the burden of, exchange-value, which is to say, it transports the possibility of being transported, converted into, or traded for something else. Yet nothing immanent in the thing as thing makes such exchange possible—there is no *Ding-an-sich* in exchange, neither use nor nature. Some mediation "must" intervene, some redefinition or metamorphosis within the things that provides the axis of resemblance or comparison (*Vergleich*) around which they may exchange. This preparatory operation within, this *perestroika* or *Gleichsschaltung* at the interior of the thing, is called abstraction. It "characterizes" the exchange. In abstraction—the operation that readies the things for exchange, that makes them exchangeable, and that exchanges them—not an atom of use-value remains. Nor is anything left of the labor that has produced them, no thing but a strange "residue." There is nothing left over but ghosts (*gespenstige Gegenständlichkeit*), as practical possibility—or should we say, as necessity.

This haunting can only be thought as the difficult (simultaneous and impossible) movement of remembering and forgetting, inscribing and erasing, the singular or the different. Difference is the reason for economy: were things not different, there would be no possible interest in exchange. "Were each of the things not qualitatively different use-values and hence not the products of qualitatively different useful labors, they would be utterly incapable of encountering each other as commodities." Exchanging something for itself would be tautology, not economy. "Heterogeneous use-values" (132/56) are the condition of the system; no substitution of identicals, only of different things in differing uses.

But this difference, the *raison d'être* of the system, is also its target. "La différence de leurs valeurs d'usage est éliminée, de même disparaît" (52): "Just as in the [exchange] values coat and linen there is abstraction from the difference between their use-values, so in the labors represented in these values, from the difference between their useful forms" (135/59). Only when this abstraction occurs can things come into relation as (exchange) values (136/60), an abstraction from use-value, as from human labor. The only "labor theory of value"[34] here reads as follows: "it is in this property of being similar or abstract [*gleich . . . oder abstrakt*] human labor that [labor] forms commodity's value" (137/61) and *only* insofar as it is abstract(ed) and no longer particular labor but its ghostly residue. But the emphasis is on "human" rather than "labor," which is to say, alike because abstract. This is the definition of humanity—abstract, similar, spectral.

This *Doppelcharakter* of the commodity requires the ghosting of an abstraction—different and alike, used and exchanged. Insofar as they are exchanged, commodities have no materiality. "In direct opposition to the coarsely sensible objectivity of the commodity body, not an atom of natural material enters into their objectivity as values." It is indeed ghostly. "You may twist and turn [*drehen und wenden; tourner et retourner*] a single commodity as you wish; it remains ungraspable as a value-thing" (138/62/55).

That (commodity) exchange is not natural but social is a commonplace, but the self-evidence of the politicizing cliché obscures its force: the analytic decomposition of the thing of value suggests that exchange is not simply possible, that the entry of different things-uses into exchange relations has no transcendental guarantee or basis at all. Exchange is at best pragmatic and thus aberrant, seeking out differences in order to eliminate them, recalling them to oblivion. A coat is not a house, and they have nothing in common, just as Achilles is not a lion. Their substitution only occurs when the uses or things are disappeared and returned as ghosts, different but alike to the extent that they are all *unfassbar* . . . or, more precisely, all words.

Although it receives its sharpest thematization only in the final section on fetishism, the analytic necessity of this linguistic turn is at stake throughout the third section of the first chapter. Measuring carefully the implications of the theory of the doubled character and the ghosting abstraction, Marx suggests that the ghost means, paradoxically, that commodity exchange is not something visible, not sensory, not something to see or feel. It has nothing sensible or phenomenal [*sinnlich*] about it, nothing "real" as philosophy or political economy has interpreted reality (within oppositions like matter/spirit, essence/appearance, real/ideal, etc.).[35] Exchange is a matter of signification, expression, substitution, and hence something that must be read. The like-ness of the ghosts is invisible, untouchable, ungraspable by human hands. So when two things, as value, "look alike," the emphasis falls on the like rather than the look. It is obvious but worth emphasizing: the economy is a system of differences or relations, relations which precede the things they relate to the extent that they are values. When things are exchanged they are not exchanged as things but as values, values within a system that traffics only in abstractions, idealizations, prejudices, *and* their ciphers or markers. Ghost: *Geist* and *Gespenst* at once.

Value is always value in a relation, in an exchange. (Recall that early in the chapter Marx stops writing "exchange-value" and substitutes simply "value.") "The simplest value-relation is evidently that of a commodity to a single heterogeneous commodity: . . . x commodity A = y commodity B" (139/62–63). The relation makes the value happen, since neither commodity brings its value with it, independent of the other. One thing uses the other as the medium of its expression as value; "the value of the linen can therefore be expressed only relatively, i.e., in another commodity" (140/63). The relation is structured as something like a dialectical staging of self-recognition through contradiction and mediation (expression) in an other (recall the example of Peter and Paul). (Exchange) value emerges only relatively, without (and as a result of the evisceration of) anything intrinsic, absolute, especially sensible or phenomenal. "In the value-relation of one commodity to another, its value-character emerges or steps forth through its own relation to the other commodity" (141–42/65). Commodities relate not as things but as values, ghostly or jellied abstractions: "it is only as value that [the linen] is related to the coat as equal in value [*Gleichwertiges*] or exchangeable with it." Nothing sensible happens here, but simply the transformation by substitution of values. Thus Marx can write that "weaving, insofar as it weaves value [which is no sensible activity], has nothing to distinguish it from tailoring" (141/64).

What allows exchange to happen is neither the labors nor the uses nor the things themselves but their abstracts, abstractions, operating as tokens (practical necessities) in a relation. Being alike is being abstract. And in relation, one thing counts as the "qualitative equal [*Gleiches*]" of the other, "as a thing of the same nature, *because it is a value*" (142/66; emphasis added). Relation is abstraction, and the "expression" or equation of one unit in the other, accomplished in the event of the abstraction, is unavoidably a matter of signification or figuration—to be read: "The coat, the body of the coat-commodity, is sheer use-value. A coat as such no more expresses value than does the first piece of linen we came across. This proves only that, within its value-relation to the linen, the coat signifies more [*mehr bedeutet*; *signifie plus*] than it does outside it, just as some men signify more when inside a gold-braided uniform than they do otherwise." (Note that the example, the figure of the coat as commodity, has begun to slip into something more literal here.) Marx presents the event of the relation, the signifying encounter, as a drama of mutual recognition, a little fable of things looking at—and like—each other and thus saying I = I thanks to the entrance of the other. But the recognition cannot, by definition, be an (aesthetic, sensory) experience; the only experience of exchange is the extinguishing of all that is phenomenal. You can twist and turn the ghosts, but you'll see or feel or hear or touch nothing of their value.

> And in the value-relation with the linen, the coat counts therefore only under this aspect, as embodied value, as value-body [*Wertkörper*]. Despite its buttoned-up appearance, the linen recognizes in it [the coat] a beautiful kindred value-soul. *C'est le côté platonique de l'affaire.* Nevertheless, the coat cannot represent value toward the linen unless value, for the latter, simultaneously assumes the form of a coat. . . . As use-value, the linen is a sensibly different thing from the coat; as [exchange] value, it is "coat-like or -identical [*Rochgleiches*]," and therefore looks like a coat [*sieht daher aus wie ein Rock*]. (143/66/58)

This appearance, this look, cannot be seen; if it were capable of being perceived phenomenally, if it could be seen, it wouldn't be a value. Value is a signification and must be read, a purely verbal "like." This is what Marx calls the "language of commodities [*der Warensprache*]," the discourse of likeness-without-likeness engaged in by commodities as soon as they enter into the abstracting-ghosting relation of exchange.

> We see then, that everything our analysis of the value of commodities previously told us is repeated by the linen itself, as soon as it enters [*tritt*] into association with another commodity, the coat. Only it reveals its thoughts in a language with which it alone is familiar, the language of commodities. . . . In order to say that its sublime value-objectivity differs from its stiff and starchy body, it says that value looks like a coat, and therefore that insofar as it [the linen] itself is a value-thing, it and the coat are like as one egg and another. (143–44/66)

Or should we say, like as two ghosts?

That all this language is a matter of fable (and that fable is a language of matter) is made clear by Marx's ironic—and rhetorically abyssal—example of the Nietzschean sheep. As for the linen, it is a figure, and a figure of figure at that: "Its existence as value appears in its likeness [*Gleichheit*] with the coat, just as the sheep-nature of the Christian [appears] in his likeness with the Lamb of God" (143/66). Thus the commodity is like something that is like something else *only as a figure*, as something that can be looked at only on paper.

It now becomes obvious why the original sentence that introduced the problem of abstraction in all its force had recourse to the strange little word "obvious," *augenscheinlich* (127/52). To the eye, it demands to be read. The look of and at the commodity is finally, if it is ever finally anything, a purely *material* vision, but material in the sense that language is material, not phenomenal or sensible. It appears, it looks like, but merely as an inscription. It appears to the eye (*Augenschein*) of a reader, but abstractly, *unfassbar*. If it turns and returns, the movement is that of the trope and the ghost, but only insofar as they are written down. That is why Benjamin could speak of the commodity as "material that is dead in a double sense, . . . anorganic matter, matter that has been eliminated from the circulation process" or, quoting Baudelaire, *oublié sur la carte*:[36] doubled, both ghost and inscription. The ghosts are there to be read, again and again.

Doing Without Knowing

Having decomposed the commodity to present it as doubled, abstracted, ghosted, aberrant, *Capital* quickly reintegrates it, if rather ironically. The mechanism of the recomposition is itself rhetorical, a fabulous movement of personification superimposed on the metaphorical abstraction. Luce Irigaray has described the process precisely: "Commodities among themselves are thus not equal, nor alike, nor different. They only become so when they are compared by and for man. And the prosopopoeia of the relation of commodities among themselves is a projection through which producers-exchangers make them replay before their eyes the operations of specul(ariz)ation."[37] To a certain extent the possibility of prosopopoeia had already begun in the text's fourth paragraph when commodities were embodied (*Warenkörper*). The ghosts of the analysis, which allow the passage to a specular system of likeness or equality (called, abstractly, "humanity") now return with a vengeance. With the entrance into the analysis of *Warensprache*, *Capital* takes its figure (body, ghost, humanity) literally, deploys it narratively, and soon commodities are walking, standing, choosing, carrying, dressing (indeed, the coat, however threadbare, wraps itself around the very commodity of which it is the privileged example [143/66]) . . . and talking commodity-talk. "The linen [as a value-form] no longer stands in social relation with only one other kind of commodity, but with the commodity-world [*Warenwelt*]. As commodity it is a citizen of this world" (155/77).

The system of commodity exchange within which these re-animated if somewhat spectrally abstract figures enter into relations with each other is itself spectacularly powerful. Having been artificially dissolved, the formalized rigor of the exchange relation (so the story goes) can be all the more thoroughly reconstructed.

Like the geometry of forms with which Marx regularly compares it, its equations or likenesses are symmetrical, mirrorlike, and totalizing. Equipped with the resources of dialectical negativity (the commodity's mediation of itself in the other as *its* other), the system maps out the time and space of the exchange and binds its terms tightly together. The exchange of commodities is a "system of formalization and notation rigorous enough to be patterned on the model of mathematical language" or, more precisely, "its model is that of analytic geometry," as Paul de Man says of Kleist's marionette theatre.[38]

Growing through a series of stages (the different "forms of value"—simple, expanded, general [recapitulated at 158/80), the isolated substitution of one thing for another is multiplied into the general system of economy ("it is an embryonic form which must undergo a series of metamorphoses before it can ripen into the price-form" [154–76]). The system begins as a simple equation, and the symmetry of the substitution allows others to be added to it infinitely, in a movement of specularization ("every other commodity-body becomes a mirror of the linen-value" [155/77]) and infinite incorporation (one thing's "isolated value-expression is transformed into the indefinitely expandable series of its different simple value-expressions" [154/76]). Although the series is entirely ad hoc, "a motley mosaic of disparate and heterogeneous value-expressions" (156/78), any equation within this endless chain of substitutions or transformations can be reversed—since all "commodities, when taken in certain proportions, must be equal [*gleich*] in value" (136/60)—and the chain "remains constantly extendable" by any new *Wertgleichung* (156/78). Being a commodity, an exchangeable thing, means being inscribed in this transformational system of crossings and reversals, illimitable in principle. The commodity is this perpetual motion machine, at least until its twists and turns are temporarily halted with the emergence of a general value-form, a commodity set apart from the rest as "immediate[ly] exchangeable with all other commodities" (161/82), a kind of zero excluded from the system in order to guarantee its totality and closure. "This form, for the first time, actually relates commodities to each other as values or lets them appear to each other as exchange values" (158/80); it is "immediate universal exchangeability" (162/84).

With the emergence of universal exchangeability arrives the moment for which *Capital* is justly most well known, the final section on "The Fetishism of Commodities and the Secret Thereof." The *Geheimnis*, though, of the section is what it says. Those who claim to understand it usually argue that *Capital*'s so-called theory of fetishism is (1) an explanation of how human beings come to relate themselves, through buying and selling (exchange), to commodities and not to each other, and (2) a reminder that every commodity is the product of a human social relation, one of "our" creations and not something to be endowed with the independent existence we tend to grant it. It is a warning to recognize our "own" offspring as such and to refuse their domination over us—because we made them. This is perhaps the central commonplace of the talk that goes on under the name of Marxism. Lukács pointed out that "the essence of commodity structure has often been pointed out." This did not stop him from repeating it: "Its basis is that a relation between people takes on the character of a thing and thus acquires a 'phantom objectivity,' an autonomy that seems so strictly rational and all-embracing as to conceal every trace of its fundamental nature: the relation between people."[39]

This interpretation is not without its basis in *Capital*, and there is even reason to see the analysis of the commodity structure as a critique with practical implications, thanks to Marx's indulgence in an analogy to religion with a decidedly negative tone: "The commodity-form . . . is nothing but the determined social relation between humans themselves, which assumes here, for them, the phantasmagoric form of a relation between things. In order, therefore, to find an analogy we must take a flight into the misty realm of religion. Here the products of the human head appear as endowed with a life of their own, entering into relations both with each other and with humans. This I call fetishism" (165/86–87). Perhaps *Capital* is saying forewarned is forearmed—against not simply the errors classically described as fetishism[40] (confusing one's creations with one's creator, fixatedly mistaking the substitute for what it replaces), but against the double danger of the commodity form: abstraction *and* reanimation. Here, warning would be preparation for action: if the danger is the aberrant totalizations and exchanges of tropes or commodities, the reader and consumer might acknowledge their existence, understand their mechanism, and by that cognitive advance stand some chance of circumscribing or regulating their impact. So the question would be: Does it suffice to become aware of the rhetorical or commodified nature of our exchanges in order to control their tendency to error, or at least in order to avoid the delusions of the fantasy apparently criticized as "fetishism"?

If Marx is any example, the answer would have to be no. Needless to say, the reading sketched here suggests that the *phantasmagorische Form* of fetishism is an exact description of the story we have just been reading. Does *Capital* conclude by denouncing the very errors it practices? Does it practice the very errors it denounces? Or does it protect itself from error and denunciation by a self-critical turn at the end? Perhaps it does none of this, and the practice of fetishism is a little more complicated than the standard definition suggests. We would do well to heed Marx's admonition to the French reader and slow down, suspend our eagerness to connect immediate questions with general conclusions, and pursue the fatiguing reading just a bit further.

The section begins:

> A commodity appears at first sight a self-evident [*selbstverständliches*], trivial thing. Its analysis brings out that it is a very strange [*vertracktes*] thing, abounding in metaphysical subtleties and theological niceties. Insofar as it is a use-value, there is nothing mysterious about it, whether we consider it from the point of view that by its properties it satisfies human needs, or that it first takes on these properties as the product of human labor. It is absolutely clear that, by his activity, man changes the forms of the materials of nature in such a way as to make them useful to him. The form of wood, for instance, is altered [*verändert*] if a table is made out of it. Nevertheless, the table remains wood, an ordinary sensible thing. But as soon as it emerges [*auftritt*,

steps forth] as a commodity, it changes into a sensible supersensible thing [*ein sinnlich übersinnliches Ding*]. (163/85)

The opening paragraph of the section conspicuously echoes the first paragraph of the chapter, rehearsing the progress it has performed. It returns us to the question of how exactly something can step forth as a commodity, how use-value is transformed into exchange-value in the process of exchange. We have reached the analytic determination that a certain abstraction must (have) take(n) place in order for exchange to occur, and that in fact abstraction is the name of what goes on in exchange. But the ghosts of the abstraction have proved to be less an answer than a practical necessity, replacing the missing measure with the prejudice of "humanity."

The turn to fetishism finally grants us the rhetorical room to theorize this placeholding prejudice. There is nothing at once particular and common that an abstraction could substitute for, no common trait: if use-values (or productive labors) have nothing in common, by definition (being *only* ways of use or working themselves), and thus requiring their radical (subatomic) erasure, then doesn't the so-called common or third term have to be substituted for nothing? The *Gespenst* that Marx calls abstraction is a substitution for nothing, which in constituting the nothing as a something that could be substituted for, institutes an originary simulation of exchange between something (common, abstract) and nothing. But the institution is structured like a substitution. It looks like the positing of an improper name (a common noun)—say "exchange value," or just "value," or "abstract human labor," or more precisely "human"—for something which has no name at all of its own. Could this positing be in any way distinguished from the act of exchange itself?

If abstraction is structured like the imposition of an improper name on something that has none of its own, then another turn to rhetoric will be helpful. The situation is that described by the rhetoricians as *catachresis*: "if for lacke of naturall and proper terme or word we take another, neither naturall nor proper, and do untruly applie it to the thing which we would seem to express," said Puttenham,[41] then we have used the figure he called "abuse, or catachresis." It exposes the symmetrical and totalized field of the trope to something that troubles its closure. Catachreses, as Paul de Man comments in "The Epistemology of Metaphor,"

> are capable of inventing the most fantastic entities by virtue of the positional power inherent in language. They can dismember the texture of reality and reassemble it in the most capricious of ways. Something monstrous lurks in the most innocent of catachreses: . . . the word can be said to produce of and by itself the entity it signifies, [one which] has no equivalence in nature. When one speaks of the legs of the table or the face of the mountain, . . . one begins to perceive a world of potential ghosts and monsters.[42]

The first chapter of *Capital* is this world of monsters and ghosts, from the first sentence's hideous assemblage to the abstraction's spectral remnant to this final section's misty fetishes. Ghosts and monsters are the (figurative) names of the commodity. And the story of these figures, the one narrated by this chapter and allegorized here under the name "fetish," runs the full tropological spectrum, from simile or metaphor to synecdoche to prosopopoeia and now to catachresis. The question is whether we're still within a continuous spectrum, or if we ever really were: is catachresis a matter of substitution, of exchange, or does it rupture the closure of the tropological system?

Can you *exchange* something for nothing? That you can get something for nothing should be clear by now, and if it isn't, then the privileged example of the fetish ought to make it so. Think of a table.[43] The vertical things which keep the flat top off the ground have no name of their own, no natural or proper signifier. But by catachresis we impose the borrowed or stolen term "legs" (or even "feet") and invent a name where before there was nothing. Which is the story of fetishism; we can pick up quoting *Capital* right where we left off:

> The form of wood, for instance, is altered if a table is made out of it. Nevertheless, the table remains wood, an ordinary sensible thing.

But as soon as it emerges [*auftritt*] as a commodity, it changes into a sensible supersensible thing [*ein sinnlich übersinnliches Ding*]. It not only stands with its feet on the ground, but, in relation to all other commodities, it stands on its head, and evolves [*entwickelt*] out of its wooden head whims [*Grillen*] more wonderful even than when of its own accord [*aus freien Stücken*] it began to dance. [The footnote adds: One may recall that China and the tables began to dance when the rest of the world appeared to be standing still (after 1848)—*pour encourager les autres.*] (163–64/85)

Whether this is good or bad is difficult to say, at this level of rhetorical complexity. After all, this turning table is not just one example among others but is, quite simply, *the* example of the commodity, the common commodity, the effective universal equivalent for all the rest. As the figure for the commodity—for the useful thing become exchangeable, for the doubled structure—the table can be substituted or exchanged for any other commodity in Marx's demonstration, "in the same way" that commodities can be exchanged for other commodities: exemplary commonplace, commodity of commodities, in more ways than one. The commodity as such (e.g., the table) is already structured like a figure, since use-values cannot be directly exchanged, having nothing in common around or across which the substitution could be organized, but must instead by mediated or figured by being transformed into so-called exchange values. The medium is the ghost, here.

The structure of this violent figure is that of catachresis, a placeholder, the opening of the tropological spectrum beyond the symmetry of an exchange whose possibility can no longer be taken for granted. Dissolved or volatilized by the reductive force of abstraction-in-exchange, use-values become exchangeable only as ghosts. Or (abstract) humanity. But these spectres are traded with a vigor and an urgency approaching that of living bodies themselves. The force of abstraction (*Abstraktionskraft*) both de- *and* re-animates commodities; we could say it "ghosts" them, giving them whatever life (*über-leben*) or animation (suspended) they have without presuming that they had any prior to the abstraction. The same *coup de force* institutes and destitutes them at once—thus violating the propriety of any "same" or "at once"—which means that "monster" would be as good a name as "ghost" for the structure Marx analyzes under the name *Ware*.

Perhaps the difficulty of the exemplary table can be measured. The table is a figure of the commodity, which is itself structured as a figure. Besides being the example of the commodity, the table is also an exemplary figure, a catachresis. And catachresis provides the example for the structure of the commodity. Thus, as they say, it could be no accident, and nothing less than a certain textual necessity, that the table steps forth (not to mention standing on feet and head, and rising off the ground altogether) as the ghostly residue of the monstrous collection of commodities which the chapter has analyzed. This table, "more wonderful even than when of its own accord [*aus freien Stücken*] it began to dance," stands here not only *on* its feet and head but *for* the commodity as such: ghost of a monster, monster of a ghost[44]—freely.

What is called exchange or substitution has always already begun with an act which can only be unthinkably different from it, an act of institution—the wild, random, uncontrolled, and utterly arbitrary positing of a status, a relation or a name to be related (*Gespenst, Menschheit*). That act can only be described as the simulation in advance, the pre-simulation or the simulacrum (the radically non-transcendental condition of possibility, non-transcendental because strictly speaking it is the condition of the *im*possibility of any exchange worthy of the name) of exchange. Abstraction would thus itself name neither the institution of exchange nor the substitution which is exchange, neither catachresis nor metaphor.

So when the question of commodity fetishism turns into the question of what is to be done, it should come as no surprise that it is figured as a problem of reading and writing: "Value, therefore, does not have its description branded on its forehead; rather, it transforms every product of labor into a social hieroglyphic. Later on, men try to decipher the hieroglyphic" (167/88). All the emphasis here is on the effort, the difficult labor of decipherment. Try as we may, though, the interpretation does not help much. Learning what we have learned from reading *Capital,* Marx says, "in no way banishes the semblance [*Schein*] of objectivity" which mists the commodity, and which locks in fetishistic pursuit (the hermeneutic gesture itself). The ghosts may be linguistic, but that does not make them any easier to read. Indeed, precisely to the extent that they are placeholders, markers, catachreses, they become more linguistic and more trouble to read. "Matter that is dead in a double sense," language (at least) twice: abstracted, inscribed.

Faced with this the interpreters (exchangers) succeed only in redeploying the double bind which structures commodity exchange: no matter how forewarned we are, thanks to the forearmaments of the knowledge of the secret of commodity exchange and its resulting fetishism, as long as exchange (language) goes on we are powerless to overcome its difficulties. And knowing only makes it more scary. *Je sais bien, mais quand même.*[45] As Marx says, this is the path of madness: "If I state that coats or boots stand in a relation to linen because the former is the universal embodiment of abstract human labor, the craziness [*Verrücktheit*] of the expression hits you in the eye [*springt ins Auge*]. But when the producers of coats and boots bring these commodities into relation with linen, . . . the relation . . . appears to them in this crazy [*verrückten*] form" (169/90).[46] "Humanity" is this madness, its subject and its object. It is not simply the ignorance of not knowing what to do; it is rather the terror of still having to do, without knowing. And we have no magic caps, only ghosts and monsters.

§ 5 The "Paradox" of Knowledge and Power: Foucault on the Bias

> What if thought freed itself from common sense and decided
> to think only at the extreme point of its singularity? What if
> it mischievously practiced the bias of *paradox*, instead of
> complacently accepting its citizenship in the *doxa*? What if it
> thought difference differentially, instead of searching out the
> common elements underlying difference?
>
> —Michel Foucault, "Theatrum Philosophicum"

If "Ça Parle," What Responds?

Writing in the pages of *L'Express* in the fall of 1986, after a half-dozen books about Michel Foucault had just appeared, the French political philosopher Alain Renault attempted to measure what were for him the disturbing implications of Foucault's "anti-humanism."[1] He associated this attack on man with the discovery of the "unconscious" as expressed in the Lacanian formula, attributed to Foucault, "Where 'it speaks,' man no longer exists [*Où 'ça parle,' l'homme n'existe plus*]." This insistence on the unconscious implies the rejection of man and "the end of humanism," because it situates thinking and acting in a time and place not entirely within the control of the self-present subject, namely, language. *Ça parle* means that I, to the extent that I speak and that my speaking figures my thinking and acting, am not in control of myself. Because something speaks from me beside(s) me, because the "I" finds its time and place in something other than itself (its immediate relation or presence to itself), it no longer speaks for itself. The logocentric determination of man as essentially speaking has been taken at its word and turned inside out, so that the subject is seen strictly as a grammatical subject, an effect of discourse. "The 'subject,' man in other words, must renounce the flatly metaphysical, even petit-bourgeois, project of mastering its discourse and claiming to be the author of its acts or ideas" (150).

The necessity of this rejection troubled Renault, who asked whether Foucault's linguistic anti-humanism "had not paradoxically engendered the contrary of what it sought": though "apparently open to diversity, . . . hadn't it contributed to the legitimation of insidious forms of intellectual terrorism?" (150). In other words, hadn't the disappearance of the subject into language removed both the moral ground of resistance and the possibility of ethico-political agency? The answer was of course yes, based on the time-honored analogies between a hermeneutics of suspicion (attributed to Foucault) and an "intellectual activity on the police model," and between the claim that "there are no facts but only interpretations" and the "revisionist" denial of the existence of the gas chambers.[2] The objection recapitulated two decades of critique in France, which had emphasized that denial of the priority accorded to subjectivity by displacing it into language (*où ça parle*) effectively withdrew from ethico-political activity any base in knowledge or truth (known facts), left it without grounds for opposition to injustice or any autonomous creative power. Grounding and subjectivity figure each other, thanks to the essential assumption of the subject's capacity to "master its discourse," to "author its acts or its ideas"—in other words, its capacity to be an author by virtue of the articulation of ideas with acts, the coordination of cognition with performance in a subject. The signature (of an "author") marks the connection of knowing with doing, the mastery of the linguistic field (discourse) in which they can come together, and the ability to sign is what is called responsibility.

This principle of reason defines the philosophical (theoretical) prejudice, whether idealist or materialist, and defines it as a thought of responsibility: action is grounded, in knowledge, or it is not responsible. Hence Renault could conclude with the customary denegations—"it is not at all a question of resuscitating the Cartesian *cogito*, even less a question of considering all our opinions and choices as products of an autonomous and sovereign freedom"—and still ask for the preservation of the responsible subject.

"If one grants that the discovery of the unconscious cannot and must not lead to a ruinous renunciation of the *ideas* of autonomy and responsibility, what is the figure of the subject that corresponds to this unprecedented situation?"[3]

The willful error of Renault's argument is of course the interpretation of the linguistic turn as a symmetrical reversal, the simple replacement of "I" with "ça" and "man" with "discourse" (this substitution being precisely what *The Order of Things* [*Les Mots et les choses*] resists with its elegant metaphor of the event of the self-effacing of man, "like a face drawn in sand at the edge of the sea [*comme à la limite de la mer un visage de sable*]," even if elsewhere this erasure is less rigorously given the status of a death or an end).[4] If the displacement of man or the subject amounts to the declaration of its disappearance (*disparition*), to the ruinous renunciation of responsibility, and thus to terror, then it is no wonder that we need new "figures of the subject." How else could one then answer the question "what remains of the subject after its deconstruction?" than with a call for a return to the subject?—and it will be no surprise if the newly restored one will look rather familiar, a pseudo-Kantian rational subject of freedom and morality.[5]

The willfulness of the error comes in Renault's stubborn refusal to consider anything of the large body of texts Foucault had devoted to the question of rights and responsibility, most importantly *Discipline and Punish* (*Surveiller et punir*), a strictly Nietzschean genealogy of the invention of the responsible subject. But already in May 1968, in an extraordinary "response to a question" about the political stakes of his work, Foucault had asked this simple question: "Is a progressive politics linked (in its theoretical reflection) to the themes of signification, origin, the constitutive subject, in brief to the entire thematic that guarantees to history the inexhaustible presence of the *logos*, the sovereignty of a pure subject, and the profound teleology of an originary destination? . . . or with its being put in question?"[6] Again the answer was clear: a progressive politics is linked with the *mise en question* of the subject and signification, because, for Foucault, this politics would assume a "perilous ease . . . were it to give itself the guarantee of an originary foundation or a transcendental teleology" (19/865–66). The ease, in fact, would be that of escaping the difficulty or risk of the political for the guarantees of "technocratic" administration or the "historico-transcendental destination of the Occident." In the end, Foucault makes this "progressive politics" conditional on "not mak[ing] man or consciousness or the subject in general the universal operator of all transformations (24/871), on withdrawing this guarantee.

Maurice Blanchot read this gesture with care: "the subject does not disappear; rather, its unity, all too determined, is made questionable. What arouses interest and inquiry is its . . . dispersal, which does not annihilate it but offers us, out of it, no more than a plurality of positions and a discontinuity of functions."[7] The gesture of dislodging the subject from any position of control, and exposing it instead to the irreducible risk or difficulty of its occupying a discursive space and time whose rules cannot be transformed at will, does not imply the symmetrical "end" of responsibility in terror but rather ("paradoxically") the asymmetrical emergence of a different responsibility.[8] The dispersal or dissemination of the subject's unity (its determination of meaning, its articulation of cognition and action), its opening onto a discontinuous "plurality of positions," simply intensifies the demand for responsibility. The subject is still in question, in more than one question, but without the security of *a* present (position) from which to respond. If "the language [we] speak, . . . even the fables [we] were told in childhood, obey rules not entirely given to [our] consciousness," what speaks and signs, what comes after the subject?[9] What responds without me when I respond, and from where and when, if I no longer control the position from which I respond? In the last sentence of the response, Foucault provides no replacement— certainly not discourse, nor power—but only the law of an indifference which continues to compel a response.

> Discourse is not life; its time is not yours. . . . In each sentence that you pronounce—and very precisely in the one that you are busy writing this instant, you who have been so intent, for so many pages, on

responding to a question in which you felt yourself so personally
concerned and who are going to sign this text with your name—in
every sentence there reigns the nameless law, the blank indifference:
"What matter who speaks [*Qu'importe qui parle*]; someone said: what
matter who speaks." Michel Foucault[10]

The signature pointedly reminds us that responsibility remains,
precisely in the *loi sans nom*, in the blank indifference of the
demand to sign or to respond and the utter impossibility of the
subject's recognizing itself in "its" response, of its assuring anything—even its own survival—with its words. If this security, the
articulation of knowing with doing in a present, were simply
possible, what urgency would demand responsibility?

Dashing the Hope

Newsweek for July 9, 1984, reported this "milestone":

> DIED. Michel Foucault, 57, opaque, paradoxical French philosopher-
> historian. . . . He reasoned that "power and knowledge directly imply
> one another," and that modern society seeks ever greater control
> through greater knowledge of individuals.[11]

The farewell echoes the objections made, in a series of important
critiques over the past several years, by some of Foucault's best
interpreters. Foucault, thanks to his innovative rethinking of the
interplay between relations of force (power) and relations of cognition (knowledge) under the term "power-knowledge," has removed
the basis for the practical political linkage of the two. Hence the
opacity and the paradox—too much, it seems, is not enough.

This objection is forcefully summarized in Jürgen Habermas's
economical little formula: "So why fight? [*warum überhaupt kämp-
fen?*]"[12] Habermas feels that Foucault "cannot answer" this question, the "question of the normative basis of his critique," precisely
because of his suspicions about the implication of knowledge in
power relations (for instance, the "normalizing" aims of power-
knowledge networks). Foucault's predicament stems from what

Habermas seems to find an admirable gesture: Foucault's consistent refusal "to give a status to the other" (to install the other and its knowledge as the negation of the same, thus reducing its alterity to manageable or integrable proportions) in order "to defend himself against a naturalistic metaphysics which idealizes counter-power into a prediscursive referent."[13] Having done so, however, Foucault apparently cannot explain how one gets to the "fight" (the exercise of force in resistance) from some "why" (a right based in reason or truth). Where Foucault would seem to have knowledge and power linked as tightly as possible, a gap or "aporia" opens up, inside the thought of power-knowledge.

Nancy Fraser diagnoses the problem as "normative confusion."[14] She is willing, perhaps more so than Habermas, to take up Foucault's "empirical insights" into the positivity of power relations, but she also worries about the tendency of these understandings to turn on themselves and undercut their own deployment. The problem is again one of crossing a gap: Fraser wants to know "how [Foucault] got from the suspension of the question of the legitimacy of modern power to [his] engaged critique of bio-power" (28). While raising the prospect that Foucault thinks he is "politically engaged yet still somehow normatively neutral" (28), she does not think normless engagement possible: his "rejection of humanism . . . puts Foucault in the paradoxical position of being unable to account for or justify the sorts of normative political judgments he makes all the time—for example, 'discipline' is a bad thing" (42). Again, the aporia seems to neutralize or anarchize action by disconnecting knowledge from the norms which translate it into force.

Charles Taylor agrees that this position is paradoxical. Foucault obviously disjoins what Taylor calls the "standard link" between power and knowledge and undermines "the familiar terrain [of] an old Enlightenment-inspired combination."[15] This standard view of the combination founds the gesture of political critique in the essentially cognitive nature of power: power, understood as domination or the imposition of constraint, works by "fraud, illusion, false pretenses" (172–73), by preventing our purposes and desires from reaching fulfillment (or perhaps even formulation) and then

masking that fact. Because dissimulation is essential to the exercise
of power, truth or knowledge (determined as unconcealment) can
reverse and erase the imposed errors and with them the domination: "the negation of the one (domination) makes essential use of
the negation of the other (disguise)" (152). Because power already
(ab)uses knowledge, critique can deploy against it "a truth that
frees us" (181).

Foucault reverses and threatens to unhinge this essential, if
negative, articulation. He brackets the truth-error distinction
within "regimes of truth," and binds these regimes to the exercise
of power. He takes the cognitive "essence" of power a little too far,
perhaps, and apparently converts a critical or dialectical negation
(based on opposition) into a sterile hierarchy, even an identity.
Because he insists on the "close intrication" of truth, rather than
error, "with systems of dominance," he can only see "truth as
subordinated to power," as "imposed by a regime of power," so that
"the regime is identified entirely with its imposed truth" (175).
Hence the familiar scheme finds itself inverted in a classic Foucaul-
tian chiasmus: the imposition of the one (domination) makes
essential use of the imposition of the other (truth). And the reverse
no longer holds: "unmasking can only destabilize [power]; we
cannot bring about a new stable, freer, less mendacious form of it
by this route" (176).

This position leaves Taylor disconcerted, though, because there
is "unmasking." Foucault's work does offer important insights into
modern politics; indeed, his analyses are actively and effectively
inscribed in contemporary struggles (recall the infamous "insurrection of subjugated knowledges"). But Foucault won't endorse these
knowledges as norms, as grounds for a programmatic political
struggle, nor will he find in them any Good to be universally
affirmed. Participating in struggles certainly involves knowledge,
but the content of the knowledge does not validate the struggle. He
offers insights, but not what Taylor calls a "critique," where the
negation or overcoming of what is criticized "promotes a good,"
where the unmasking is the "route" to better forms of power (152).
Foucault worries about insurrections posed in terms of the truth

that frees us. And this resistance to totalization, to affirming some powers over others based on their relative "gain in truth or freedom" (162), in turn disorients Taylor. It leads him to the breaking point, "the break in Foucault's thought, the point that disconcerts, where he adopts a Nietzschean-derived stance of neutrality between the different historical systems of power, and thus seems to neutralize the evaluations that arise out of his analyses" (176).

Foucault's neutralization of the link between power and knowledge on this level, while on another he seemingly intricates them to the point of identity, disturbs these three critics. The rigor of their work is to let us measure just what is at stake in the "standard link." Foucault's strange hyperbolization *and* neutralization leaves him in a difficult predicament, as Taylor sees it: "He dashes the hope . . . that there is some good we can *affirm* as a result of the understanding [his] analyses give us. And by the same token he seems to raise a question of whether or not there is such a thing as a way out. This is rather paradoxical" (152).[16]

It is a testimony to the urgency of the issues that Taylor and the others choose not to linger hopeless in this aporetic paradox, but rather present it as a question requiring immediate resolution: either Foucault has rewritten the standard definitions of "power" and "knowledge," or he is incoherent. As the possibility of another "semantic field" (173) for these familiar philosophemes is not raised, the conclusion is unavoidable.[17] If Foucault cannot "free his position of this paradox, seemingly linked with the impossible attempt to stand nowhere" (166), then his "position ultimately is incoherent" (181). Paradox, aporia: hopes dashed, no way out.

We can endorse these conclusions, take them at their word, but not the reasoning that leads to them. Let us agree that Foucault's work on forms or local centers of power-knowledge tells the story of a certain unhinging, a break in coherence, a difficulty of coincidence, even as it insists that nothing more than a dash or a hyphen keeps power and knowledge apart. But the paradox does not arise from confusion, irresponsibility, or evasion, or even from what Taylor injudiciously calls "the fog emanating from Paris in recent decades" (172). Perhaps Foucault was right when he warned in *The*

History of Sexuality, Volume I (*La Volonté de savoir*) that "this word *power* is likely to lead to a number of misunderstandings."[18] Where there is incoherence, it does not come about because Foucault identifies or hierarchizes power and knowledge, or because he resists affirmations, but rather because he has put the existing "semantic fields" of power and knowledge, and with them their relations, in question . . . because, in a "word," of the hyphen, the "-" which separates and joins power and knowledge.

If this ineffaceably rhetorical little placeholder "dashes [our] hopes" for the familiar (negative) combination, if it seems to deface the picture of a good future we can affirm with(in) our present understanding, if its paradox or aporia leaves us with no way out, then it is no accident that this difference of the relation comes to be thought in rhetorical (paradox, aporia) and temporal (affirmation, hope) terms.[19] For much of Western thought, the burden of making the passage from knowledge to power and back has fallen on discourse, language insofar as it is rhetorical—trope and persuasion, cognitive and active, constative and performative. And the crossing within rhetoric inevitably raises in its turn(s) the problem of time and timing. One thing is clear—we cannot begin to address these questions without suspending the presupposed semantic fields of "power" and "knowledge," without reading the hyphen, its rhetoric, its temporality, its militant materiality.

Rhetoric of Paradox

What is a paradox? And what is at issue in calling the power-knowledge relation "paradoxical"? Beginning to address this requires a detour through the field of rhetoric, because the question of paradox is nothing if not rhetorical. We understand rhetoric here as a way of approaching language which emphasizes the interplay between its cognitive possibilities (constative, informative, descriptive statements) and its active capabilities (its pragmatic, performative, or perlocutionary forces) or, in other words, the intersection and interference between trope and persuasion.[20]

What is a trope? In the section on rhetoric at the beginning of

Raymond Roussel, Foucault turns to the eighteenth-century rhetorician Dumarsais to define language in terms of its "internal movement," as a system of transformations in which a word or phrase can be detached from one meaning or signification to settle on another, "as if it had turned on itself to trace around a fixed point a whole circle of possibilities (the 'meaning,' as they said)." For Dumarsais, " 'words are often turned away [*détournés*] from their primitive meaning to take on a new one which more or less diverges from it but that still has a relation to it. This new meaning of words is called their tropological meaning, and we call this conversion, this detour which produces it, a trope.' " Foucault adds: "it is in this space of displacement (the 'turn' [*tour*] and the 'detour,' as Dumarsais says) that all the figures of rhetoric are born."[21]

Thus in Aristotle's example "Achilles is a lion," the word "lion" is metaphorically detached from its four-legged wild referent and re-applied to the Homeric hero, turned around the fixed axis of resemblance which compares the two creatures in terms of their shared strength and ferocity. The trope makes something known, provides knowledge about Achilles which can be verified or falsified, and expands the reserve of possible descriptions. "Lion" means something new, now, but it only means it to the extent that it preserves its bond to the "primitive meaning." The resourcefulness by which language turns "its own poverty into wealth" in this economy of re-use works on a principle of substitution: words change places, stand in for each other, cross over from one meaning to another. The hegemony of meaning is far from being questioned: on the contrary, rhetoric is designed to exploit the exchangeability of words to expand the horizon of meaning.

The economy of paradox is exemplary, then, in that it recovers the negativity of a connection for the purpose of conveying a positive meaning more emphatically. The turn depends not on a comparison—resemblance, contiguity, or comprehension—but on the absence of such axes, on the lack of connection, on opposition. So when Pierre Fontanier, early in the nineteenth century, came to update Dumarsais's treatise, he included the figure of *paradoxisme*, which his precursor had omitted, with this definition: "an artifice of language by which ideas and words which are ordinarily opposed and self-contradictory find themselves reconciled and combined such that, while seeming to conflict and mutually exclude each other, they strike the intellect with their most surprising agreement and produce the truest, deepest, and most energetic meaning."[22] Fontanier summarized by reference to etymology: from the Greek *para*, against or counter to, and *doxa*, opinion or belief, a paradox is an idea which contradicts a more generally accepted idea, on purpose. The trope "links together words which appear to and, if taken literally, really would contradict each other, and thanks to this very contradiction, through implied or underlying intermediary ideas, . . . admirably escapes it to a more perfect harmony" (264). Richard Lanham has recently proposed this economical definition: "a seemingly self-contradictory statement, which yet is shown to be (sometimes in a surprising way) true."[23]

Common to these definitions is not only the persuasive effect of surprise produced by the trope but also the dialectical trick with which it is accomplished. The rhetorical paradox presents an opposition in order to dissolve it. The operation is based on a binary system: appearance or reality, semblance or essence, explicit or implicit, false or true, where the extremity of the opposition on the level of the first term (literal) leads one to grasp a unity on the level of the second (figurative). Paradox, for the rhetoricians, is a matter of appearance ("seeming") and its erasure, and the trope works by exaggerating the appearance (of conflict) and then removing it. Because the ideas or words are symmetrically opposed, one can take the other as its own negation and reveal the underlying (presupposed but not yet explicit) mediations which bring them together. But the paradox is required in order to bring the conflict to the point of self-resolution. Because one wants so much to say "either-or," to hold to the *doxa* that one must be true and the other false, the experience of the truth of the paradox forces the acceptance of "both-and," the transcendence of exclusion. The contradiction heals itself, once its differences find mediation; for Fontanier, the questions of paradox are: "how to re-establish one by the excess of the other" and "will we find, in order to supplement [the gap] between them, something implied which re-connects one to the other, effacing their contrariety and incompatibility?"[24] In a true paradox, a paradox of truth, the answer will be yes. Then the paradox, always self-effacing, can step aside to allow the underlying truth of harmony to present its more perfect union. The conflict is a step toward unity, an instrument of the truth of the whole, a transference all the more powerful since it proceeds by negation.[25]

But, rhetorically speaking, there are at least two paradoxes. Buried in or alongside each of these definitions is another, more radical, version of the contradiction where the difference cannot be eradicated or integrated. Fontanier refers to it as the risk of literal-ism, of failing to read figuratively: read *à la lettre*, without recourse to something "implied," a contradiction will reveal "nothing but pure gibberish, nothing but a bizarre and monstrous coupling of discordant and senseless words [*vide de sens*], or of words at cross-purposes [*à contre-sens*]."[26] This paradox suffers from a kind of communication breakdown: the different terms can find no com-mon ground, no shared center, no third term or tongue into which they can be translated and their differences overcome. What is lost, without recourse to semblance, is the ability to recover the contra-diction as a symmetrical one, to show that it never really was a contradiction but only an agreement waiting to be uncovered, a meaning waiting to be forcefully underlined. Without the nega-tivity of appearance, Fontanier suggests, there is only the absence of meaning, or worse, *contre-sens*, active conflict, counter-sense, something working against or interfering with meaning. Where, in the case of the aesthetic paradox, the excess of one established the other, and the gap became the measure, here the excess is itself excessive. The coupling is forced: where it ought to provide just the extra energy to secure the effect of unification, here it proves unrecoverable. The negative appearance which in the first case drives the conflict toward harmony cannot be overcome. The transfer interferes. The either-or persists, and resists not only its collapse into both-and but also any decision between the terms. They remain linked, but incompatible, without common reason or truth to unite them. Since this paradox cannot be erased in the experience of contradiction, but was designed from the start to be erased, it can only be excluded as monstrosity, stuttered nonsense or anti-sense.

The conflict between these definitions is structured like a paradox, but which one? This paradox of paradox reminds us that we cannot always overcome our differences, and since paradox always requires difference, it will always be haunted by the threat that the difference will not go away, that the necessary "excess" or divide will remain, to overflow the bounds of symmetry. This difference can hinge, and unhinge, the relation—or better, can do neither simply. But how can we tell the difference between the differences—between the excess that re-establishes a relation and the excess that leaves the connection monstrously open—when the exemplars of our decision itself are what we must decide between? And we must decide: each paradox is precisely the error denounced by the other and cannot tolerate the coincidence. This second-order paradox or aporia, the paradox of paradox, would thus name the difficulty and necessity of distinguishing these moments of transference and interference, of paying heed to the demands of cognitive unification (what is the truth of the contradiction?) without effacing the active interference of language (the "monstrous coupling of discordant and senseless words"), in other words, of language as at once and neither knowledge and/nor power, of word as meaning and as force at an unrecoverable remove from meaning, and word as neither. "At once"?[27]

Power Hyphen Knowledge

Foucault was none too kind to those who mistook the hyphen as a sign of transparency:

> When I read—and I know it has been attributed to me—the thesis "knowledge is power" or "power is knowledge," whichever, I begin to laugh, since studying their relation is precisely my problem. If they were identical things, I would not have to study them and I would be spared a lot of fatigue as a result. The very fact that I pose the question of their relation proves clearly that I do not identify them.[28]

What is at stake in the "paradox" of power-knowledge, I will argue, is nothing more, but also nothing less, than the rhetoric and the temporality of the hyphen, the mark which joins and separates knowing and doing, cognition and force. But what sort of paradox is it?

Fraser, Habermas, and Taylor find it impossible, confused, incoherent. But Foucault's critics are certainly not the only ones to become transfixed by his re-elaboration of the problem.[29] There is abundant evidence on all sides of the investments made in securing the links between cognition and action, as well as of the force of a reassuring or orthodox view of the relation. The difficult hyphen which joins and separates the two words has come to function as a kind of phantasmatic blank space, to be filled in with the hopes and desires of the interpreter.[30]

Readers more sympathetic to Foucault share the obsession but are sometimes less elegant. Garth Gillan and Charles Lemert, to take just one example, treat "power-knowledge" as Foucault's proper name, "the concept with which he is uniquely identified." And they take the hyphen between the words to mean that they are "fused" or even the same thing. "To know *is* to exercise the power of . . . domination; hence, power-knowledge." "Cognitive relations *are* the exercise of power." "*This* [disciplinary] *knowledge is a power.*" "*Knowledge must be power.*" "The effectiveness of power is knowledge. And the effectiveness of knowledge is . . . power."[31]

This is probably not what Foucault had in mind, and certainly is not what his texts say. As he pointed out in one of his last interviews, responding to a question about these kinds of interpretation, "if I had said, or meant to say, that knowledge was power, I would have said so, and having said it, I would have had nothing more to say—once they were identified, why should I work so hard at showing their different relations?"[32] What is at stake is "the question of their relation." The hyphen does not conflate, nor does it mark a covert dissimulation. It is a mark of a linguistic, discursive, rhetorical predicament, an unfolding political paradox.

Foucault used the phrase *pouvoir-savoir* (I believe for the first time) as the "working hypothesis" in the course he gave at the

Collège de France in 1971–72. His course description made the stakes clear from the start:

> relations of power (with the struggles that traverse them and the institutions that maintain them) do not merely facilitate or obstruct knowledge; they are content neither to favor or stimulate it, nor to falsify or limit it; . . . the problem is thus not solely to determine how power subordinates knowledge and makes it serve its ends nor to determine how it superimposes itself on it and imposes on it ideological contents and limitations. No knowledge can be formed without a system of communication, of recording, of accumulation, of displacement—which is itself a form of power. . . . No power, on the other hand, can be exercised without the extraction, appropriation, distribution, or retention of knowledge. At this level, there is not learning [*connaissance*] on one side and society on the other, or science and the state, but rather the fundamental forms of "*pouvoir-savoir*."[33]

The hyper-negativity of this introduction—its insistence on the rhetoric of neither-nor and rejection of a two-sided both-and—and the ultimate condensation of the question of the relation in the enigmatic hyphen, should have warned away from the start those who hoped to recognize in it the familiar schemas of subordination or superimposition. And when Foucault spelled things out a bit more in *Discipline and Punish*, the relation was only complicated by its treatment under the heading of *s'entrelacer*, to interlace, entangle, intertwine. "A knowledge [*savoir*] . . . is formed and entangled with the practice of the power [*pouvoir*] to punish."[34] The stakes of the entanglement were translated in a hesitant but nevertheless imperative mode:

> perhaps . . . we must abandon a whole tradition that lets us imagine that there can only be knowledge where power relations are suspended and that knowledge can only develop outside of its injunctions, its demands, and its interests. . . . We must admit rather that power produces knowledge . . . ; that power and knowledge directly imply or implicate one another; that there is no power relation without the correlative constitution of a field of knowledge, nor is there knowledge that does not presuppose and constitute at the same time power relations. These [are] "power-knowledge" relations. (27/2)

The polemical, both philosophical and political, burden of the *pouvoir-savoir* entanglement or knot can now be grasped in some detail. Foucault demands that we give up the thought that power and knowledge are not always already implicated in each other. There is no exteriority or exclusion, no outside of uncontaminated innocence, no margin, no free space alongside one in which the other can play unaffected. Neither do they come together over time, as if first independent and then joined. Neither power nor knowledge relations operate without having already presupposed the operation of the other. Just as one cannot speak a truth to power which would itself be free of power relations, so too effects of power are not merely the accidental by-products of the independent constitution of knowledge. Power does not work simply by impos-ing constraints or contents on knowledge, just as knowledge does not merely mask, serve, or expose power. Power's role cannot be limited to facilitation or to obstruction—while such effects do occur, the fundamental mechanisms of power relations are not negative. The exteriority required for such structures is lacking. Thus, where knowledge is concerned, power relations do not simply say "no." On the contrary, according to Foucault's hypoth-esis, they stimulate, excite, incite knowledge. Power and knowledge are tangled up in the knot of a "not-without." Each presupposes the other: no knowledge without power, no power without knowl-edge. No outside, no priority.

This logic (such as it is) of the "not-without" reappeared in *The History of Sexuality, Volume I* (*La volonté de savoir*), where Foucault called it the "rule of immanence": "between techniques of knowl-edge and strategies of power there is no exteriority" (98/129–30). The constitution of a field of knowledge depends on the institution of a possible object within power relations, and, vice versa, power takes as its target only what is capable of being invested by cogni-tive relations. The force of this structure of co-implication and presupposition threatens to eliminate any substantive difference between power and knowledge.

Although Foucault's rhetoric of reversal is well known, this attempted erasure of border lines does not simply invert the "tradi-tion's" models, but exceeds them. There is a turning, but not the conversion of power and knowledge into each other. While Foucault erases the exteriority of the opposition between power and knowledge, intricates them as closely as a hyphen will allow, the account of their complicity (of the effacement of opposition) in turn reiterates a new disjunction as it overcomes the other. The erasure of the attempted erasure leaves nothing but the residue or the excess of an interior, a divided, mutual "interiority" marked by a hyphen in the knotted space of the intertwining. There is an "interior" here, but not the antithesis or the opposite of the exterior, not the inside *of* the outside.

What remains? The double erasure leaves a hyphen, a "difference." In fact, without the difference there would be no articulation. No exteriority, but power and knowledge are nevertheless "articulated with each other on the basis of their difference," linked in "incessant comings and goings" which refuse stabilization (98/130). The "interior" is differentiated, folded and pocketed, multiply tensed. "In" it, power and knowledge relations are somehow superimposed on each other, make each other possible, without either being reducible or subordinate—and certainly not identical—to the other. Difference without exteriority or precedence. Resisting identity as much as opposition, with their difference as their hinge, power and knowledge inhabit each other, parasitize each other, get inside each other—but into a double inside without outside. Neither one, without the other. Each is the other's inside: such are the comings and goings of their coincidence, their "immanence."

What makes this difficult structure possible, to the extent that it is possible? Foucault has a direct—which does not mean easy—answer: discourse, what is said, *ce qui se dit*. Quickly, we could say: discourse makes the difference. "It is *within discourse* that power and knowledge come to articulate themselves" (101/132–33; emphasis added). Consider the example, privileged by Foucault, of confession [*l'aveu*], an event in language invested by relations at once of power and of knowledge. It is a "form of knowledge-power": "a technique for producing truth" which "unfolds within a power relationship" (58, 61/78, 83). And it is discursive—not by accident, but necessarily. One cannot confess without language, without speaking or writing, without the event of utterance. As much as one might like to ignore this linguistic moment, it cannot be evaded: the differential relations of power-knowledge are entangled within, not without, discourse, made possible by linguistic structures and events.

But if the answer to the question "where and when are power and knowledge articulated?" is "in discourse," what does the discursivity of the coincidence imply? A rhetoric, a temporality, and . . . a fragility.

What is discourse such that the vertiginous structure (condensed in the hyphen) of difference without exteriority, of the comings and goings of the double reversed interior, is possible? For starters, discourse does something: "parler, c'est faire quelque chose," as Foucault says in *The Archeology of Knowledge*, "to speak is to do something, to do something other than express what one thinks [or] translate what one knows." "Discourses are made of signs, but what they do is more than use these signs to designate things."[35] So the analysis of discourse must address it as an "operation," a "technology," and "not at all [as] a system of representations."[36]

That operation is extraordinarily complex, as might be expected. Return to the confession, that peculiar ritual of discourse addressed to a demand that it be at once performative ("*j'avoue*, I confess") and constative ("that my truth is"). The rhetoricity of a speech activity which requires that two radically different gestures (one, the avowal, a matter only of performance, to be judged simply in terms of its accomplishment or failure; the other, the avowed, a question of knowledge, to be judged in terms of its truth value) coincide in the same utterance, places strange burdens on the language which must articulate it. What is the tense, the timing or the tension, of an abysmal utterance like "if I tell the truth about myself, as I am now doing" (as Foucault precisely put it in an interview)?[37] What *I* can say this, and when? A performative does not have to describe itself, but this one does: not only does it do what it says, but it says what it does it says. And the constative saying *is* the performative doing—it makes the description possible by doing it, and what it does is nothing other than describe itself doing, the performative. Thus the *I* has to multiply itself, cite itself, and cite itself citing: as I am doing now. The temporal structure of this "now," which gives the time within the "same" utterance for at least two *I*'s, requires a kind of internal hinge or fold, exceeds the present (the first-person present) on which it seems to depend. The present of the confession divides itself and its subject: hence the inevitable problem, which Foucault says attended necessarily upon the generalization of confessional techniques or rhetorics, of "the presence of consciousness to itself" and the jeopardy into which it is put by the material event (the *énoncé*) of language said. The subject differs "itself" in the "same" utterance, but the utterance must also allow the confession to take place, as a "ritual of discourse where the subject who speaks [*qui parle*] coincides with the subject of the utterance [*de l'énoncé*]."[38] Discourse must be dense enough, sufficiently interfolded, to enable the different speech acts, with their uncoordinated *I*'s and times, to coincide and to remain different.[39] But the necessity of these folds, of internal differentiation, suggests that discourse may not exactly be a locus of stability.

Foucault did not hesitate to draw out the implications of the discursivity, the difference, of the hyphen in "power-knowledge," to a radical point: the complex rhetoricity and temporality opened up in the discursive ritual where power and knowledge are entangled puts the possibility of that articulation in question. This is perhaps the thought avoided by many of his interpreters, if not by Foucault:

> It is within discourse that power and knowledge come to articulate themselves. And for this very reason, we must conceive discourse as a series of discontinuous segments, whose tactical function is neither uniform nor stable. . . . We must allow for a complex and unstable play in which discourse is perhaps at once the instrument and effect of power, but also an obstacle, a stumbling-block, a point of resistance.[40]

Because they require language to happen—its rhetoric and its temporality—the relations of power and of knowledge can always be disengaged, as can the relation between power and knowledge.

Because the articulation between power and knowledge is discursive, then, the link can never be guaranteed. The same discourse that transports the relation can undermine, block, distort, disable it. If the vehicle of the coincidence is discourse, the transference between the two cannot be totalized, unified, integrated, or otherwise stabilized. It is unpredictable. When discourse must be thought as a "series of discontinuous segments," interference always already remains a possibility and a threat. The play of the difference, not bound to itself by exteriority or ultimate continuity, opens the relation to the chance or *alea* of disarticulation. "Discourse transports [*véhicule*] and produces power; it reinforces it, but it also undermines it, exposes it, renders it fragile or breakable and makes it possible to thwart it" (101/133). The link between knowledge and power can always not take place, because of its place. The discourse which makes it possible also undermines it, precisely because power and knowledge are different: not identical, without exteriority or priority, heterogeneously interiorized. Coincidence is not copresence, so that the difference which allows the articulation, as opposed to identity or exteriority, clears a space and a time for a certain disjunction.

In a sense, the question of the relation between power and knowledge has received two answers: "articulation," so interlocked that we cannot take for granted the possibility of telling them apart, and "heterogeneity," so different that we cannot not distinguish them. The two depend on each other. Telling the difference becomes urgently necessary (and Foucault's texts militate against this error of confusion as rigorously as possible) to the precise extent that it is radically impossible (it is the same rigor of these texts to refuse the opposition). The texts erase the difference they insist on, and erase their insistence in reiterating the difference.

The problem here is not just that these two conclusions must both be drawn from Foucault's texts, or that they co-exist in some ambiguity or "seeming" paradox, but that they are at odds, cut obliquely across each other. We cannot simply decide between them, or for both. To choose one version of the relation—transference or interference—is to commit exactly the error the other version has already undone. This leaves us reading the hyphen between *pouvoir* and *savoir*. The "answer" to the question of the relation is the meaningless little syntactical plug which holds the words together and apart. The relation remains in question, divided between the asymmetrical answers Foucault's texts offer. The difference is not merely between interfering answers, but between an answer (there is a relation, governed by such and such a law) and an interference with the very possibility of an answer. This interference of interference, which is not symmetrical, cannot be mistaken for the semantic richness of the question or the paradoxical profundity of the aesthetic situation. It is strictly undecidable and traps the reader of the question in an uncomfortable double bind: the hyphen of *pouvoir-savoir* must, and cannot, be read, other than as the material marker of an unreadable gap.

In other words, if the coincidence is already so difficult that it answers to no other law than that of ceaseless, twisting, comings-and-goings, then the rupture or breakdown which threatens the vehicle cannot be structured as a simple failure but must instead be the possibility of an uncontrolled acceleration or spin. It is this possible spin, within language, that we would call rhetoric, a paradox of paradox. Its infolded timing and spacing makes politics, as the stuttering coincidence of power and knowledge, knowing and doing, possible, and dangerous.

Difficult Coincidences

Politically speaking, where does this leave Foucault? In an aporia of hopeless neutrality, a paradox of normless engagement, an "impossible attempt to stand nowhere"? If the very structure which makes the passage between power and knowledge possible also threatens it with disarticulation, discontinuity, and heterogeneity, what sort of politics is possible? Can the rhetorical and temporal paradox be erased—can Foucault free his "position" of paradox? Or would *that* be to efface the very possibility, and necessity, of politics as such? Foucault insisted that the problem was not one of positions but of politicizations: "The problem is not so much to define a political position (which comes down to a choice on a pre-constituted chessboard) but to imagine and bring into existence new schemas of politicization."[41] Let us practice the peculiar bias, the slant, of paradox and approach these questions obliquely. Politically.

In the last days of December 1981, Jacques Derrida, visiting Prague to meet with dissident philosophers, was arrested and jailed for twenty-four hours by Czech authorities. After his release he was asked by colleagues in Paris to draw a lesson in the politics of philosophy from the episode, and we are told that "among other things, he insisted on the difficulty there is in making an ethico-political gesture (supporting the resistance of the Prague philosophers, who demand respect for human rights and articulate that with a philosophy of the subject, the person, individual liberty, etc.) coincide with a philosophical labor governed by the necessity of deconstructing precisely such philosophemes."[42] The questions which have recurrently structured our reading find themselves addressed here with considerable force, and repeat themselves: how does knowledge ("the necessity of deconstruction") coincide with the action or power of an ethico-political gesture? Where and when, if it can, does this coincidence occur? What are the stakes of its (non-)occurrence? If it does occur, how and why is it "difficult"? What is the law, and the force, of the coincidence in its difficulty?

It may seem surprising, or unjustified, or at least difficult, to make Derrida and Foucault coincide around this question of their knowledge and their power, especially given their explicit and very public differences, but in fact the structure only reiterates our rhetorical problematic. After all, as Shoshana Felman has pointed out, "systems of thought are not necessarily opposed in the same way their authors are: it is always possible to have chosen the wrong adversary. To be sure, differences, sometimes radical ones, do exist: but these differences, being asymmetrical, often elude the simple structure of opposition."[43]

Let us put this asymmetry to the test of example. Foucault has his own difficult coincidences. A few months before Derrida's Prague affair, on June 19, 1981, at a press conference in the Geneva

Intercontinental Hotel, Foucault joined with activists from two international "humanitarian" organizations (Médecins du Monde and Terre des Hommes) and others, in a "Comité International contre le Piraterie," to announce a new human rights initiative in defense of Vietnamese boat people. Western officials and Vietnamese eyewitnesses had described tens of thousands of people, fleeing Vietnam but not yet received as refugees elsewhere, being attacked in the Gulf of Thailand by pirates and kidnapped, raped, tortured, and murdered. In the face of inaction by governments and the incapacity of existing international organizations, the actor Yves Montand said, "we cannot let this massacre happen." So, under the sign of a Rilke verse, "All terrifying things / Are perhaps only helpless things / Awaiting our help," the group proposed sending a fleet of nongovernmental naval vessels—including a new ship of its own—into the area to protect the boat people and dissuade the pirates.

Foucault, who frequently involved himself in these doctors' unorthodox politico-humanitarian initiatives, used the opportunity to theorize the gesture of the action itself. He never published his statement, but after his death the newspaper *Libération* did, under the title "Face aux gouvernements, les droits de l'Homme." (Although this text provides one of its rare theoretical elaborations, Foucault's militancy was often conducted under the banner of "rights": with the women's health movement, for the right to abortion, to contraception, and to the free use of one's body; with the gay liberation movement, for the right to choose one's sexuality; with the labor union CFDT, for the worker's right to a healthy job; with the Information Group on Prisons, for the right to know about prison conditions; with Solidarity, for the rights and liberties of people living under Polish martial law; and so on.)[44] The brief text, which I translate here in its entirety, retains considerable force of surprise.

> We are here only as private individuals, who have no other claim to speak, and to speak together, than a certain shared difficulty in accepting what is happening.

I know full well, and we have to face facts, that there is not much we can do about the reasons which lead men and women to prefer leaving their countries over living in them. That fact is simply beyond our reach.

Who, then, has commissioned us? No one. And that is precisely what establishes our right. It seems to me that we must bear in mind three principles which, I believe, guide this initiative, like the many others which have preceded it (the *Île de Lumière*, the *Cap Anamour*, the *Avion pour le Salvador*, but also Terre des Hommes, Amnesty International).

1. There exists an international citizenry, which has its rights, has its duties, and promises to rise up against every abuse of power, no matter who the author or the victims. After all, we are all governed and, to that extent, in solidarity.

2. Because they claim to concern themselves with the welfare [*bonheur*] of societies, governments have arrogated to themselves the right to draw up a balance sheet, to calculate the profits and losses, of the human misfortune [*malheur*] provoked by their decisions or permitted by their negligence. It is a duty of this international citizenry always to make an issue of people's misfortune, to keep it in the eyes and ears of governments—it is not true that they are not responsible. People's misfortune must never be a silent remainder of politics. It founds an absolute right to rise up and to address those who hold power.

3. We must reject the division of tasks which is all too often offered to us: it is up to individuals to become indignant and speak out, while it is up to governments to reflect and to act. It is true that good governments like the hallowed indignation of the governed, provided it remains lyrical. I believe that we must realize how often, though, it is the rulers who speak, who can only and want only to speak. Experience shows that we can and must reject the theatrical role of pure and simple indignation which we are offered. Amnesty International, Terre des Hommes, Médecins du Monde are initiatives which have created this new right: that of private individuals actually to intervene in the order of international politics and strategies. The will of individuals has to inscribe itself in a reality over which governments have wanted to reserve a monopoly for themselves—a monopoly which we uproot little by little every day.[45]

Was it unjust of this text's posthumous editor at *Libération* to suggest that it "could be *une Nouvelle déclaration des Droits de l'homme*"? Its principles—its "rights" and "duties"—certainly recall those of the Western humanist tradition, which Foucault is widely believed to have rejected. Individuals, as citizens, have rights and obligations against or in the face of abusive rulers—governments which have attempted to reserve to themselves the power to speak and to act.[46] This nongovernmental citizenry can and must intervene, verbally and actively, against abuses of power, and not merely get indignant—here, in order to assert and to address the misfortune of others, whether they are Vietnamese boat people or Spanish militants condemned to death in Franco's courts.[47] That responsibility includes assigning the responsibility for misfortune to governments, no matter how they attempt to account for it, to explain it away, or otherwise to evade it. But another, unprecedented, intervention is also required: actually, *effectivement*, inventing and undertaking strategies and tactics of acting in international politics, where governments have hitherto at once monopolized and squandered the rights and means to act. Their arrogation of speech and action must be wrested away, by reordering or reinscribing political reality—by claiming the right to do, and by doing, what they will not.

If these terms are more or less standard, the rhetorical strategies or style with(in) which they are deployed are not so familiar. This declaration reinscribes its all too easily recognized philosophemes using some rather unorthodox gestures, which displace the self-evidence of their context. Foucault follows a peculiar course, one which would appear at first to be negative but which we will argue is not positive, but affirmative. The first sentence exemplifies this strategy. It mimes a certain self-positioning, a presentation of credentials, an establishment of a right or claim to speak, only to remove it or relocate it otherwise: What entitles us to do this? "We . . . have no other claim to speak . . . than . . . a difficulty," a difficulty with what is happening, with the present and the prospect that it will be the future too. This difficulty entitles not a position, nor even the lack of a position, but the affirmation of a fold within the present.[48] No sooner does the affirmation say its *yes*, initiate itself into the difficulty, than it is echoed by the second *yes* of a pledge. "This international citizenry . . . promises to rise up against every abuse of power." The initiative affirmation takes the performative character of a promise, a future-oriented speech act which does what it says. Once the difficulty—in its intolerable and irreducible difficulty—is affirmed, the initiative co-signs itself with a promise which projects it(self) and opens (into) a future, a pledge which binds the difficulty in the present to an unforeseeable future created in the act. The declaration is this promise, this engagement, and the promise is the affirmation of the difficulty and its future. The promise requires the declaration: what it says it does it could not do without saying.

This complicated little text submits its rights and obligations to the same initiative rhetoric of difficulty. The citizenry must resist the reduction of others' misfortune to *un reste muet*, a mute trace or leftover of politics and its calculations. The threat of that double effacement, the chance that misfortune will be left wordless, and not simply the misfortune itself, calls for active and insistent assertion. "People's misfortune must never be a silent remainder of politics. It founds an absolute right to rise up and to address those who hold power." Against the possibility of that effacement insists the imperative that it be addressed, a duty to act, to speak, and to write. The gesture of address affirms the right to memory of a future survival, a *reste*, where it might otherwise be effaced and its effacement silenced. The name and the trace must be preserved, kept in word and act of memory, so that the people of the name will not themselves be erased in the silent, calculated, oblivion of politics. What remains after the calculation, the remainder of the operation, is misfortune: an unmasterable and uneliminable remnant, which in its stubborn excess "founds an absolute right" and creates an obligation to respond.

The misfortunate ones, though, have not delegated this noble task or the authority to perform it to anyone, have not ceded their rights or (what remains of) their voices to this committee, have not chosen Foucault or anyone else in Geneva to speak on their behalf.

They, and their reasons, are beyond reach. Where is this right "founded," then? In the name of whom or what is it exercised? "Who, then, has commissioned us? No one. And that is precisely what establishes our right [*Personne. C'est cela justement qui fait notre droit*]." Because there is no one, there is a right. The committee (like the other initiatives to which Foucault refers) was never elected, represents no one, has no mandate or authority. There is no original owner or possessor of rights, no self-present source here mediated or represented in its (temporary and ultimately accidental) absence. Uprooting the monopoly claimed by those who have been delegated that authority and those rights (we are all already governed), the initiative of the initiatives, their institutive performance, has pragmatically "created," in fact, this new right: to speak and to intervene, outside or beyond this logic of delegation, where there is no one. In a gesture not unlike the one Derrida has called a *coup de droit*, the initiative initiates its new right, makes or creates it, based on no one: *no one* "articulates and conjoins the two discursive modalities, the to-be and the ought-to-be, constative and prescriptive, fact and right [*le fait et le droit*]."[49] No one . . . makes our right. The invention, the intervention, creates the right to intervene, enacts the right to act, initiates the right to initiate.

What is this "new right"? Is it a "norm"? How can we read this direct, if complicated, articulation of an ethico-political gesture with a warped vocabulary of rights and obligations? The reading is particularly difficult given Foucault's elaborate critique of the term "right," the apparently "rejectionist" critique which leads his interpreters to worry about "normative" aporias and confusions. His insistence here on a "founded" "absolute right" seems retrograde (i.e., limited to an Enlightenment-inspired critique of governments by the assertion of the rights of a misfortunate humanity they have tried to forget) and perhaps embarrassing. Is not Michel Foucault the most committed opponent of the discourse of rights, the operator of the theoretical guillotine which decapitates not only the king as political power principle but the individual, the human, and the humanism of human rights as well? Was not man's face erased from the sand at the edge of the sea in the final words of *Les mots et les choses*? Doesn't "right" belong precisely to the juridical vocabulary of power as sovereignty out of which Foucault tried to twist? Did not "power-knowledge" replace "right"? Doesn't "right" presuppose as the object of its legitimation or the target of its claims exactly the conception of power as negative, repressive, interdictive, against which Foucault tried to rethink power as positive, provocative, and productive (of exactly the subject, indeed, which would claim its rights and thus secure the play of power)? Did not Foucault contend that right in the West is the King's right and demand with distinctive epigrammatic economy that we "cut off the King's head"?[50]

The answer to these questions is of course yes. Again and again. Foucault measured his distance from and suspicions of a theory of right most extensively in two January 1976 lectures at the Collège de France. "Right should be viewed," he said, "not in terms of a legitimacy to be established, but in terms of the methods of subjugation that it instigates."[51] His philosophical objections to the discourse of rights took the form of a certain hesitation with regard to the thought of the proper which underwrites it. Right is proper to Man as such: as individual, man has rights, man's own rights. This property depends in its turn on a thought of presence. Possession requires the presence of the subject to itself; self-possession founds all other property and proprieties. On that basis, rights can also be delegated, transferred, or represented. The discourse of right elaborates the rules governing such exchanges, culminating in a theory of political representation. "Power is taken to be a right," said Foucault, "which one is able to possess like a commodity, and which one can in consequence transfer or alienate, either wholly or partially, through a legal act that establishes a right, such as takes place through cession or contract."[52] This means that the history of the theory of right is its deployment in defense of, and then in the assault on, kings and their sovereignty. In the West's thought of the political, "it is a question of the king, his rights, his power, the eventual limits on his power"; to that extent, says Foucault, its "essential function" was nothing other than "to efface the domination intrinsic to power," either by justifying or by putting limits on the king's or the state's power (95/177). Challenges made in the name of rights to regimes which abused them, said Foucault elsewhere, "did not put in question the principle that right should be the form of power and that power always had to be exercised in the form of right."[53]

Foucault proposed undoing, reversing, exposing the elimination of the fact of domination in the theory of right, to show "how right is, in a general way, the instrument of this domination—which scarcely needs saying—but also to show the extent to which and the forms in which right . . . transmits and brings into play relations not of sovereignty but of domination." "My general project," he said, "has been, in essence, to reverse the mode of analysis followed by the entire discourse of right, . . . to invert it"—to show, not which rights (whether divine, individual, or human) are legitimate, justified and authorized, but rather, how force relations have been enabled and naturalized in the name of "right."[54]

This inversion undid more than the effacement of domination. It changed the very terms of the analysis. The "short-circuiting or avoidance" of the question of the legitimate right to exercise power, in favor of specifying just what asymmetries of force "right" made possible, led the analysis to "the point where power exceeds the rules of right which organize and delimit it and extends itself beyond them."[55] These so-called "disciplinary mechanisms of power," Foucault said in *The History of Sexuality, Volume I*, are "irreducible to representation by right." The discourse of right is "absolutely heterogenous to new procedures of power, which operate not by right but by technique, not by law but by normalization, not by punishment but by control, which are exercised on levels and forms which exceed [*débordent*] the state and its apparatuses."[56]

Yet the discourse of right continues to provide the "code" for interpreting or analyzing the mechanisms of a power which has overrun or exceeded its conceptual limits, into a "horizon which of necessity has nothing in common with the edifice of right." In spite of the fact that disciplinary power is "impossible to describe in the terminology of the theory of sovereignty," right continues to serve as the model or code for its investigation and legitimation. Foucault's "inversion" aims to expose the unreliability of this code: "a system of right [has been] superimposed upon the mechanisms of discipline in such a way as to conceal its actual procedures, the element of domination inherent in its techniques, and to guarantee to everyone, by virtue of the sovereignty of the State, the exercise of his proper sovereign rights." Modern democracies have taken over the code of right while operating new mechanisms of discipline: on the one hand, there are no kings but only networks of disciplinary *quadrillage*; on the other, there remains "a discourse, an organization of public right." But rights (whether of kings or the "people" who replace them as sovereign) and discipline are "incompatible," "radically heterogenous." "And this *quadrillage* cannot, in any case at all, be transcribed into this right, which is, however, its necessary accompaniment."⁵⁷

Their coincidence or superimposition, "not so much the linking as the perpetual exchange and encounter of mechanisms of discipline with the principle of right" (107/188), proves difficult for the analysis of and the struggles against existing power relations. The discourse of right—precisely to the extent that it is simply inverted or undone and its effacement of the imbalance of power relations made legible—reasserts itself, comes back to haunt the analysis and the struggle as an unreliable but unshakable code. The reversal, while bringing the fact of domination to light and pointing to the disciplines' *débordement* of the rules of right, cannot prevent its recurrence and indeed threatens to retain the very terms which it had exposed as inadequate.

> Against disciplinary mechanisms . . . we find ourselves in a situation where the only, apparently solid recourse available to us today lies precisely in a return to the theory of right. . . . When today one wants to object in some way to the disciplines and all of the effects of power and knowledge that are linked to them, what is it that one does, concretely, practically? What do the *Syndicat de la Magistrature* or other similar institutions do? What do they do if not precisely invoke this right, this famous, formal bourgeois right, which is in reality the right of sovereignty? But I think that we are in a kind of blind alley or bottleneck [*goulot d'étranglement*] here, that we cannot continue to function indefinitely in this way. (107–8/189)

The extreme difficulty of this "blind alley" is not merely that there is no way out, that the path is closed off at one end. In that situation it would suffice merely to reverse directions, learn from one's mistakes, and find a new alley. The aporia Foucault finds us in is complicated by the fact that we have no place or room to turn, that we are in a sense blind (to) ourselves, and that we cannot go on like this: faced with the irreducibility of discipline to right, with their radical heterogeneity, what do we do in our struggle against disciplines if not invoke this very, incompatible right? Foucault may pose this as a "rhetorical question," but it should not be taken lightly. He provides no answer, and not because the answer is too obvious. The predicament we are written into by "right" is not easily escaped or even avoided. The disciplines have theorized and codified themselves in the incommensurable language of right. We know, negatively, that the code is inadequate, in error, and that we must invert and expose it. But the reversal fails to exorcise the code, and attempts to deploy it (reversed or not) against the disciplines only tighten the bind. The heterogeneity of the problem and its only available answer provokes a kind of mutual interference and multiplies the difficulty. Against the disciplines the only recourse is a return to the very code of right which the analysis of those disciplines has discredited, doubling the blindness in and of the alley. The blindness of the alley incites, and is in turn hyperactivated by, our own blindness: right inscribes us in a double bind, a double blind, a double blind alley.[58]

In a sensitive reading of this problem, Habermas has accurately if critically characterized Foucault's predicament here as another aporia. He appreciates the attempt to resist a simple inversion of the discourse of human rights: "the humanistic critique . . . which bases itself on the obsolete opposition between legitimate and illegitimate powers, . . . etc., and fights against instances of exploitation [or] . . . repression is in danger of reinforcing the humanism that has been brought from heaven down to earth and has congealed into normalizing violence."[59] This objection, he says, suffices as long as the point is merely tactical, "if the only concern is the mobilization of counter-power," but it does not answer the question "Why fight?" Still, since the "answer" would have to provide new standards of justice and a rationale for struggle, there is a certain necessity to Foucault's hesitation in the double blind alley: "if one tries to obtain the implicitly used standards out of the indictments against the disciplinary powers, one encounters known determinations from the explicitly rejected normativistic language game" (6–7/751).

Given this aporia—the unreliability and persistence of the term "right"—one might expect Foucault simply to reach for another vocabulary, a code proper to discipline (technique, normalization, control, etc.), responding to his own imperative: "we must build an analytic of power which will no longer take right as its model and code."[60] But Foucault takes the predicament seriously: having revealed a "position" to be aporetic, one cannot simply change language games and make the aporia vanish. An aporia (from *a-poros*, without passage, impassable) is something one cannot get out of, and this radical absence of possible choices characterizes the double blind alley. The difficulty is not one of political naïveté, simplicity, or ignorance, and cannot be dissolved by a technical, terminological measure. Thus, in the final paragraph of the same lecture, whose horizon necessarily had nothing in common with right, Foucault surprisingly concluded that there was no alternative to right, or only alternative rights. Even if he had tried to overturn or turn away from the classical right of sovereignty, this reversal was only one turn in a double gesture, coincident with a different mo(ve)ment, a reinscription of the "same" term in new possibility:

> In fact, sovereignty and discipline, the right of sovereignty and disciplinary mechanics, are two absolutely constitutive pieces of the general mechanisms of power in our society. To tell the truth, in order to struggle against the disciplines, or rather against disciplinary power, in the search for a nondisciplinary power, the direction in which we must turn is not toward the old right of sovereignty; it would be in the direction of a new right, one which would be anti-disciplinary, but at the same time liberated from the principle of sovereignty. (108/189)

The recovery or rewriting of the term "right" is important and not common: in the next, and final, sentences of the lecture, in fact, Foucault explicitly rules out any recuperation of the word "repression," "no matter what critical use one would make of it." "Right" receives no such stigma, and is indeed reserved for "new" possibilities.

New rights, but how and when? How is this possible? What is the difference between the "right" of the "entire discourse of right" to be undone and the "right" of the "new right" to be actively put back into play? How does Foucault negotiate this twisting into and out of right? We should not hesitate to assimilate the "new right" of this lecture to the one(s) enunciated or initiated in Geneva. But that goes no distance toward freeing Foucault's position of the paradox involved in *at once* making the practical gesture with the word "right" *and* submitting the same word to the theoretical and rhetorical work of decapitation, undoing, and reinscription.

How does the ethico-political gesture of supporting the resistance and protest of people, with its reference to *les droits de l'Homme*, coincide with the philosophical necessity of problematizing or "short-circuiting" the model of rights, the very terms in which the gesture is made?

Rights Without Right, on the Bias

For Kant, in the *Metaphysics of Morals*, right was a matter of straightness: "Right (*rectum*) is, as the straight, opposed not only to the curved, but also to the oblique."[61] But what if politics had no choice but to practice the bias—as prejudice, as sidestep, as cut across the grain—of paradox?

Needless to say, I am not proposing Foucault's "new right" as a model, a formula, or a theoretical example to be reapplied elsewhere, as if one could analyze the (political or philosophical) difficulties of an "old" term and then replace it with a new one which would do its job better. It is neither philosophically nor politically correct(ed). The right enunciated as a theoretical possibility and initiated at Geneva marks, in its difficulty, a permanent political predicament. It does not avoid or transcend, but only repeats with emphasis, these difficulties. It displaces and temporalizes its terms, and plays them out as the paradox of "right": a claim based in the affirmation of a difficulty in the present and seconded by a promise to a future (a double bond); a remainder threatened with silence whose right to a future is opened in assertive memory; and a *coup de droit*, the initiation of the right to initiate, the intervention of a right to intervene, where there is no one. These are not classical rights, but they recall or remember them and offer implicitly a theory of right beyond sovereignty. They retheorize rights, claim a certain right to "right": they guard a link with that past while twisting or knotting it almost beyond recognition, opening it out of its present onto its future difficulties.[62] These paradoxically folded binds inscribe within them that temporal predicament—ahead of and behind themselves. The double blind alley, then, cannot be ignored: we must negotiate with the rights we have, even "after" their problematization. Because rights, as such, disperse any attempt at totalization: they disperse not only the rigid inscription of rights within a system of classical sovereignty but also the negative work of controlling or even merely circumscribing their unreliability. We recall the futures of a right beyond right, a right without right, only by making reference or gesturing to the "rights" we have. There is "no way out," because there is no "out"— not because the present is somehow self-enclosed or self-identical, or because rights are a thing of the past, but because the present differs from itself and thus makes politics necessary. The only way out is out of politics altogether.

What is the law or the force of persistence and resistance which allows the hyphen—whether between power and knowledge, the gesture and its deconstruction, or the two "rights"—to be marked, erased, and remarked? What governs the materiality of the hyphen which we read, efface, and rewrite as if only stutteringly unable either to respect or reject it? What is the necessity of negotiation? The law is, according to Foucault, that "there is no general law indicating the types of relation."[63] Perhaps only a rhythm, the intolerable tension of the alteration . . . of different hyphens. Earlier we characterized this tension of the "at once" as an internal heterogeneity, or an infolding. Politics, though, demands that this infolding be unfolded, that it be deployed across time. Foucault suggests this in two discussions of the political uses of "rights": on defending gay rights, "it is important to have the possibility—and the right—to choose your own sexuality. . . . Still, I think we have to go a step further. . . . Not only do we have to defend ourselves, but we have to affirm ourselves."[64] Which is to say, affirm something which can only be affirmed and not defended—because it is not (yet). Likewise, on rights in prison: "There are immediate measures to take . . . in order to eliminate all the abuses of rights in the way the law is applied. . . . But then [*ensuite*]—or rather, at once [*tout de suite*]—it's a question of taking up everything again, at the roots. . . . We must try now to rethink the entire thing: not at all to avoid the real, but rather never to accept anything 'self-evident' as given."[65] That can only happen in a future, but a future which is inscribed as a difference within the non-presence of the present, a rhythm modulating and opening the present to a difference which seems to incapacitate its present even as it hyperactivates the future already within it.[66] The terms, though, cannot be found anywhere else. The paradox repeats itself: "on peut être en face et debout,"[67] but not without difficulty. The politics is in the negotiation of the difference between *ensuite* and *tout de suite*, in the inscription of the affirmative "step further" into the defense.

Hence Foucault's formulation of the temporal task of political criticism:

> It is fruitful in a certain way to describe that-which-is by making it appear as something that might not be, or that might not be as it is. . . . It does not consist in a simple characterization of what we are but, instead, by following lines of fragility in the present, in managing to grasp why and how that-which-is might no longer be that which is. . . . [The present] is a day like any other, or rather, a day which is never quite like any other.[68]

This thought of divisions "within" the present, its internal displacement or fragility, opens politics onto its futures. It disqualifies the metaphoric extension by "likeness" of the present into a future all its own, imagined as enough "like" this present to replace it. (It is in this sense that we take Foucault's claim that "imaginer un autre système, cela fait actuellement encore partie du système.")[69] What opens up is a time never quite like any other. Not the future of the present, not a future good to be hoped for from a position (or negation) in the present, but the promise and the affirmation of the future, of future*s*, as other, as never quite like any other, as what is only possible or, better, what is (always) not yet possible: what might no longer be what is. But this negative-future-conditional event can just as little be passively awaited as actively imagined—it does not happen in a future present: it will always have already violently interfered with the presence of our present and our position(s) within it. We imagine, we see or hear, nothing here; reading is our task. So Foucault calls the event a *caesura*, an anti-rhythmical (rhetorical) interruption,[70] "the straight line of the future that again and again cuts the smallest thickness of the present, that indefinitely recuts it starting from itself." Interrupting the symmetrical exchanges that organize the subject and its "minutely present unity"—the likenesses of cognition—the caesura opens it in the encounter with the difficult and always particular (singular) text of the political. Not to some new thing, something newly present, but to a strange repetition. If the caesura "is less a cut than an indefinite fibrillation," then what repeats—"fissured by this arrow of the future that carries it forward by always causing its swerving"—"recurs as singular difference; and the analogous, the similar, and the identical never return."[71] This affirmation of the (never quite like any) other, another other than our own, and of the event of the other, can only be an appeal to the future or the excess of "another law and another force beyond the totality of this present" (Derrida). It demands, says Foucault, "an affirmative thought whose instrument is disjunction" (185/899).

Foucault was once bold—or ironic—enough to call this interference a "truth," a reading in and of the future. "What I am trying to do is provoke an interference between our reality and the knowledge of our past history," he said in an interview. "Two years ago there was turmoil in several prisons in France, prisoners revolting. In two prisons, the prisoners in their cells read my book. They shouted the text to other prisoners. . . . I hope that the truth of my books is in the future."[72]

Where and when could one possibly "stand" to make, or respond to, this call of the future? Nowhere? Never? Is it possible? Does the hyphen prevent this possibility, or does it mark the timing and the spacing of an unavoidable, however paradoxical, coincidence as difficulty? What are the (anti-)rhythms and the sites that unfold in the dash? What sort of decision can be made between a philosophical effort and a political gesture in discord? Can either one be forgotten and the other pursued with impunity, as if each were not precisely the error denounced by the other, the error which it can only undo? The fact that these are (not simply) rhetorical questions does not make them any less urgent or easier to bear.

The philosophical labor is an effort of understanding which produces a negative knowledge concerning the risks and stakes of a set of terms ("right," "individual," etc.). Exposure of the unreliability of this discourse demands its undoing, its reversal or decapitation. But the order of action, the gesture of intervention in the existing relations of force, is not paralyzed or incapacitated by this knowledge, just as it does not remain untouched. A gesture is made, something gets inscribed "in a reality," people interfere or actually "intervene in the order of . . . politics." But not without difficulty, or perhaps even paradox. The interest of Foucault's "declaration" is finally not simply that he supports human rights while deconstituting or problematizing them, but how he performs their difficult coincidence while refusing to allow either gesture to escape unscathed. The purity or propriety of the philosophical work is undone by the reinscription of the undermined term in a struggle theorized in already-deconstructed terms, while the ethico-political gesture finds itself robbed of any extra-political or philosophical authority.

So Foucault does neither of the two things simply, or at least not in the style to which they are accustomed. The coincidence is difficult, and its difficulty cannot be forgotten in the excitement of the coincidence. Each moment of the double gesture undoes the other; they do not derive from, nor do they ground, each other. They are articulated on the basis (the nonbasis) of their difference, and the difference will always threaten to turn into disarticulation, just as the paradox will always have already collapsed. The difficulty of coincidence is the necessity of negotiation, its inevitability and its impossibility. It is political because it is impossible. If negotiation were merely possible, politics would be unnecessary. But there are double binds, everyday, which is why politics is difficult, and which is why politics is not programming. Difficult as it is, the coincidence will always have already taken place—future anterior—more or less, like it or not. But it is a coincidence, in something like the everyday sense—it cannot be programmed, guaranteed in advance with any certainty, predicted or predictated. A truly temporal predicament: utterly without guarantees, except that it will happen. Only in this sense is what we call the "relation" of power-knowledge a paradox: it must maintain or support an intolerable and insupportable difference without opposition or resolution. The unpredictability, the bias or the obliquity, of the relation is the risk, the predicament, and the chance, of politics as of reading. It is difficult.

No More Morals

When Foucault argued in Geneva that this new right to intervene was based simply on a difficulty in accepting what was happening, that it was delegated by no one and stemmed from nothing already given, he defined a radical theory of rights as such. Not the classical rights of individuals, the inalienable rights of man, or the rights said to find their ground in human nature, but rather, a theory of rights as the condition of a radically democratic politics, rights without limit and end, rights as the irreducible claim and gesture of the political as such. Claude Lefort has argued that "rights are constitutive of politics," and we need only add that politics is here thought and experienced as a paradox, in the strictest sense, an ungrounded or aporetic predicament: the experience of "the legitimacy of a debate on the legitimate and the illegitimate, a debate necessarily without any guarantor and without any end."[73] Rights, because they are based on nothing more, or less, than discourse, on the claims we make to them, are essentially unlimited, which is to say, inessential and irreducible. Hence the "unpredictable adventure" of the right to rights, as Lefort argues: "The idea of human nature, which was so vigorously proclaimed at the end of the eighteenth century, could never capture the meaning of the undertaking inaugurated by the great American and French declarations. By reducing the source of right to the human utterance of right, they made an enigma of both humanity and right."[74]

This enigma, the political predicament itself, has no subject, and it cannot give rise to the agonized existential choice of something human encountering its fate. It can no more be decided by a subject, suspended over the abyss of its freedom and called to choose between irreconcilable ends, than it can be referred to a calculation or a technical rule. This angst of the decision can emerge only against the background of a possible (correct) answer, and the security of that possibility (and its pathos) escapes us in politics. The articulation never quite takes place, at least not within a subject responsible for synchronizing knowing and doing. Its freedom begins in the chance that opens where calculation gives way. There is always too much or too little knowledge to meet the demands of action, or the reverse.

Too often, a demand for politics takes the form of an evasion of the political. Lefort insists that the strictly political meaning and force of rights emerges only when they are divorced from the horizon of the subject or the individual; human rights are not individual rights. The category of the individual, shared by liberalism and its radical critics, serves to shelter something from the aberrations and confusions of the political, of the enigma of the human utterance of right. I have argued that the political urgency and force of Foucault's claims comes precisely in their refusal to seek this extra-political standpoint, a ground in the subject, knowledge, or the realities of power. That is why Foucault's would-be "political" critics, who decry the erasure of the subject and its rights, miss what is most interesting, and most political, about his work. For instance:

> Without any way of conceptualizing juridical subjectivity, Foucault's recommendation of collective resistance has such a blind and un-

differentiated character as to be almost politically irresponsible. He provides us, ultimately, with no way of distinguishing the resistance of the women's movement or the Polish Solidarity movement from, say, the Ku Klux Klan or Jim Jones' People's Temple.[75]

It is not clear why, especially after reading Foucault, one would require a theory of subjectivity or of power in order to tell the KKK from Solidarity. Philosophy or theory does not need to perform these tasks for us. Indeed, the political character of the differentiation, the political difference itself, arises in the removal of these foundational concepts or general rules ("ways") for distinguishing. What is here called "irresponsible" is the structure of political responsibility as such. The demand for the theory of "juridical subjectivity" functions as way of hiding from the call for just the political decision that seems to be appealed to. The reference to subjectivity or ground, in this sense, constitutes nothing less than an evasion of the political.

This has been Lefort's most unforgiving and shocking claim, that the modern or democratic experience of politics is precisely the invention of rights *as* the removal of foundation, "the general contradiction that arises when the social order no longer has any basis."[76] Rather than bemoan this loss of foundation, or criticize those who point to it as disingenuous or nihilistic, we can see in it the necessity of the political:

> Democracy is instituted and maintained by the *dissolution of the markers of certainty*. It inaugurates a history in which people undergo the experience of a final indeterminacy as to the foundation of power, law, and knowledge, and as to the foundation of relations *between self and other*, at every level of social life (everywhere that division, and especially the division between those who held power and those who were subject to them, could once be articulated as a result of a belief in the nature of things or in a supernatural principle). (19/29)

The condition of politics is this impossibility of society: "the markers of certainty which once allowed people to situate themselves in a relation to one another in a determinate manner have disappeared."[77] When society cannot be totalized, when it has no foundation and no given order or principle capable of comprehending or organizing it as a totality, then there is politics. Although Foucault never referred to Lefort that I know of, he assumed this analysis and once, memorably, made very clear that it was the premise of his investigation of power:

> Nothing is fundamental. That is what is interesting in the analysis of society. That is why nothing irritates me as much as these inquiries—which are by definition metaphysical—on the foundations of power in a society or the self-institution of a society, etc. These are not fundamental phenomena. There are only reciprocal relations, and the perpetual gaps between intentions in relation to one another.[78]

Because society doesn't exist, because nothing is fundamental, there is politics—rights and responsibilities, decisions without subjects or guarantees.[79]

Nothing finally orients such decisions, not even the "strategy" to which Foucault so often referred; politics would instead be the experience of strategy without finality, pure tactics, the bias of a "slalom."[80] Yet we remain responsible, before this demand, before the other (something must be said, known, or done), simply before. Decidability and the pain of its failure are equally ways of evading this call, just as "political positions," to the extent that they are "choices on an already-constituted chessboard," are nothing but alibis for responsibilities.[81] When the coincidence is called for and troubled, troubled just to the extent that it is necessary, then we are responsible. In the withdrawal of the ethico-political position, of a ground or a last instance to which we might appeal, we are left in the predicament of a singularity that resists incorporation into any program or law, without the guidance of a moral.[82] Displacing the instruction in what is to be done was what Foucault called "fictions," but not simply fictions, because they are examples without rules. Blanchot could not have imagined a more precise explanation from Foucault: "In other words, I am a fabulist composing fables whose morals it would be imprudent to wait for."[83]

Conclusion:

No Man's Land—Ideology, Between Ethics and Politics

What we call ideology is precisely the confusion of linguistic with natural reality, of reference with phenomenalism. It follows that, more than any other mode of inquiry, including economics, the linguistics of literariness is a powerful and indispensable tool in the unmasking of ideological aberrations, as well as a determining factor in accounting for their occurrence.

—Paul de Man, "The Resistance to Theory"

No One

Who's there? Who speaks, reads, acts, takes responsibility or claims rights, if not me? Again and again over the preceding chapters we have read the answer: *no one*. The non-responsive *nay* of the arriving sentinel and the enigmatic *personne* at the start of Foucault's Geneva declaration can stand in here for a generalized de-constitution of the subject in the experience of responsibility. So, no one takes responsibility? And still we answer, make our claims, unfold ourselves? As it turns out, we have argued here that an experience we might call *de-facilitation*—difficulty (in the strongest sense), unease, or impossibility—is the condition or, more exactly, what Levinas calls the "uncondition," of anything worthy of the name responsibility. No one authors, masters, or organizes this difficulty; indeed, the grammar, as Nietzsche might have said, is misleading here, for this impossibility marks the incapacity of any notion of subjectivity to approach the question of responsibility. "No one" is not a new name or placeholder for what used to be called the "subject"—the oblique negation tells us that, if there is responsibility, then it coincides with the undoing of this very place and time. Nothing teaches this predicament better than reading, reading exposed to the difficulties of its own rhetorical circumstance. Responsibility passes by way of the undecidable.

What is it to say then, yes, finally, I take responsibility, I am responsible? Perhaps we are overtaken by our responsibility, taken by our over-responsibilities, by others, but nothing could be more irresponsible than the immodest self-certainty of one who rests content in the good sense of a responsibility properly assumed. We will never be rid of what Derrida calls a "surplus of responsibility."[1] Like rights, responsibilities are unlimited and unguaranteed—if they are anything at all. Which means that this "no one" implies, with or without paradox, a certain endlessness. Because the ground is lacking, because the claim or the response comes to pass without the security of an authoritative cognitive position, nothing guarantees that what we accomplish will remain finished, once and for all inscribed in reality. This removal of grounds, objective and subjective, gives to our decisions the quality of contingency that makes them strictly political. "No one" means, then, no last instance, no final solutions, what Giorgio Agamben has recently called "means without ends"—"the sphere of pure means or gestures (i.e., means which, while remaining such, are freed from their relation to an end), as the properly political sphere."[2] Or as Richard Rorty said somewhere: in politics, time will tell, but epistemology won't. And time will tell many different stories. Politics is the name we give to this endlessness, to the irresolution of differences, to the happy and traumatic impossibility of totality.[3]

And what are the stories told here? What about this "no one"? Does its anonymity figure the generalized or universalized abstraction of the citizen, rather than the singularity of the subject? Am I narrating here the passage from private individual to public citizen, the emergence from the simplicity of what used to be called "the bourgeois self" into the activism of a robust new post-subjective agency? Or even worse, into the emptiness of the "member of society," the man of the crowd erased in the bland homogeneity of a contentless anyone? Does the insistent reference here to language bring us out of the confines of privacy into a shared public space of discourse, since "speech as such and thought as such, independent of any particular individual, prove to belong to no one," as Claude Lefort says?[4]

Yes and no. *No one*, in a word, is not just *anyone*. There would be little interest in deconstructing the responsible subject only to replace it with the homogeneous openness of the public sphere, the bright enlightenment of *Öffentlichkeit*. What needs to be deconstructed is precisely the *opposition* between public and private, the formal symmetry that secures each over against the other and the reciprocal determinations that have kept them locked together through the history of metaphysics. And what needs to be opened up are the differences and the alterity within each, crossing, traversing, and dividing the terms of this paralyzing doublet. Only in this opening—the mutual impossibility of individual and society—can we begin to think about what articulates ethics and politics, singularity and community.

"Ideology" has long been the conceptual hinge which has secured the distinction, and the movement, between private and public, subject and others. Trying to account for the ways in which individuals are said to be brought into conformity with "larger social structures," the category has generally served to prop up the distinction at precisely the point of its maximum vulnerability. Thanks to the fact that we can think them together, as mediated in ideology, the opposition between private and public spheres is allowed to go largely unchallenged. But what becomes of theories of ideology when "society is impossible" and the subject is dispersed across incommensurable "subject positions"?

Ghosts of Ideology

They come back. Not only the ghosts and phantoms that regularly reappear, for instance, whenever Marx returns to the question of ideology and fetishism, but more simply the strange afterlives of the concept of ideology itself, its singular success in outliving, and indeed living on, the announcements of its demise.[5] What, after all, could be more ideological than the claim to be putting an end to ideology? There is no ideology without this wish for and promise of an end, an end to itself, and then its remaining, returning, all the more unaccountably and powerfully. And thus no ideology that would not present itself as illusion.

In the days and nights that follow what is unquestionably the collapse of the Soviet Union, this auto-spectralization of the ideological demands new attention—not only does its merely empirical persistence or its resistance alone earn it the right to our questions, but its theoretical status, its relation to a certain philosophical past, merits a return as well. Simply put, is it possible to extricate a concept of ideology from the themes of illusion, apparition, and error (tied, in opposition, to truth) that have governed its manifold appearances? Can a concept of ideology be detached from the narrative of a mistake and its undoing, an inversion and its correction—from the narrative of life and death which always issues in the phantasmatic return that constitutes the banal history of ideology? That a reading of irreversible error and of ongoing inversion can put the most critical political questions at stake should be clear by now—but does it serve as a theory of ideology? And what is the necessity, here and now, of a theory of ideology?

The most powerful such theory today is not German but Slovenian, in the work of Slavoj Žižek.[6] The final sentence of the introduction to *The Sublime Object of Ideology* promises "a new approach to ideology, allowing us to grasp contemporary ideological phenomena . . . without falling prey to any kind of 'postmodernist' traps (such as the illusion that we live in a 'post-ideological' condition)" (7). "The idea of the possible end of ideology is an ideological idea *par excellence*" (2). This eagerness to dispel illusions—here, the ideology of the post-ideological—captures with admirable economy the aporias at the heart of this complex reinvigoration of ideology critique. It marks Žižek's commitment to something like the classical project of a theory and critique of ideology, even as the particular instance of illusion here has a doubly exemplary status: would eluding the illusion of the end of ideology, the ideological illusion itself, avoid falling into the trap of that illusion? Answering that question—and this is his most prominent rhetorical strategy, answering the question—will be the aim of Žižek's work, and of my brief recapitulation of it. Žižek confronts, then, not just the dream of the end of ideology but the question of whether or not a theory of ideology is itself a thing of the past, another sort of specter. He answers no, and the theory that emerges with that negation can best be seen as a direct rejection of the claim that the concept of ideology, whether understood as false consciousness or as interpellation, is too bound up in a metaphysics of the subject, Hegelian or Heideggerian, as consciousness or as *Dasein*, that appears increasingly questionable today. Žižek's gesture is not to forsake the category of subjectivity but rather to suggest new ways of reading the relation between cognition and action, between knowing and doing, which has been the greatest stake of the theory of the subject, new ways that—by refusing to take the possibility of the articulation or the passage between knowledge and deed for granted—open a chance to think the conditions of a political time and space finally irreducible to any subjectivity. And yet, if Žižek succeeds in a striking rearrangement of our understanding of politics as the failed articulation between knowing and doing, his investment in presenting this as a theory of ideology, and of ideological misrecognition, commits him in the last instance not simply to a view of politics as aberrant but more importantly to the search for a certain kind of control over that danger. He proposes what we could call an ethics of the political, an extrapolitical effort to protect the political, to preserve the conditions for political-ideological action—but one which hesitates in the face of just that action.

"Ideology," writes Žižek, is "a social bond" (124), a relation linking people to one another in the aftermath of the address that has constituted them as subjects and inscribed them in that bond. It is also a mistake—although not a simple one, since the conditions for the correction of the error are constituted by the error and thus belong to it. Žižek's analysis begins with Marx's elegant formula for what they both call the "fetishistic inversion" (16), the effect that Marx famously compared to that produced in a camera obscura: "*sie wissen das nicht, aber sie tun es*—they do not know it, but they are doing it" (28). Ideology is, in this sense, the blinding of consciousness to its actions, the mistake of taking an effect for a cause or a particular for a universal. The promise of the *but* (*aber*) that articulates mis-knowing with doing is of course that it might be undone, by more or better knowing, by the de-inversion of sight and the clarification of consciousness. This scene presupposes a subject and a consciousness prior to the act in question, and thus pins all its hopes on the conversion of the upside-down image. The subject would be the neutral ground for this symmetrical exchange, and thus not only the site but the implied end of ideology.

This theory is not exactly Žižek's. Seeking at once to explain how it is not simply wrong and to hold onto a theory of ideology, Žižek proposes a reversal of a different order: following the formula for fetishism not of Marx but of Freud—*je sais bien, mais quand même* . . . , "I know very well, but still . . ." (18). If fetishism is an illusion, it is a constitutive and not an accidental one, an illusion that makes for a certain kind of sight. The default here is not on the side of knowledge, but rather is built into the act itself in spite of—or more accurately, thanks to—cognitive clarity. "We are fetishists in practice, not in theory" (31). Žižek insists, though, that the practice is still mistaken, an active misrecognition or inversion, a sort of simulation of a cognitive error in the event of doing. Here the *but* no longer allows the easy reversal of clarification, but it still signals an opposition, the symmetrical contradiction re-established by the arrival of an "as if "—"I know very well, but nevertheless I act as if I didn't." In fact, I am able to act as if I don't know precisely because I do know, because my clarity of cognition, my consciousness of my knowledge, or my knowledge of my consciousness, blinds me to the reality of my action. Consciousness blocks the correction of the error because it recognizes no error; the error—for instance, acting as if worker and manager met as equally free partners, while both know that one exploits the other—occurs in our action, not prior to it or layered over it, as if the action itself were the subject of the misrecognition. What we know and what we do remain isolated from each other, because another sort of knowing has emerged within doing itself.

Following Althusser, at least for some distance, Žižek interprets this basic ploy of ideology as an interpellation, the address from the other that constitutes its addressee as respondent and subject. Before the subject, there is a call that opens it as consciousness. The address is ideological, which is to say, in error, not only because it produces the effect of illusion but because it covers its own tracks. We are not subjects, and yet we are converted. Žižek diverges from Althusser, though, in his insistence that the internalization of the interpellation "never fully succeeds." The address arrives as a sense-less injunction, an order to obey by responding, and in that act offers the possibility both of following the order and of making sense of it retrospectively. Our answer comes, says Žižek, uncon-sciously, from the automaton in us that responds because it must—and, in answering, we take hold of our name and our address (mechanically, automatically, externally), we recognize ourselves as something that responds for a reason, on a ground, responsibly. This internalization of the exterior, comprehension of the sense-less, integration of the traumatic, makes us subjects—subjects of an originary error. So the "but" in "I know very well, but still . . ." means that everyday ideological behavior—I know, but I act un-consciously, routinely, according to a memorized ritual, and the fact that I know protects me from my blindness—repeats the response to the originary injunction, as the radical independence of unconscious action from conscious cognition. Rather than mark-ing a symmetrical reversal, the "but" has now, it seems, been reinscribed asymmetrically . . . except that the action is still under-stood as an illusion ("the illusion is on the side of doing," says Žižek [32]), because of the misrecognition that inverts the externality of obedience into the interiority of belief.

The mistake is confirmed as such precisely because the internal-ization or the identification never fully succeeds, always leaving what Žižek calls a "residue, a leftover, a stain of traumatic senseless-ness sticking to it"—a remainder that, since it cannot be integrated or made sense of and since it is protected by consciousness from consciousness itself, emerges as "the very condition" of our uncon-ditional submission to the ideological injunction. It can neither be known or done away with, only obeyed: "this non-integrated surplus of senseless traumatism" produces our unconditional submission to the command (43). Thus Žižek can provisionally define ideology as "a totality set on effacing the traces of its impossibility"—that is, the residue—and the fetishism proper to it as the concealment of the lack on or around which this network is articulated (49).

> Ideology is not a dreamlike illusion that we build to escape insupportable reality; in its basic dimension it is a fantasy-construction which serves as a support for our "reality" itself: an "illusion" which structures our effective, real social relations and thereby masks some insupportable, real, impossible kernel ([i.e.] . . . "antagonism": a traumatic social division which cannot be symbolized). (45)

So, "on the side of . . . what people are doing," the ideological "mistake" is reinscribed, as erasure and concealment of a gap, as an error and its cover up.

As Žižek unfolds his analysis, the language of a critical epistemology becomes more and more pronounced, even if a regime of quotation marks emerges hygienically: from illusion and reality, to "illusion" and "reality." The identity of the ideological field is made possible by a signifier—the *point de capiton*—that stops the sliding of the proto-ideological signifiers and fixes their meaning (87). This name that totalizes the field, analogous to the name with which we are addressed in the ideological interpellation, is a signifier without a signified, a "purely performative" event whose "signification coincides with its own act of enunciation" (99). But if this name holds the field together, "supports the identity of the object," it is only at the cost of opening "a discontinuity in reality" (95)—because it refers to nothing but its own task of totalization— and hence of opening the possibility of its own undoing. Žižek again calls it an error, open to detection and isolation: "The properly ideological dimension is therefore the effect of a certain error of perspective: the element . . . through which the signifier's non-sense erupts in the midst of meaning is perceived as a point of extreme saturation of meaning, as the point which gives meaning to all the others and thus totalizes the field of (ideological) meaning. . . . In short, *pure difference is perceived as Identity*" (99). As soon as this point is given a face or a figure, the epistemology is evident. But here, the figure is a figure: like an anamorphosis, Žižek continues, when we look at it "from the right . . . perspective, we are able to recognize in it the embodiment of a lack, a chasm of non-sense in the midst of ideological meaning" (100).

Ideology is thus the conversion of performative into constative or trope, and the critical analysis of ideology consists in "detecting" the performative operation lurking behind the tropological illusion (99). The emergence of this illegitimate passage, the exposure of the residue or surplus of the name's non-sense behind the trope's significance, gives rise to the final ideological maneuver—the figure of fantasy that offers us a non-sensical kernel of "enjoyment" as the substitute for this empty space. If the ideological identification cannot but fail, the fantasy is offered in compensation and as a further block on the deconstruction of its aberrant substitutions and fixings. Thus, concludes Žižek, the "critique of ideology" consists not just in this " 'deconstruction' of the spontaneous experience of [ideological] meaning" (125), but in addition—since the ideological operation has already accounted for its own susceptibility to this simple undoing ("fantasy is a means for an ideology to take its own failure into account in advance" [126])—goes on to "extract the kernel of enjoyment, to articulate the way in which an ideology implies, manipulates, produces a pre-ideological enjoyment structured in fantasy" (125). And it turns out that this second gesture is structured somewhat like the first, because the figure of fantasy is "a screen masking a void," a figure for the "inconsistency" or the "impossibility which prevents society from achieving its full identity as a closed, homogeneous totality" (127). Unlike the first-order trope, a traditional "metaphoric/metonymic displacement" (126), this one is radical: "fantasy is not to be interpreted, only 'traversed': all we have to do is experience how there is nothing 'behind' it, and how fantasy masks precisely this 'nothing'" (126). There is a name for this other aberrant name—the rhetorical handbooks would call it a catachresis—and Žižek offers a supplementary maneuver of ideology critique, another deconstruction, to identify it: "to detect, in a given ideological edifice, the element which represents within it its own impossibility" (127).

In a strange way, then, Žižek remains overcommitted to this task he calls, in quotes, "deconstruction"—and the defensive critique he offers of Derrida and of "post-structuralism" all over *The Sublime Object* reminds us that his interpretation of that word diverges widely from Derrida's (e.g. 153–55)—overcommitted and excessively confident in its demystificatory powers. But this double deconstruction (the first "discursive," the second "beyond interpellation" [124–25]) has an odd outcome. The determination of politics as ideology, and hence as mistake or aberration (even at the extreme of "figure for nothing," of the catachrestic positivization or figure for the void of society's inability to correspond with itself), finally implies the abandonment of the political field for an elsewhere from which those errors can be denounced. That this abandonment aims to protect the political field from its totalization by any given politics only adds another turn to the spiral of error.

The decisive gesture comes with Žižek's announcement in the very first pages of *The Sublime Object* that the theory of the subject he will offer "implies" what he calls an "ethics," if one paradoxically grounded in a certain facticity: "the fact that we must not obliterate the distance separating the Real from its symbolization" (3).[7] We must not erase, in other words, the residue or the surplus that exceeds ideological interpellation, the undecidability or the impossibility of full identification to which the ideological address gives rise and responds. Thus the ethics is one of respect, respect for the fact, for the distance, and for the fact of distance: against the obliteration of the separation, against the erasure of the gap or remainder that persists between cognition or meaning and that which provokes it. The fact at the origin of this ethics, then, is not the fact of the real but rather of its retreat from or resistance to any final statement of the facts. There is, as Žižek says, "no final solution"—and there ought not to be (5).[8]

But since this deadlock, the antagonism marked by the fissure, is a fact, it demands respect, the recognition if not the cognition due to that which maintains itself at the distance of ethical singularity. The autonomy of this gap, the transcendence of the real, must, that is to say, be acknowledged precisely because it cannot become an object for knowledge, and because it is always becoming one. If "we must not obliterate the distance," it is only because we always do, in the everyday operation of politics and ideology—the aberrant passage from performative to trope, from mindless obedience to mindful identification, from void to fantasy. (Recall one of the definitions of ideology: "a totality set on effacing the traces of its impossibility" [49].)

Politics and ideology, according to Žižek, are this erosion of distance, and the only protection available is an *ethics of the political*—a higher-order injunction (thou shalt not obliterate the distance), this time not in the name of sense but of its blockage, on behalf of antagonism. Do not efface the traces of impossibility. Evidently for Žižek such an injunction could not be issued within ordinary politics, as it is a fact and not an illusion, what he elsewhere calls a "stupid, traumatic, inconsistent fact," one whose "authority is without truth" (38). The responses to this incomprehensible imperative, this ethical law, seem to have a chance of adequately addressing it. In holding onto the distance, to the open possibility of the political, Žižek proposes that "the thing to do is" to "recognize," "accept," "acknowledge," "come to terms with" the originary cleft or fissure or negativity that structures the possibility of the political (in all its different versions: the relations between men and women, humans and nature, or within democracy). We must try to "patch things up," "articulate a *modus vivendi*" with the originary trauma of the real's excess over our symbolizations (5). Antagonism is "fundamental," and so "we can save democracy," for instance, "only by taking into account its own radical impossibility." Even if, as he elegantly puts it, "we always live in an interspace and in borrowed time, every solution is provisional and temporary, a kind of postponing of a fundamental impossibility," nevertheless that postponement can be governed, regulated, by reference to just this ground or fundament, at least to the fact of its insistently disruptive effects on our ideological constructions (6).

"The only thing man can do," Žižek says—"the thing to do"—is to acknowledge the antagonism, not to try to overcome it and thus fall prey to the ideological illusion, the teleological or just logical lure of totality—of erasing the traces. Facing the fact has a kind of tired resignation, or perhaps a resigned heroism. The reality of impossibility will interrupt whatever else we do, in any event, so we might as well get used to contingency, give in, and "accept" the impossibility of reconciling differences . . . in a word, the only thing to do is reconcile ourselves to the irreconcilable. What this comes down to, then, is this: for Žižek, politics is a matter of meaning and knowledge, of closing and fixing, and thus inevitably of mistakes, while ethics involves a respect and a tolerance, a recognition rather than a misrecognition, and is finally not subject to the deconstruction reserved for tropo-ideological errors. Žižek's ethics thus has the most unlikely of implications. It seals off the political from politics, imagines yet another end to ideology, and takes its place as the latest name for the ghost of ideology.

It is in this sense that we can understand Žižek's critique of what he disparages as the "post-structuralist" dimension of Laclau and Mouffe's radical democratic theory. Worried about their unholy flirtation with the notion that "so-called 'reality' is a discursive construct; every given identity, including that of a subject, is an effect of the contingent differential relations, etc.," Žižek emphasizes instead the Lacanian formulation that "society doesn't exist." Thus, "far from reducing all reality to a kind of language-game," the good Lacanian part of *Hegemony and Socialist Strategy* understands that "the socio-symbolic field is conceived as structured around a certain traumatic impossibility, around a certain fissure which cannot be symbolized."[9] I have argued here that "linguistic" deconstruction is co-extensive with an insistence on the impossible—this impossibility is encountered in discourse, in textuality in the largest sense. In trying to evade this aporia, Žižek finds himself forced back to an extremely traditional notion of an ethics, even "toward an ethic of the Real." So he praises, to my mind incorrectly, Laclau and Mouffe for "articulating the contours of a political project based on an ethics of the real, . . . an ethics of confrontation with an impossible, traumatic kernel" (259). The desire to found politics on ethics and the belief in the "going-through" of the confrontation—as if we could shake hands or slug it out with the impossible, could articulate our modus vivendi with all that refuses to go away in the trauma—marks the limits of Žižek's very powerful argument, at the moment of its maximum interest. What is most radical about Laclau and Mouffe is that they *don't* offer an ethics outside of, let alone as the basis of, a politics—politics is irreducible to some foundational ethics, which is why both ethics and politics continue to be inescapable, necessary, and open to our ongoing intervention.

What would happen if this "ethical" acknowledgment worked, if we did finally take account of or come to terms with contingency and traumatic incomprehensibility? If this lonely hour of another last instance will just as surely never come, what does it mean to propose an ethics over against the constitutive aberrations, the ideological illusions and inversions, of politics? What differentiates the "solution," which Žižek so rightly rejects, from the acknowledgment, the coming to terms, the acceptance? Ideology, and the wish to be done with it, is a strictly constitutive feature of the political, *because* the social totality cannot succeed in establishing itself once and for all, because there is no simple reconciling oneself with this impossibility. There is neither escape from nor reconciliation with this difficulty. The impossibility is the condition of political action. If reconciling, accepting, acknowledging were possible—if we could just come to terms with antagonism, *différance*, undecidability, dissemination—then politics would be over. Ethics suffers from, lives on, and responds to the same difficulties.

Un-ending

Perhaps Žižek is just too dialectical here. He announces that "the most consistent model of [the] acknowledgment of antagonism is offered by Hegelian dialectics" (6), and who could disagree? Our question is about the acknowledgment: How can we take measure of the distance that we must not obliterate? Here one might return to him the reproach Žižek directs at Derrida: his argument is "too 'theoretical,'" which is to say that it "does not affect the place from which we speak" (15). The interest of the example is the persistence of the notion that a formal or fundamental structure, a "model," needs to be overlaid on the aberration and the afformativity of the political, as of the ethical. I borrow the word "afformative" from Werner Hamacher's reflections on "a politics of pure mediacy," a politics of means "that do not serve as means to ends situated outside the sphere of mediacy."[10] Žižek's Hegel could use a little more mediation, indeed, nothing but media, means without ends. Mediation is aberration, error, but error without possible reversal, without end. The danger of opposing ethics to politics, private to public, is the lure of a dialectic that can protect us, in the end, from "falling prey to" ideological traps.

So the fables read here, fables whose morals it would be imprudent to wait for, are not simply narrating a passage from private to public, self to others—certainly not from ethics to politics. The recourse to ethics too often designates a fear of politics, a desire to be done with it and its aporias. In their radical disorientation, then, ethics and politics, as we speak of them here, are irreducibly risky. My interest here—signaled by the recurrence in this analysis of the term "ethico-political"—has been to expose the enigmas of each to the other. "No one" is at once, and neither, public and private; the ghosts whose irreducibility I have tried to insist on are public, and private, and neither. The phantom public sphere, says Lefort, belongs to no one, and we could say the same for our private phantoms: privacy is nothing other than all that remains inaccessible in and to ourselves . . . the secrets and the traumas, even the responsibilities, which no one, least of all me, possesses but is rather possessed by.[11] The ethico-political occupies a kind of "no man's land," as Lyotard says, the public-private sphere of a certain inhumanity that undergirds without grounding:

> If we do not preserve this inhuman region where we can encounter this or that something, that which completely escapes the exercise of rights, we do not deserve the rights granted to us. What use is the right

to freedom of expression if we have nothing to say but what has already been said? And how can we have any chance of finding a way to say what we don't know how to say if we don't pay attention to the silence of the other inside us? This silence stands as an exception to the reciprocity that characterizes rights, but it is its legitimation. We should indeed accord an absolute right to this "second existence," because it is what provides the right to have rights. Yet since it has nothing to do with rights, it will always have to make do with an amnesty.[12]

In language, the line of demarcation between public and private is redrawn, passing through them, exposing each to its impossibility and hence to the irresolution and the necessity of ethics and politics. In the dark, crossing, without security and without end.

Reference Matter

Notes

Introduction

1. Jacques Derrida, "Passions: An Oblique Offering," trans. David Wood, in Wood, ed., *Derrida: A Critical Reader* (Oxford: Blackwell, 1992), 23; *Passions* (Paris: Galilée, 1993), 65. Throughout this book I have silently modified existing translations from French and German whenever necessary. Where double page citations are given, the first refers to the English translation, the second to the original text.

2. Throughout this book I use the terms "ethics" and "politics" more or less interchangeably, often (as here) in the phrase "ethico-political," distinguishing them less one from the other than together from the discourse of grounds, morality, and good conscience. The formula "ethico-political" comes either from Derrida (*Limited Inc*, trans. Samuel Weber [Evanston: Northwestern Univ. Press, 1988], 97; "Limited Inc," in *Limited Inc* [Paris: Galilée, 1990], 180) or from Foucault ("On the Genealogy of Ethics," in Paul Rabinow, ed., *The Foucault Reader* [New York: Pantheon, 1984], 343, or, in the same volume, "Politics and Ethics," 376–77).

3. Claude Lefort, "The Question of Democracy," in *Democracy and Political Theory*, trans. David Macey (Minneapolis: Univ. of Minnesota Press), 19; "La question de la démocratie," in *Essais sur le politique* (Paris: Seuil, 1986), 29.

4. For instance, Tzvetan Todorov, "Against All Humanity," *Times Literary Supplement*, October 4, 1985, 1094: "I can personally testify that Paul de Man was a delightful man, and that Stanley Fish still is. I am not saying that they themselves are inhuman; I am merely saying that it is

impossible (without being inconsistent) to defend human rights out of one side of your mouth while deconstructing the idea of humanity out of the other." But "inhumanity" is just the question, or rather, what comes out of the other sides of your mouth—why should there be just two sides, after all? Human rights only become political when "the idea of humanity" becomes contestable, when appeals to human nature or some secure ground lose their authority—which is to say, when we start to take inhumanity seriously, rather than simply using it as an epithet. The ongoing effort of Luc Ferry and Alain Renault to replace "man as such" or "human nature" with humanity as a "regulative idea" or a "symbolic value" seems a little desperate in this regard (Ferry and Renault, "How to Think about Rights," trans. Franklin Philip, in Mark Lilla, ed., *New French Thought* [Princeton: Princeton Univ. Press, 1994], 152). Human rights only become viable as ethico-political theory and practice when the symbolic value of "humanity" is exposed to its deconstruction, not when it is blindly and reactively re-posited.

5. Claude Lefort, "Human Rights and the Welfare State," in *Democracy and Political Theory*, 37; "Les droits de l'homme et l'Etat-providence," in *Essais sur le politique*, 51.

6. Jean-François Lyotard, "The General Line," in *Political Writings*, trans. Bill Readings and Kevin Paul Geiman (Minneapolis: Univ. of Minnesota Press, 1993), 111; "Ligne génerale," in *Moralités postmodernes* (Paris: Galilée, 1993), 110.

7. Derrida, "Passions," 23–24/66–68.

Chapter 1

1. William Shakespeare, *Hamlet*, ed. Harold Jenkins (Arden Shakespeare, London: Methuen, 1982).

2. This analysis of the strange coincidence of performative and constative, as well as the formulation "it does what it says it does," owes a lot to what remains one of the most concise and articulate demonstrations of the power of deconstructive reading for political theory and practice, Jacques Derrida's "Declarations of Independence," trans. Thomas Keenan and Thomas Pepper, *New Political Science* 15, *Between Literature and Politics* (Summer 1986): 7–15; "Déclarations d'Indépendance," in *Otobiographies: L'enseignement de Nietzsche et la politique du nom propre* (Paris: Galilée, 1984), 11–32. Lurking in the neighborhood of all references to the king and his bodies is of course Ernst H. Kantorowicz, *The King's Two Bodies* (Princeton: Princeton Univ. Press, 1957), especially

when supplemented by Claude Lefort and Michel Foucault, to whom I will turn shortly. My thinking about "tonight" was prompted by Werner Hamacher's contribution to "Interventions," trans. Adam Bresnick, *Qui Parle* 1, no. 2 (Spring 1987): 39.

3. Jacques Derrida, "Signature Event Context," in *Limited Inc*, trans. Samuel Weber (Evanston: Northwestern Univ. Press, 1988), 21; "Signature Evénement Context," in *Marges: de la philosophie* (Paris: Minuit, 1972), reprinted in *Limited Inc* (Paris: Galilée, 1990): 50.

4. Jacques Derrida, "Force of Law," trans. Mary Quaintance, in Drucilla Cornell et al., eds., *Deconstruction and the Possibility of Justice* (New York: Routledge, 1992), 26; *Force de loi* (Paris: Galilée, 1994), 58. Derrida's essay was first published in *Cardozo Law Review* 11, nos. 5–6 (July–August 1990): 919–1045.

5. ["Tayacan"], *Psychological Operations in Guerilla Warfare*, with essays by Joanne Omang and Aryeh Neier (New York: Vintage, 1985); based on a translation by the Language Services of the Congressional Research Service, Library of Congress, first published in book form as *Operaciones Sicologicas en Guerra de Guerrillas: CIA warfare manual, English translation* (New York: Options for the Future, 1984). Omang identifies the author as "a CIA agent who called himself John Kirkpatrick" (27).

6. I learned much from teaching this text together with Barbara Johnson, who has analyzed its rhetoric of "covert operations" powerfully in "Apostrophe, Animation, and Abortion," *Diacritics* 16, no. 1 (Spring 1986): 29–47.

7. Carl Schmitt, *The Concept of the Political*, trans. George Schwab (New Brunswick: Rutgers Univ. Press, 1976); *Der Begriff der Politischen* (Berlin: Dunker und Humbolt, 1979; orig. pub. 1932). Crucial to any understanding of Schmitt's text is Jacques Derrida, *Politiques de l'amitié* (Paris: Galilée, 1994), and Chantal Mouffe, *The Return of the Political* (London: Verso, 1993).

8. Ryszard Kapuściński reports one Angolan soldier's description of this nonfrontal character of the front in that country's civil war as follows: "so the front doesn't consist of a line here, but of points, and moving points at that . . . we are a three-man potential front now, traveling northward" (*Another Day of Life*, trans. William R. Brand and Katarzyna Mroczkowska Brand [New York: Penguin, 1988], 83).

9. Stanley Fish, "Force," in *Doing What Comes Naturally* (Durham: Duke Univ. Press, 1989), 517.

10. Paul de Man, *Allegories of Reading* (New Haven: Yale Univ. Press, 1979), 107.

11. Emmanuel Levinas, *Otherwise Than Being or Beyond Essence*, trans. Alphonso Lingis (The Hague: Martinus Nijhoff, 1981), 99–129; *Autrement qu'être ou au-delà de l'essence* (The Hague: Martinus Nijhoff, 1974), 125–66. Compare Jacques Derrida's comments in "At this very moment in this work here I am," trans. Reuben Berezdivin, in Robert Bernasconi and Simon Critchley, eds., *Re-Reading Levinas* (Bloomington: Indiana Univ. Press, 1991), 20, 31–32; "En ce moment même dans cet ouvrage me voici," in *Psyché* (Paris: Galilée, 1987), 170, 182–83.

12. Maurice Blanchot, *The Writing of the Disaster*, trans. Ann Smock (Lincoln: Univ. of Nebraska Press, 1986); *L'écriture du désastre* (Paris: Gallimard, 1980).

13. Levinas, *Otherwise*, 185/233. For an exemplary reading of this "me voici" (and much more in Levinas), see Jill Robbins, *Prodigal Son/Elder Brother* (Chicago: Univ. of Chicago Press, 1991), esp. 78–79. Robbins emphasizes that this response precedes the call to which it responds. Derrida has proposed an extensive interpretation of sacrifice and responsibility in *The Gift of Death*, trans. David Wills (Chicago: Univ. of Chicago Press, 1995); "Donner la mort," in Jean-Michel Rabaté and Michael Wetzel, eds., *L'éthique du don* (Paris: Métailié-Transition, 1992), 11–108. Jean-François Lyotard has a helpful section on Levinas and "obligation" in *The Differend*, trans. Georges Van Den Abbeele (Minneapolis: Univ. of Minnesota Press, 1988), 110–15; *Le différend* (Paris: Minuit, 1983), 163–69. Of course, we await Robert Bernasconi's promised *Between Levinas and Derrida*; in the meantime, see his "Levinas and Derrida: The Question of the Closure of Metaphysics," in Richard Cohen, ed., *Face to Face with Levinas* (Albany: State University of New York Press, 1986), 181–202; "The Trace of Levinas in Derrida," in David Wood and Robert Bernasconi, eds., *Derrida and Différance* (Evanston: Northwestern Univ. Press, 1988), 17–44; and "The Ethics of Suspicion," *Research on Phenomenology* 20 (1990): 3–18. See also John Llewelyn, *Emmanuel Levinas: The Genealogy of Ethics* (New York: Routledge, 1995).

14. Levinas does write that "in responsibility . . . is only this unlimited passivity of an accusative which does not issue out of a declension it would have undergone starting with the nominative" (*Otherwise*, 112/143). But we have to ask whether the forceful rhythm of the declension can just be ruled out by fiat like this, whether the accusative doesn't always come back to an undeclined noun.

15. Fabio Ciaramelli calls attention to the disparity between Blanchot and Levinas on the question of individuality, but not in the most helpful of ways. In short, Levinas puts the emphasis on the constitution of the individual in being-taken-hostage, while Blanchot underlines the effect of dis-individualization. Ciaramelli accuses Blanchot of "distort[ing] radically Levinas' understanding of the hostage's condition (or uncondition)," and of "destroy[ing] . . . the basis of ethical discourse in Levinas's sense" ("Levinas' Ethical Discourse," in Bernasconi and Critchley, eds., *Re-Reading Levinas*, 105, n. 76). I read Blanchot's interpretation of the hostage as a rigorous pursuit of the thinking that Levinas sets underway but sometimes shies away from. "That the other has no other meaning than the infinite aid [*recours*] which I owe him—that he should be the unlimited call for help [*secours*] to which no one other than I can answer—does not make me irreplaceable, still less does it make me unique. But it makes me disappear in the infinite movement of service where I am only temporarily singular and a simulacrum of unity: I cannot draw any justification . . . from a demand that is not addressed to anyone in particular, that demands nothing of my decision and that in any case exceeds me to the point of disindividualizing me" (Blanchot, *Disaster*, 21/39).

16. See, in addition, Blanchot's further considerations of this paradoxical responsibility, and its banality (*Disaster*, 22/41, and esp. 25–27/45–47).

17. For a different interpretation of television and the hostage, see Jean Baudrillard, "The Timisoara Syndrome," *D* 2 [Columbia Documents of Architecture and Theory] (1993): 61–70. Writing of the 1989 overthrow of the Ceaucescu regime in Romania, much of which happened on television, he argues that "the Romanians took themselves hostage by manipulating their own revolution on screen, but they took us hostage as well, we who absorbed this fiction of a revolution and this fiction of information—we bore the same responsibility as those who fomented it. Or rather, there isn't any responsibility anywhere. The question of responsibility can no longer even be asked" (65). Needless to say, I contend that only in the experience of simulation and hostage taking can the conditions of something like a responsibility be formulated, and that the passage of contemporary politics across our television screens makes this all the more urgent. *Videogramme einer Revolution*, Harun Farocki and Andrei Ujica's 1992 compilation film about the Romanian uprising, makes this massively clear.

18. I have advanced some arguments about light, Enlightenment, and the public sphere in a series of texts published elsewhere, among them: "Light Weapons," *Documents* 1/2 (Fall–Winter 1992): 147–53; "Windows: Of Vulnerability," in Bruce Robbins, ed., *The Phantom Public Sphere* (Minneapolis: Univ. of Minnesota Press, 1993): 121–41; and "Live from . . . ," in Elizabeth Diller and Ricardo Scofidio, eds., *Back to the Front* (Caen: F.R.A.C. Basse Normandie, 1994), 130–63.

19. Louis Althusser, "Ideology and Ideological State Apparatuses," in *Lenin and Philosophy*, trans. Ben Brewster (New York: Monthly Review Press, 1971): 172–75; "Idéologie et appareils idéologiques d'Etat," in *Positions* (Paris: Editions Sociales, 1976), 111–14.

20. Zakia Pathak and Rajeswari Sunder Rajan, "'Shahbano,'" in Judith Butler and Joan Scott, eds., *Feminists Theorize the Political* (New York: Routledge, 1992), 257–79. Gayatri Chakravorty Spivak has presented an elegant reading of this text in conjunction with the case of Salman Rushdie in "Reading *The Satanic Verses*," in *Outside in the Teaching Machine* (New York: Routledge, 1993), 217–41.

21. Richard Dienst, *Still Life in Real Time* (Durham: Duke Univ. Press, 1994).

22. This call or *Ruf* sounds, of course, throughout Heidegger's *Being and Time* (trans. John Macquarrie and Edward Robinson [New York: Harper and Row, 1962]; *Sein und Zeit*, 15th ed. [Tübingen: Max Niemeyer, 1979) most notably in sections 56–59, where Heidegger insists that the "alien voice" of the call "'says' *nothing* which might be talked about, gives no information about events" (*Being*, 321, 325/277,280). This call of conscience has been attended to by Christopher Fynsk, in *Heidegger: Thought and Historicity* (Baltimore: Johns Hopkins Univ. Press, 1986), 41–54, and later by Avital Ronell in *The Telephone Book* (Lincoln: Univ. of Nebraska Press, 1989), especially 47–83 and 419 n. 25: "the call of the other is essentially anonymous" (59). Also of help are Hamacher, "Interventions," and Samuel Weber, "The Debts of Deconstruction and Other Related Assumptions," in Joseph H. Smith and William Kerrigan, eds., *Taking Chances* (Baltimore: Johns Hopkins Univ. Press, 1984), 33–65.

23. Jacques Derrida, "Ulysses Gramophone," trans. Tina Kendall and Shari Benstock, in Derek Attridge, ed., *Acts of Literature* (New York: Routledge, 1992), 299; *Ulysse gramophone* (Paris: Galilée, 1987), 127: "*Yes*, the condition of any signature and of any performative, addresses itself to some other which it does not constitute, and to which it can only begin

by *asking*, in response to a request that is always anterior, by asking it to say *yes*. . . . the *yes* addresses itself to some other and can appeal only to the *yes* of some other—it begins by responding" (299, 301/127, 130).

24. Hamacher, "Interventions," 37.

25. I will return to the question of ideology and responsibility in the concluding chapter, but I am referring to the pioneering work on radical democracy by Ernesto Laclau and Chantal Mouffe, *Hegemony and Socialist Strategy*, trans. Winston Moore and Paul Cammack (London: Verso, 1985), here in particular to their discussion of "subject positions" (109) and the "no man's land" (111). They have extended this work in: Laclau, *New Reflections on the Revolution of Our Time* (London: Verso, 1990); Laclau, ed., *The Making of Political Identities* (London: Verso, 1994); Mouffe, *The Return of the Political*; and Mouffe, ed., *Dimensions of Radical Democracy* (London: Verso, 1992); as well as in a number of uncollected essays. On ideology, I will turn later to the related investigations by Slavoj Žižek, especially *The Sublime Object of Ideology* (London: Verso, 1989). See also Andrew Ross's "Discussion of Ernesto Laclau and Chantal Mouffe, *Hegemony and Socialist Strategy*," *m/f* 11–12 (1986): 99–106, and "The Politics of Impossibility," in Richard Feldstein and Henry Sussman, eds., *Psychoanalysis and . . .* (New York: Routledge, 1990), 113–25, especially the concluding phrase, on more mail headed to multiple addressees: "they sent their income tax returns, their parking fines, and their other love letters elsewhere." Some interesting remarks on the way "the problem of responsibility is dispersed into . . . particular sites, positions, statuses and agents" can also be found in Parveen Adams and Jeff Minson, "The 'Subject' of Feminism," *m/f* 2 (1978): 53.

26. Jean Rhys, *Wide Sargasso Sea* (1966), in *The Complete Novels* (New York: W. W. Norton, 1985), 548.

27. The allusion is to the conference "Deconstruction and the Possibility of Justice," at the Cardozo Law School in New York City in October 1989.

28. Jacques Derrida, "Passions: An Oblique Offering," trans. David Wood, in Wood, ed., *Derrida: A Critical Reader* (Oxford: Blackwell, 1992), 15; *Passions* (Paris: Galilée, 1993), 41.

29. Michele Barrett, *The Politics of Truth: From Marx to Foucault* (Stanford: Stanford Univ. Press, 1992), 166.

30. J. Hillis Miller, *The Ethics of Reading* (New York: Columbia Univ. Press, 1987). Whatever modifications to his thinking I seek to propose, I must thank Hillis Miller, who presided over the first incarnation of this

book as a dissertation, for all that I have learned from him. Christopher Norris has also provided an exemplary summary of another version of this position, in terms not of ethics but of politics: "De Man's texts quite explicitly *ask* to be read in this 'political' mode. They insist that the field of rhetorical tensions is always ('contrary to what one might think') a space where the politics of reading is inevitably brought into play. . . . The 'burden' of politics, as de Man conceives it, is a negative labor (like that of deconstruction) relentlessly trained upon its own liability to error and delusion. . . . If the political unconscious is structured like a language, then the politics of reading is both more error-prone *and* more radically unsettling than criticism (Marxist and otherwise) can easily allow" (*The Contest of Faculties* [New York: Methuen, 1985], 44–45).

31. "The Authority of Reading: An Interview with J. Hillis Miller," conducted by Martin Heusser and Harold Schweizer, in Miller, *Hawthorne and History* (Oxford: Basil Blackwell, 1991), 136.

32. Miller, *Ethics of Reading*, 4.

33. "The Authority of Reading," 164–65.

34. Miller, *Ethics of Reading*, 59.

35. Whatever my differences with Miller's interpretation of the ethics of reading, they have nothing in common with the retrograde criticisms offered by Vincent Pecora, who seems to think that Miller's arguments can be reduced to slogans like "obey the law" and "things can't help being the way they are." Miller has no such desire for guarantees of "cosmically clean hands," a wish attributed more properly to the neo-universalism of Pecora's analysis ("Ethics, Politics, and the Middle Voice," in Claire Nouvet, ed., *Yale French Studies* 79, *Literature and the Ethical Question* [1991]: 215, 217).

36. Simon Critchley, *The Ethics of Deconstruction* (Oxford: Blackwell, 1992), 46.

37. Paul Smith, "Laclau and Mouffe's Secret Agent," in Miami Theory Collective, ed., *Community at Loose Ends* (Minneapolis: Univ. of Minnesota Press, 1991), 104. Smith makes similar arguments in *Discerning the Subject* (Minneapolis: Univ. of Minnesota Press), 1988. Another oft-cited version of this complaint can be found in S. P. Mohanty, "Us and Them: On the Philosophical Bases of Political Criticism," *Yale Journal of Criticism*, 2, no. 2 (Spring 1989): 1–31.

38. Alan Kennedy, *Reading Resistance Value* (New York: St. Martin's Press, 1990), ix.

39. Drucilla Cornell, "Post-Structuralism, the Ethical Relation, and

the Law," *Cardozo Law Review* 9, no. 6 (August 1988): 1587–628. Cornell offers similar arguments in a number of places, for instance toward the end of the chapter "The Feminist Alliance with Deconstruction," in *Beyond Accommodation* (New York: Routledge, 1991), 113–18.

40. Laclau and Mouffe, *Hegemony and Socialist Strategy*, 125.

41. See Joan Copjec, *Read My Desire* (Cambridge: MIT Press, 1994), on the extimate: "not only rejected from but internal to the subject, . . . they are in us that which is not us" (129).

42. This remark comes in a discussion of Derrida's "hesitancy to name the ethical desire that pushes deconstruction forward," but it has a certain exemplary value.

43. Jill Robbins emphasizes this: "in Levinas's account, . . . there is response before (or even in the absence of) there being anyone to respond to. In this asymmetrical call and response, there is neither reciprocity nor meeting nor even necessarily understanding" (*Prodigal Son/Elder Brother,* 79). And later: "there is an asymmetrical relationship to an absolute singularity. Yet, despite Levinas's insistence on this point, we do not get away from the universal altogether. As Derrida reminds us, in Levinas's descriptions, 'the relation to the other also passes through the universality of law' " (144).

44. As Werner Hamacher has pointed out, the tropes are capricious here: "the performative act of promising a possible understanding must be structured as an epistemologically illegitimate rhetorical figure, as metalepsis, in order to be carried out. For what is announced by the promise only for the future—a possible understanding—is asserted to be already effective in the present. The rhetorical figure of confounding a future with a present . . . is unavoidably a figure of deceit, insofar as that which it implicitly states to be present can be opened up only by the illocutionary act as futurial" ("LECTIO : de Man's Imperative," trans. Susan Bernstein, in Wlad Godzich and Lindsay Waters, eds., *Reading de Man Reading* [Minneapolis: Univ. of Minnesota Press, 1989], 197).

45. Although our interpretations of this impossibility differ slightly, I second Renata Salecl's association of it with a theory of democracy, in her *The Spoils of Freedom* (New York: Routledge, 1994): "Democracy . . . maintains a split between law and justice: it accepts the fact that justice is 'impossible,' that it is an act which can never be wholly grounded in 'sufficient (legal) reasons' " (97).

46. Jacques Derrida, "Violence and Metaphysics," in *Writing and Difference*, trans. Alan Bass (Chicago: Univ. of Chicago Press, 1978), 80;

"Violence et métaphysique," in *L'écriture et la différence* (Paris: Seuil, 1967), 118.

47. Michel Foucault, *The History of Sexuality, Volume I: An Introduction*, trans. Robert Hurley (New York: Random House, 1978), 145; *La volonté de savoir* (Paris: Gallimard, 1976), 190–91. I pursue this argument more fully in Chapter 5, where it is finally a matter of a "new right" altogether.

48. This instrumentalist or utilitarian, sometimes simply pragmatic, notion of rights means that the radicality of the democratic mutation goes unrecognized in too much analysis today. It even threatens one of the most exciting efforts to rethink rights, that of Patricia Williams, "The Pain of Word Bondage," in *The Alchemy of Race and Rights* (Cambridge: Harvard Univ. Press, 1991), 146–65. Criticizing the "abandonment" of rights which she sees as characteristic of the Critical Legal Studies movement, or its recognition that "rights may be unstable and indeterminate," she opts initially to affirm the value of talk about rights: "Although rights may not be ends in themselves, rights rhetoric has been and continues to be an effective form of discourse for blacks. The vocabulary of rights speaks to an establishment that values the guise of stability, and from whom social change for the better must come (whether it is given, taken, or smuggled). Changes argued for in the sheep's clothing of stability ('rights') can be effective, even as it destabilizes certain other establishment values (segregation). The subtlety of rights' real instability thus does not render unusable their persona of stability" (149). (I will return to the sheep and its clothing in the next chapter.) As the chapter continues, though, Williams's argument demonstrates that speaking of rights is not simply one vocabulary that we can use or not use at will, and equally that the "real instability" (or the structural limitlessness) of rights—far from undermining their force—gives them their radical politicality. Rather than discarding rights, she concludes, "society must *give* them away. Unlock them from reification by giving them to slaves. Give them to trees. Give them to cows. Give them to history. Give them to rivers and rocks" (165).

49. Claude Lefort, "Politics and Human Rights," in *The Political Forms of Modern Society,* trans. Alan Sheridan, ed. John B. Thompson (Cambridge: MIT Press, 1986), 239–72; "Droits de l'homme et politique," in *L'invention démocratique* (Paris: Fayard, 1981), 45–86; and "The Question of Democracy" and "Human Rights and the Welfare State," *Democracy and Political Theory,* trans. David Macey (Minneapolis: Univ.

of Minnesota Press, 1988), 9–44; "La question de la démocratie" and "Les droits de l'homme et l'Etat-providence," the first two chapters of *Essais sur le politique* (Paris: Seuil, 1986), 17–58. On human rights, see also in general: the work of Ernesto Laclau and Chantal Mouffe, referred to above; Jean-François Lyotard and Jacob Rogozinski, "The Thought Police," trans. Julian Pefanis, *Art & Text* 26 (Sept.–Nov. 1987): 24–31; "La police de la pensée," *L'Autre Journal* 10 (December 1985): 27–34; Emmanuel Levinas, "The Rights of Man and the Rights of the Other," in *Outside the Subject*, trans. Michael B. Smith (Stanford: Stanford Univ. Press, 1993), 116–25; "Les droits de l'homme et les droits de l'autrui," in *Hors sujet* (Montpellier: Fata Morgana, 1987), 173–87; Etienne Balibar, "What is a Politics of the Rights of Man?" and " 'Rights of Man' and 'Rights of the Citizen,' " in *Masses, Classes, Ideas*, trans. James Swenson (New York: Routledge, 1994, 39–59, 205–25; " 'Droits de l'homme' et 'droits du citoyen' " and "Qu'est-ce qu'une politique des droits de l'homme," in *Les frontières de la démocratie* (Paris: La Découverte, 1992), 124–50; Rosalyn Deutsche, "Agoraphobia," in *Evictions: Art and Spatial Politics* (Cambridge: MIT Press, 1996); Barbara Johnson, ed., *Freedom and Interpretation* (New York: Basic Books, 1993); Stephen Shute and Susan Hurley, eds., *On Human Rights* (New York: Basic Books, 1994), esp. Jean-François Lyotard, "The Other's Rights," 135–47; Olwen Hufton, ed., *Historical Change and Human Rights* (New York: Basic Books, 1995); and Derek Jones and Rod Stoneman, eds., *Talking Liberties* (booklet to accompany Patricia Llewellyn / Wall to Wall, prod., *Talking Liberties*; London: Channel Four Television, 1992).

50. Lefort, "Politics and Human Rights," 256–57/67.

51. Lefort, "Human Rights and the Welfare State," 37–38/51.

52. Hannah Arendt, *The Origins of Totalitarianism*, 2d ed. (Cleveland: Meridian Books, 1958), 296. As he says, Lefort borrows the expression in "Human Rights and the Welfare State," 37/51.

53. Paul de Man, "Wordsworth and the Victorians," in *The Rhetoric of Romanticism* (New York: Columbia Univ. Press, 1984), 83–92.

54. Let me be clear: what is interesting about this claim is that it does not issue from a subject. The cry is not the demand of a subject for its rights, but just the contrary, the ungrounded inauguration of the right to rights. Joan Copjec makes an important argument about the irreducibility of rights to "a series of demands, fully expressible in language and fully known to the subject who insists on them": "what the reduction of rights to demands results in is the elimination of the question . . . of the

subject's attachment to what language cannot say, to the unspeakable double that is the indestructible support of our freedom" (*Read My Desire*, 137). In "The Subject Defined by Suffrage," *Lacanian Ink* 7 (spring–summer 1993): 47–58, Copjec argues that the "right to rights" is in effect a translation of Lacan's "desire to desire."

55. Laclau, *New Reflections on the Revolution of Our Time*, 92. The question is precisely that of ideology: "the ideological would not consist of the misrecognition of any positive essence, but exactly the opposite: it would consist of the non-recognition of the precarious character of any positivity, of the impossibility of any ultimate suture." Alan Keenan's sympathetic critique of this volume is instructive: "he risks promoting a new political myth—that of a democracy as a sort of 'antagonistic harmony,' a steady-state of conflict that somehow never threatens to become war—without, however, telling us much about how such a state could be achieved" ("The Difficult Politics of Democracy," *PoLAR* 18, no. 1 [May 1995]: 82).

56. No current thinker has pushed the question of this commonality and of community farther than Jean-Luc Nancy; see e.g.: *The Inoperative Community*, trans. Peter Connor et al. (Minneapolis: Univ. of Minnesota Press, 1991); *La communauté desoeuvrée* (Paris: Christian Bourgois, 1986); Eduardo Cadava et al., eds., *Who Comes After the Subject?* (New York: Routledge, 1991); Nancy's special issue of *Après le sujet qui vient, Confrontation* 20 (Winter 1989); and "Of Being-in-Common," trans. James Creech, in Miami Theory Collective, ed., *Community at Loose Ends* (Minneapolis: Univ. of Minnesota Press, 1991): 1–12.

Chapter 2

NOTE: The epigraph is the closing moral of *The Gliders*, dir. Paul Terry, in the animated series *Aesop's Film Fables*, produced by Fables Pictures, 1922 (available in the film collection of the Museum of Modern Art, New York).

1. A short list of the most important recent texts on the fable would have to begin with the pioneering work of Jacques Ehrmann, "Problems of Narrative 1: The Minimum Narrative," trans. Jesse Dickson, *SubStance* 1, no. 2 (Winter 1971–72): 3–14. It should continue with: A. Kibédi Varga, "L'invention de la fable," *Poétique* 25 (1976): 107–15; Louis Marin, "La bête, l'animal parlant, et l'homme," *Traverses* 8 (1977): 36–47; "L'action juste comme reste," *Traverses* 11 (1978): 82–93; *Le récit est une piège* (Paris: Minuit, 1978), whose chapter on Perrault is translated as

"Puss-in-Boots," *Diacritics* 7, no. 2 (summer 1977): 54–63; as well as three chapters in *La parole mangée* (Paris: Méridiens Klincksieck, 1986): 39–88; *Food for Thought*, trans. Mette Hjort (Baltimore: Johns Hopkins Univ. Press, 1989): 27–84; Michel Serres, "Le jeu du loup," in *Hermès 4: La distribution* (Paris: Minuit, 1977): 89–111; "Knowledge in the Classical Age: La Fontaine and Descartes," in *Hermes*, trans. Josué Harari and David Bell (Baltimore: Johns Hopkins Univ. Press, 1982): 15–28; Béatrice Didier, ed., *L'animal fabuleux, Corps écrit 6* (May 1983); Joan DeJean, "La Fontaine's Crafty Parable," in *Literary Fortifications* (Princeton: Princeton Univ. Press, 1984), 76–95; Hans Robert Jauss, "The Alterity and Modernity of Medieval Literature," trans. Timothy Bahti, *New Literary History* 10, no. 2 (winter 1979): 181–227; Jean Starobinski, "Fable et mythologie aux XVIIe et XVIIIe siècles," in *Le remède dans le mal* (Paris: Gallimard, 1989): 233–62; Ross Chambers, *Room for Maneuver* (Chicago: Univ. of Chicago Press, 1991), 47–101; Annabel Patterson, *Fables of Power* (Durham: Duke Univ. Press, 1991); Alexander Gelley, "The Pragmatics of Exemplary Narrative," in Gelley, ed., *Unruly Examples: On the Rhetoric of Exemplarity* (Stanford: Stanford Univ. Press, 1995), 142–61.

2. Patterson, *Fables of Power*, 5, 42.

3. Marin, *Le récit est une piège*, 32.

4. "Exemplary Tales: Narrative Examples and Moral Meanings" was Gelley's title for the original incarnation of a collective project (panels, and finally a book) that gave rise to an earlier version of this chapter.

5. I presuppose here a critical literature on the example that has grown up over the last twenty years, two examples of which would be the special issue of *Diacritics* 11, no. 2 (summer 1981), containing Derrida's "Economimesis," Andrzej Warminski's "Reading for Example," and a piece of Werner Hamacher's "Pleroma," and the volume edited by Alexander Gelley, *Unruly Examples*.

6. Jacques Derrida, "Limited Inc a b c," *Limited Inc* (Paris: Galilée, 1990), 61–197; "Limited Inc a b c," in *Limited Inc*, trans. Samuel Weber (Evanston: Northwestern Univ. Press, 1988), 29–110.

7. Joseph Jacobs, *The Fables of Aesop* (New York: Schocken Books, 1966; orig. pub. 1894), 93–94. Jacobs refers to the source of this version as "Extravagantes v. 15" in Caxton, although the version of that fable in Caxton differs from his in rather extraordinary ways (see the last note to this chapter). Jacobs also points to Matthew 7:15, which in the King James version reads: "Beware of false prophets, which come to you in sheep's clothing, but inwardly they are ravening wolves."

8. Recall the 1992 rap music disk from the group called Black Sheep,

titled *A Wolf in Sheep's Clothing*. The first single and video, "The Choice is Yours," posits the choice in the refrain as "you can go for *this*, or you can go for *that*." The video track offers two possible images for each choice, and withdraws the incorrect one to make the lesson clear.

9. La Fontaine, fable 3.3, in *The Fables of La Fontaine*, trans. Marianne Moore (New York: Viking Press, 1954), 60; *Oeuvres complètes*, vol. 1 (Paris: Gallimard/Bibliothèque de la Pléiade, 1954), 75–76.

10. Jacques Derrida, "Psyche: Invention of the Other," trans. Catherine Porter, in Derek Attridge, ed., *Acts of Literature* (New York: Routledge, 1992), 324–25; "Psyché: Invention de l'autre," in *Psyché* (Paris: Galilée, 1987), 24.

11. *Derrida*, "Limited Inc," (75–76/143).

12. Ibid., 90/167.

13. G. W. F. Hegel, *Aesthetics: Lectures on Fine Art*, vol. 1, trans. T. M. Knox (Oxford: Oxford Univ. Press, 1975), 387; *Vorlesungen über die Aesthetik*, vol. 1, *Theorie Werkausgabe*, vol. 13 (Frankfurt am Main: Suhrkamp, 1970), 497.

14. Ibid. On Hegel's interpretation of prose and the fable, see Paul de Man, "Hegel on the Sublime," in Mark Krupnick, ed., *Displacement: Derrida and After* (Bloomington: Indiana Univ. Press, 1983), 139–53, and "Dialogue and Dialogism," in *The Resistance to Theory* (Minneapolis: Univ. of Minnesota Press, 1986), 106–14.

15. "The Life: The Book of Xanthus the Philosopher and Aesop His Slave, or The Career of Aesop," trans. Lloyd W. Daly, in Daly, ed., *Aesop Without Morals* (New York: Thomas Yoseloff, 1961), 29–90; the Greek manuscript is printed as "Vita Aesopi: Vita G," in Ben Edwin Perry, ed., *Aesopica*, vol. 1 (Urbana: Univ. of Illinois Press, 1952), 35–77.

16. Philippe Lacoue-Labarthe, "The Fable," trans. Hugh Silverman, in *The Subject of Philosophy* (Minneapolis: Univ. of Minnesota Press, 1993), 11; "La fable," in *Le sujet de la philosophie* (Paris: Aubier-Flammarion, 1979), 25. See also Jean-Luc Nancy, "Mundus est fabula," trans. Daniel Brewer, *MLN* 93, no. 4 (May 1978): 635–53; "Mundus est fabula," in *Ego sum* (Paris: Flammarion, 1979), 95–127; and Andrzej Warminski, "Towards a Fabulous Reading: Nietzsche's 'On Truth and Lie in the Extramoral Sense," *Graduate Faculty Philosophy Journal* 15, no. 2 (1991): 93–120.

17. On this mirror, see Francis Ponge, "Fable," in *Tome premier* (Paris: Gallimard, 1965), 144, and Derrida's readings of it in "Psyche"; "Declarations of Independence," trans. Thomas Keenan and Thomas Pepper, *Between Literature and Politics, New Political Science* 15 (summer 1986):

7–15; "Déclarations d'Indépendance," in *Otobiographies: L'enseignement de Nietzsche et la politique du nom propre* (Paris: Galilée, 1984), 11–32; and briefly in *Signéponge/Signsponge*, trans. Richard Rand (New York: Columbia Univ. Press, 1984), 102–3. Another extraordinary fable of a mirror is, of course, Jacques Lacan, "The Mirror Stage as Formative of the Function of the I," in *Ecrits: A Selection*, trans. Alan Sheridan (New York: Norton, 1977), 1–7; "Le stade du miroir comme formateur de la fonction du Je," in *Ecrits* (Paris: Seuil, 1966), 93–100.

18. Horace, *Satires*, book 1, satire 1, trans. Niall Rudd (Harmondsworth: Penguin Books, 1987), 41: "change the name and you are the subject of the story." Lynne Tillman's novel *Cast in Doubt* (New York: Poseidon, 1994), esp. 151, 182–83, 215, 236–37, offers a brilliant interpretation of this motto and much else.

19. Maurice Blanchot, *The Writing of the Disaster*, trans. Ann Smock (Lincoln: Univ. of Nebraska Press, 1986), 13; *L'écriture du désastre* (Paris: Gallimard, 1980), 28.

20. Emmanuel Levinas, *Otherwise Than Being or Beyond Essence*, trans. Alphonso Lingis (The Hague: Martinus Nijhoff, 1981), 118; *Autrement qu'être ou au-delà de l'essence* (The Hague: Martinus Nijhoff, 1974), 151.

21. Blanchot, *Disaster*, 18/35.

22. Jacques Derrida, *The Other Heading*, trans. Pascale-Anne Brault and Michael B. Naas (Bloomington: Indiana Univ. Press, 1992), 41; *L'autre cap* (Paris: Minuit, 1991), 43. Derrida insists that the values of responsibility and exemplarity are indissociably bound, politically tied, around the problem of identity: "No cultural identity presents itself as the opaque body of an untranslatable idiom, but always, on the contrary, as the irreplaceable *inscription* of the universal in the singular, the *unique testimony* to the human essence and to what is proper to man. Each time, it has to do with the discourse of *responsibility*: I have, the unique 'I' has, the responsibility of testifying for universality. Each time, the exemplarity of the example is unique. That is why it can be put into a series and formalized into a law" (73/71–72). Compare, also, the remarks on responsibility in "Towards an Ethic of Discussion": "A decision can only come to pass beyond the calculable program that would destroy all responsibility by transforming it into a programmable effect of determined causes. There can be no moral or political responsibility without this trial and this passage by way of the undecidable. Even if a decision seems to take only a second and not to be preceded by any deliberation, it is structured by this *experience of the undecidable*" (*Limited Inc*, 116/210).

23. Friedrich Nietzsche, *On the Genealogy of Morals*, trans. Walter

Kaufmann (New York: Vintage Books, 1969), 57, 58; *Zur Genealogie der Moral: Eine Streitschrift, Sämtliche Werke: Kritische Studienausgabe in 15 Einzelbänden,* ed. Giorgio Colli and Mazzino Montinari, vol. 5 (Berlin: de Gruyter, 1988; orig. pub. Leipzig, 1887), 291, 292–93.

24. The rest of Nietzsche's animals—in "On Truth and Lie," "How the True World," *Zarathustra,* and even the birds of prey in the *Dithyrambs of Dionysus*—will have to be left aside here as well.

25. *Caxton's Aesop,* ed. R. T. Lenaghan (Cambridge: Harvard Univ. Press, 1967), 165–66. The German and Latin sources of Caxton's translation can be found in *Steinöwels Aesop,* ed. Hermann Oesterly, in *Bibliothek des Literarischen Vereins* 117 (Tübingen: L. F. Fues, 1873), 243–44. The fable numbered 98 by Steinhöwel ("Fabula prima de aquila et corvo," "Die erste fabel von dem adler, lamp, und rappen") can also be found, in different versions, as: "Eagle, Jackdaw, and Shepherd" (Daly, ed., *Aesop Without Morals,* no. 2); "Le Corbeau Voulant Imiter l'Aigle" (La Fontaine, *Fables,* book 2, no. 16); "The Jackdaw Who Would Be an Eagle" (Babrius no. 137, *Babrius and Phaedrus,* trans. Ben Edwin Perry, Loeb Classical Library [Cambridge: Harvard Univ. Press, 1965], 180–81; and Handford no. 69, in *Fables of Aesop,* trans. S. A. Handford (Harmondsworth: Penguin Books, 1964), 73. The versions differ significantly.

26. For a striking parallel, see Caxton's version of the "wolf in sheep's clothing," in which a wether dresses up as a guard dog, only to be forced to chase a marauding wolf and lose its borrowed skin. The wolf "forthwith retorned ageynste him / and demaunded of hym / what beest art thow / And the wether ansuered to hym in this maner / My lord I am a wether whiche playeth with the / And the wulf sayd / . . . I shalle shewe to the / how thou oughtest not to play so with thy lord / And thenne the wulf took and kylled him / and deuoured and ete hym / And therfore he that is wyse must take good hede / how he playeth with him whiche is wyser / more sage / and more stronge / than hym self is" (*Caxton's Aesop,* 161).

27. Nancy, "Mundus est fabula," 652/121.

28. For a further refinement of this argument, see Mikkel Borch-Jacobsen's essay on multiple personalities, "Who's Who," trans. Douglas Brick, in Joan Copjec, ed., *Supposing the Subject* (London: Verso, 1994), 45–63: "I switch, I am" (61).

29. Blanchot, *Disaster,* 18/35.

30. Levinas, *Otherwise,* 106/134–35.

31. Recall Barthes's famous example of an example, itself a fable, in

Mythologies: "I open my Latin grammar, and I read a sentence, borrowed from Aesop or Phaedrus: *quia ego nominor leo.* I stop and think. There is something ambiguous in this proposition: on the one hand, the words in it do have a simple meaning: *because my name is lion.* And on the other hand, the sentence is evidently there in order to signify something else to me . . . and it tells me clearly: I am a grammatical example designed to illustrate the rule of the agreement of the predicate. . . . I conclude that I am faced with a particular, greater, semiological system, since it is co-extensive with the language: there is, indeed, a signifier, but this signifier is itself formed by a sum of signs, it is in itself a first semiological system (*my name is lion*). Thereafter, the formal pattern is corectly unfolded: there is a signified (*I am a grammatical example*) and there is a global signification, which is none other than the correlation of the signifier and the signified; for neither the naming of the lion nor the grammatical example are given to me separately." ("Myth Today," *Mythologies*, trans. Annette Lavers [New York: Hill and Wang, 1972], 115–16); "Le Mythe, Aujourd'Hui," *Mythologies* [Paris: Seuil, 1957], 222–23). Derrida pushes this example beyond the hegemony of grammar and its logic: "this example of agrammaticality . . . proving unmistakably, by virtue of its function, that a graft is always possible; just as every phrase endowed with grammaticality that is cited in a certain context, for example in a grammar book, can also signify: I am an example of grammar" ("Limited Inc," 81/153).

32. Philippe Lacoue-Labarthe, *Heidegger, Art and Politics*, trans. Chris Turner (Oxford: Blackwell, 1990), 81; *La fiction du politique* (Paris: Christian Bourgois, 1987), 124.

33. Philippe Lacoue-Labarthe, "Typography," trans. Eduardo Cadava, in *Typography*, ed. Christopher Fynsk (Cambridge: Harvard Univ. Press, 1989), 129; "Typographie," in Sylviane Agacinski et al., *Mimesis: Des Articulations* (Paris: Aubier-Flammarion, 1975), 260.

34. Derrida, "Desistance," trans. Christopher Fynsk, intro. to Lacoue-Labarthe, *Typography*, 29; in Derrida, *Psyché*, 625.

35. Handford no. 36, *Fables of Aesop*, 38.

Chapter 3

1. Geoffrey Bennington, "Deconstruction and the Philosophers (The Very Idea)," in *Legislations* (London: Verso, 1994), 45.

2. See Isaiah Berlin, "Two Concepts of Liberty," in *Four Essays on Liberty* (New York: Oxford Univ. Press, 1970), 118–72.

3. Jacques Derrida, "The Principle of Reason," trans. Catherine Porter and Edward P. Morris, *Diacritics* 13, no. 3 (Fall 1983): 20; "Les pupilles de l'Université," in *Du droit à la philosophie* (Paris: Galilée, 1990), 497–98.

4. On impossibility, see Robert Bernasconi, "Deconstruction and the Possibility of Ethics," in John Sallis, ed., *Deconstruction and Philosophy* (Chicago: Univ. of Chicago Press, 1987), 135: "*the ethical relation is impossible and 'the impossible has already occurred' at this very moment.* . . . To acknowledge this is to submit the demand for an ethics, not to instruction, but to deconstruction. And the *possibility* of ethics is referred, not to its actuality, but to its *impossibility.*" Geoff Bennington calls our attention to the last sentence of Bernasconi's text: "we find the ethical enactment above all in the way deconstruction ultimately refuses to adopt the standpoint of critique, renouncing the passing of judgments on its own behalf in its own voice" (Bernasconi, "Deconstruction," 136). As Bennington notes, "here the 'ultimately' is vital," since precisely what is at stake is the necessity and unavoidability of responding" (Bennington, *Legislations*, 60, n. 73).

5. Drucilla Cornell, "Post-Structuralism, the Ethical Relation, and the Law," *Cordozo Law Review* 9, no. 6 (August 1988): 1616. In "Violence and Metaphysics," in *Writing and Difference*, trans. Alan Bass (Chicago: Univ. of Chicago Press, 1978), 80; "Violence et métaphysique," in *L'écriture et la différence* (Paris: Seuil, 1967), 118–19, Derrida insists simply that "the impossible has *already* taken place" ("l'impossible a *déjà* eu lieu").

6. English page references are to: Marquis de Sade, *Justine, Philosophy in the Bedroom, and Other Writings*, trans. Richard Seaver and Austryn Wainhouse (New York: Grove Press, 1965), 329; French quotations are from the Pauvert edition of Sade's complete works: *Oeuvres complètes du Marquis de Sade*, Vol. 3, *Justine, Opuscules politiques, La philosophie dans le boudoir* . . . (Paris: J.-J. Pauvert, 1986), 525.

7. Michel Foucault, "Language to Infinity," in *Language, Counter-Memory, Practice*, ed. Donald F. Bouchard (Ithaca: Cornell Univ. Press, 1977), 62; "Le langage à l'infini," *Tel Quel* 15 (autumn 1963): 50.

8. Maurice Blanchot, "L'inconvenance majeure," intro. to Sade, *Français, encore un effort* . . . (Paris: J.-J. Pauvert, 1965), 7–51; reprinted as the preface to Sade, *Oeuvres Complètes VIII: Dialogue Entre un Prêtre et un Moribund, Oxtiern, et Ecrits Politiques* (Paris: J.-J. Pauvert, 1966), 187–219; partially translated by June Guicharnaud as "The Main Impropriety (Excerpts)," *Yale French Studies* 39 (1967): 50–63. Blanchot later republished this essay as "Insurrection, the Madness of Writing," in *The Infinite Conversation*, trans. Susan Hanson (Minneapolis: Univ. of Min-

nesota Press, 1993), 217–29; "L'insurrection, la folie d'écrire," *L'entretien infini* (Paris: Gallimard, 1969), 323–42. References are to the version in *L'entretien infini,* except on three occasions (including this one) where I quote passages from a headnote which Blanchot removed subsequent to the first publications; these references are to the 1966 publication of "L'inconvenance majeure," 189.

9. Blanchot has just warned us that, although this pamphlet has a certain "place à part" in Sade's work, "we must never be content with reading [Sade's *oeuvre*] fragmentarily, we must always read it in its entirety" ("L'inconvenance majeure," 189).

10. Jacques Derrida, "Signature Event Context," in *Limited Inc,* trans. Samuel Weber and Jeffrey Mehlman (Evanston: Northwestern Univ. Press, 1988), 21; "Signature Evénement Context," in *Limited Inc* (Paris: Galilée, 1990), 50. See in this regard the helpful articulation of the difference between reading and interpretation in Andrzej Warminski, "Prefatory Postscript: Interpretation and Reading," *Readings in Interpretation* (Minneapolis: Univ. of Minnesota Press, 1987), xxvii–lxi.

11. Blanchot, "La raison de Sade," in *Lautréamont et Sade* (Paris: Minuit, 1963; orig. pub. 1949), 18; "Sade," trans. Richard Seaver and Austryn Wainhouse, in Sade, *Justine, Philosophy in the Bedroom, and Other Writings,* 38.

12. Blanchot defined "what Dolmancé calls *apathie* [as] a state of high tension and clear insensibility" ("Insurrection," 223/332). Paul de Man approached a definition of the ethical as precisely this resistance to pathos (*Allegories of Reading: Figural Language in Rousseau, Nietzsche, Rilke, and Proust* (New Haven: Yale, 1979), pp. 198, 206–7).

13. Blanchot, "Insurrection," 217/323.

14. Ibid.

15. On calling a cat a cat, see Blanchot, "Literature and the Right to Death," trans. Lydia Davis, in *The Work of Fire* (Stanford: Stanford Univ. Press, 1995), 311, 325; "La littérature et le droit à la mort," in *La Part de feu* (Paris: Gallimard, 1949), 314, 327. Often the names desired are those of body parts: "EUGENIE—. . . And these balls, what is their use, what are they named? MADAME DE SAINT-ANGE—The technical term is genitals" (201/397); or "EUGENIE—I'm dead, I'm shattered . . . I'm destroyed. But explain to me, please, two words that you've pronounced and that I don't understand: first of all, what does *womb* signify?" (206/402).

16. Blanchot, "Insurrection," 218/324–25.

17. Blanchot, "L'inconvenance majeure," 189. For another, even more

explicitly fabulous, example, see the tale of the wolf and the lamb in *Justine*, 608/176–77.

18. Sade offers another version of this critique in "Yet Another Effort, Frenchmen" (321/517). Lest we imagine ourselves to have simply outgrown this fable, consider Umberto Eco's response to a question about the political economy of contemporary universities: "Do you know what neoteinia is? Well, it's the period during which an animal lives under parental protection: a cat, for example, has a neotenic period of about three months. The mother licks it, feeds it, protects it, but after three months the kitten has become a professional cat and goes out into the world to be a cat. In tribal society, neoteinia lasts around sixteen years, after which young men and women go through initiation rites. In our industrial world, the neotenic period is getting longer and longer. We have raised it to the age of thirty. It is even possible to find students in the neotenic phase when they're forty" ("Interview," with Adelaida Lopez and Marithelma Costa, *Diacritics* 17, no. 1 [Spring 1987]: 47). It is worth noticing the remarkable frequency with which this metaphysics of maturity, authorizing itself by an appeal to animal nature or sometimes to the primitivity of the "tribal"—the unquestioning identification of full ethico-political subjectivity with independence and autonomy, understood as liberation from parental constraint—arises in debates on the politics of the university or of pedagogy. Jacques Derrida offers an exemplary warning in this regard: "It is by insisting upon the 'natural,' by naturalizing the content or the forms of instruction, that one 'inculcates' precisely what one wishes to exempt from criticism. GREPH must be particularly careful in this respect, since its tactics could expose it to the risk of naturalist mystification: by demanding that the age at which a young person begins the study of philosophy be lowered, and that the scope of instruction be extended, there is a risk of being understood . . . as suggesting that once prejudices and ideologies have been erased, what will be revealed is the bare truth of an infant always already ready to philosophize and *naturally* capable of doing so" ("The Age of Hegel," trans. Susan Winnett, in Samuel Weber, ed., *Demarcating the Disciplines: Philosophy, Literature, Art* [Minneapolis: Univ. of Minnesota Press, 1986], 6–7; "L'Age de Hegel," in GREPH, *Qui a peur de la philosophie?* [Paris: Flammarion, 1977], 77–78).

19. It goes without saying that, in general, the possibility of a narrative articulation between parent (more exactly, *mother*) and child (daughter) is put at stake in *Philosophy in the Bedroom*. Angela Carter's reading—

"The School of Love," in *The Sadeian Woman* (London: Virago, 1979), 116–36—makes clear that "the basis of the plot is Eugénie's relation to her mother" (117) and that relation insofar as it is a narrative forms the primary target: "If the daughter is a mocking memory to the mother—'As I am, so you once were'—then the mother is a horrid warning to her daughter. 'As I am, so you will be' " (124). For Carter, "the violation of the mother . . . demonstrates and creates Eugénie's autonomy but it also limits her autonomy" (131) to the extent that it returns her to the father. Our reading will take some issue with this understanding of freedom as autonomy, but not with Carter's conclusion: "the Sadeian libertine cannot forgive the mother; . . . his whole life is a violent protest against an irreversible condition because, though it is easy to stop living, it is impossible to erase the fact of one's birth" (135). The status of this protest and the impossible erasure, though, remains difficult to read. On the question of the child's relation to the mother, see also Cathy Caruth, "Past Recognition," *MLN* 100, no. 5 (December 1985): 935–48, a reading of the Blessed Babe passage in Wordsworth's *Prelude* as "the narrativization of a less *knowable* relation, which may even be disruptive of narrative as such" (946).

20. See de Man's discussion following " 'Conclusions': Walter Benjamin's 'The Task of the Translator,' " in *The Resistance to Theory* (Minneapolis: Univ. of Minnesota Press, 1986), 97, and "Anthropomorphism and Trope in the Lyric," in *The Rhetoric of Romanticism* (New York: Columbia Univ. Press, 1984), 241–42.

21. The most radical version of this thought of irrelation is still de Man's in "Shelley Disfigured," where he argues that " *The Triumph of Life* warns us that nothing, whether deed, word, thought, or text, ever happens in relation, positive or negative, to anything that precedes, follows, or exists elsewhere, but only as a random event whose power, like the power of death, is due to the randomness of its occurrence. It also warns us why and how these events then have to be reintegrated in a historical and aesthetic system of recuperation that repeats itself regardless of the exposure of its fallacy" (*The Rhetoric of Romanticism*, 122).

22. Quoting Hegel, Blanchot used "Le Règne animal de l'Esprit" as the original title of "La Littérature et le droit à la mort," in *Critique* 18 (November 1947): 387–405; he cites the phrase in that essay (302/307).

23. Blanchot, "Sade," 62/40.

24. Mme. de Saint-Ange specifies the opposition on which this exposure rests as that between (natural) birth and (fictive) work: "it is not

for that end that we are born; those absurd laws are the work of men and we must not submit to them." Or, more richly: "One fucks, dear love, in all cases because we are born to fuck, because by fucking we fulfill the laws of nature, and because every human law that would contravene those of nature is made for nothing but contempt" (226/422).

25. Immanuel Kant, "What is Enlightenment?," in *Foundations of the Metaphysics of Morals and What is Enlightenment?*, trans. Lewis White Beck (New York: Macmillan, 1959), 83; "Beantwortung der Frage: Was ist Aufklärung?," in Ehrhard Bahr, ed., *Was ist Aufklärung* (Stuttgart: Reclam, 1974), 9. Even Kant could not resist a good animal story, a story of the bad example of freedom: "That the step to maturity is held to be very dangerous by the far greater portion of mankind . . . is seen to by those guardians who have so kindly assumed superintendence over them. After the guardians have first made domestic cattle dumb and have made sure that these placid creatures will not dare take a single step without the harness of the cart to which they are tethered, the guardians then show them the danger which threatens if they try to go alone. Actually, however, this danger is not so great, for by falling a few times they would finally learn to walk alone. But an example of this failure makes them timid and ordinarily frightens them away from all further trials" (83/9). The links between Kant and Sade are important, but I leave them aside here. See, for two exemplary readings, Jacques Lacan, "Kant with Sade," trans. James Swenson, *October* 51 (winter 1989): 55–104; "Kant avec Sade," *Ecrits* (Paris: Seuil, 1966), 763–90; and the "Juliette" chapter in Max Horkheimer and Theodor Adorno, *Dialectic of Enlightenment*, trans. John Cumming (New York: Continuum, 1991), 81–119; *Dialektik der Aufklärung*, in Adorno, *Gesammelte Schriften*, vol. 3, ed. Rolf Tiedemann (Frankfurt am Main: Suhrkamp, 1981), 100–140.

26. Berlin, "Two Concepts of Liberty," 142–43.

27. Charles Taylor's disappointing defense of this position, in "What's Wrong with Negative Liberty," *Philosophy and the Human Sciences*, vol. 2 of *Philosophical Papers* (Cambridge: Cambridge Univ. Press, 1985), 211–29, finally ends up doing nothing more than repeat this summary, and with it the very metaphysics of subjectivity and transparency that any rigorous thought of freedom, to the extent that it encounters a linguistic moment, cannot help but trouble: freedom "require[s] me to have become something, to have achieved a certain condition of self-clairvoyance and self-understanding. I must be actually exercising self-understanding in order to be truly or fully free" (229).

28. The analysis of this structure reveals it as thoroughly rhetorical and strictly catachretic: "All our ideas are representations of objects that strike us: what can represent to us the idea of God, who is plainly an idea without an object? Is not such an idea . . . just as impossible as effects without causes? Is an idea without prototype anything other than a chimera?" (304/499). The corollary is remarkable: if there must be laws, as Sade contends here that there must, "let us substitute for this unworthy phantom-imposing simulacra" (301/496).

29. Blanchot, "Sade," 54–55/33.

30. Quoted without citation by Blanchot in "Quelques remarques sur Sade," *Critique* 3–4 (August–September 1946): 243. Of course, one does not have to read more than a few pages of Sade to find such phrases: "that is contrary to all the laws of nature, and [nature's] is the sole voice that must direct all the actions in our life" (309/504), or "now that we have broken with the host of religious errors that captivated us, and that, brought closer to nature by the quantity of prejudices we have recently annihilated, we listen only to [nature's] voice" (316/511), and so on.

31. Geoffrey Bennington's discussion of law and nature in Sade has been helpful in clarifying many of the questions raised here, as has his earlier reading of the pedagogical stakes of the fable (*Sententiousness and the Novel* [Cambridge: Cambridge Univ. Press, 1985], 192–209, 80–90).

32. Blanchot, "Sade," 62/39–40.

33. De Man, "Anthropomorphism and Trope," 250. De Man, who earlier associated Sade with "certain aspects of Baudelaire" around the theme of "the lost experience of natural unity" ("Image and Emblem in Yeats," *The Rhetoric of Romanticism*), reads Baudelaire in this much later essay in a way that could not be more useful for our reading here: "Enumerative repetition disrupts the chain of tropological substitution at the crucial moment when the poem promises, by way of these very substitutions, to reconcile the pleasures of the mind with those of the senses. . . . That the very word on which these substitutions depend would just then lose its syntactical and semantic univocity is too striking a coincidence not to be, like pure chance, beyond the control of author and reader" (207).

34. I am effectively in agreement with the reading offered by William Connolly, who argues in *Political Theory and Modernity* (Oxford: Basil Blackwell, 1988), that Sade's strategy is "to sever the connection between God and nature, by revealing through the endless repetition of examples how impossible it is for each to hear the same voice of God there, and

then to endorse, perhaps ironically, a standard of nature devoid of God." This is no simple separation: for Connolly, without God "nature no longer has . . . law (as command) inscribed in it," because law is "design, purpose, or end." While Sade demonstrates in fact that law needs no *telos*, that it *is* law because it simply commands, Connolly is nevertheless right to conclude that "nature now allows anything and everything." This "everything" ultimately leads to "either an ironic repudiation of nature as a guide to morality or an ironic endorsement of it because it authorizes those actions its own moralists [Hobbes and Rousseau] tried to condemn" (77–78). I would only add that this "ironic" nature not only allows but demands everything, and as law is perhaps more difficult to repudiate or endorse than it appears.

35. De Man, *Allegories of Reading*, 269.

36. The phrase "law of the law" seems to come from Derrida: see "Violence and Metaphysics," 111/164, as well as Hamacher's reading in "ʟᴇᴄᴛɪᴏ : de Man's Imperative," trans. Susan Bernstein, in Wlad Godzich and Lindsay Waters, eds., *Reading de Man Reading* (Minneapolis: Univ. of Minnesota Press, 1989): 179. See also Derrida, "The Law of Genre," trans. Avital Ronell, in Derek Attridge, ed., *Acts of Literature* (New York: Routledge, 1992), 221–52; "La loi du genre," *Parages* (Paris: Galilée, 1986), 249–87.

37. Blanchot, "Quelques remarques sur Sade," 248.

38. See also "Violence and Metaphysics," 128/188, on "the irreducible violence of the relation to the other" which opens that relation.

39. Blanchot, "Sade," 65/42.

40. De Man, "Anthropomorphism and Trope," 249–50.

41. Blanchot: "The world of Sade is constituted by the entanglement of two systems: in one, beings are equal, each counts equally. But in the other . . . not only are individuals not equal, but the inequality is such that there are no relations, no reciprocity, possible among them" ("Quelques remarques sur Sade," 244).

42. Nature, thought as fable, functions here as it does in de Man's reading of Rousseau: "Rousseau calls natural any stage of relational integration that precedes in degree the stage presently under examination. . . . The deconstruction of a system of relationships always reveals a more fragmented stage that can be called natural with regard to the system that is being undone. Because it also functions as the negative truth of the deconstructive process, the 'natural' pattern authoritatively substitutes its relational system for the one it helped to dissolve. In so doing, it conceals the fact that it is itself one system of relations among

others, and it presents itself as the sole and true order of things, as nature and not as structure. But since a deconstruction always has for its target to reveal the existence of hidden articulations and fragmentations within assumedly monadic totalities, nature turns out to be a self-deconstructive term. It engenders countless other 'natures' in an eternally repeated pattern of regression. Nature deconstructs nature, hence the ambiguous valorization of the term throughout Rousseau's works. Far from denoting a homogenous mode of being, 'nature' connotes a process of deconstruction redoubled by its own fallacious retotalization" (*Allegories of Reading*, 249).

43. Oddly, this coincides with Luce Irigaray's call " 'Frenchwomen,' Stop Trying" (*This Sex Which Is Not One*, trans. Catherine Porter [Ithaca: Cornell Univ. Press, 1985], 198–204; " 'Françaises,' ne faites plus un effort," *Ce Sexe qui n'en est pas un* (Paris: Minuit, 1977), 195–202). "Nature" has always been men's; women, their property. If nature is questioned, revealed as that of men alone, and women find themselves "attracted by something other than what their laws prescribe," then "—perhaps—it's a matter of *your* 'nature.' " And yet. No more effort means no more nature. "Don't even go looking for that alibi. Do what comes to you, what pleases you: without 'reason,' without 'valid motives,' without 'justification' " (203/202). This doing without, without ground, is just what we mean by another effort (of reading, politics). We translate: *plus d'un effort*.

44. Blanchot, "Insurrection," 218/324.

45. Sade, *Juliette*, trans. Austryn Wainhouse (New York: Grove Press, 1968), 1193; *Histoire de Juliette* 2, in *Oeuvres complètes du Marquis de Sade*, vol. 9 (Paris: Pauvert, 1987), 582. Blanchot quotes this in "Insurrection," 229/342.

46. Compare Foucault on the "prétention de tout dire" ("Language to Infinity," 61/49). The project of *tout dire* has become emblematic of a certain revolutionary freedom, and indeed of a modern experience of democracy and of literature. I am implicitly tracking this phrase here only across Sade and his best readers, but it has a rich history in the literature of the French Revolution and Rousseau, among others, as far as Foucault's analysis of the "incitement to discourse" in *The History of Sexuality, Volume I*, and Lacan's claim that "saying it all is literally impossible" (*Television*, trans. Denis Hollier, et al. [New York: Norton, 1990], 3; *Télévision* [Paris: Seuil, 1974], 9). As Derrida has argued, "the institution of literature in the West, in its relatively modern form, is linked to an authorization to say everything, and doubtless too to the

coming about of the modern idea of democracy" (" 'This Strange Institution Called Literature,' " interview with Derek Attridge, in *Acts of Literature*, 36–37; cf. "Passions: An Oblique Offering," trans. David Wood, in Wood, ed., *Derrida: A Critical Reader* [Oxford: Blackwell, 1992], 23; *Passions* [Paris: Galilée, 1993], 65, on the "right to say everything" and responsibility). Here I would also note my disagreement with Geoffrey Bennington's offhand comment on this phrase in his reading of Sade and the "transgression of nature": "by asserting that philosophy *must* say everything, Sade implies that it *can* say everything" (*Sententiousness and the Novel*, 178). In failing to coordinate the imperative with the claim to a right, and, indeed, in neglecting all mention of rights, Bennington reduces the imperative to a "demand for totalization" and is able to translate it as "recuperate all excesses." He reads this demand in stark contradiction to an equally powerful drive to "exceed all totalities," and sees "this constitutive aporia" as the motor "which generates Sade's writing as endless" (180). My argument is that no "contradiction" is necessary to produce this aporia: it resides as the heart of the claim to this right, the right to claim rights in an unlimited and illimitable (endless) effort. (Bennington also offers an unrelated, but very interesting, reading of "the drive to 'tout dire,' which commands the scene of writing in other texts by Rousseau," in the context of the condemnation in *Emile* of the use of fables with children, 89–90.)

47. Laclau, *New Reflections on the Revolution of Our Time* (London: Verso, 1990), 60, and "Negotiating the Paradoxes of Contemporary Politics," interview with David Howarth and Aletta Norval, *Angelaki* 1, no. 3, *Reconsidering the Political* (January 1995): 49.

48. Berlin, "Two Concepts," 118, distinguishing between the technical and the political. In spite of their unfortunate tendency to rely on phrases like "the human condition," Berlin's pages on the singularity of politics— as at once "the necessity and agony of choice" and the resistance to "the very desire for guarantees" that choice seems to demand—are remarkable (168–72).

49. Bennington, *Sententiousness and the Novel*, 199.

50. Blanchot, "Literature and the Right to Death," 318/321–22.

Chapter 4

1. Karl Marx, "Theses on Feuerbach," in Karl Marx and Friedrich Engels, *Collected Works*, vol. 5 (New York: International Publishers,

1976), 5; "Thesen über Feuerbach," in Karl Marx and Friedrich Engels, *Werke*, vol. 3 (Berlin: Dietz, 1958), 7.

2. Recall that Engels changed things considerably: in his version, the crucial phrase reads "es kommt *aber* darauf an" (Marx and Engels, *Collected Works*, 5: 8; *Werke*, 3: 535).

3. Paul de Man, *Allegories of Reading* (New Haven: Yale Univ. Press, 1979), ix.

4. "Martin Heidegger: An Interview," trans. Vincent Guagliardo and Robert Pambrun, *Listening* 6, no. 1 (winter 1971): 35; "Martin Heidegger im Gespräch," in Richard Wisser, ed., *Martin Heidegger im Gespräch* (Freiburg: Karl Alber, 1970), 69. Richard Dienst has offered a compelling reading of Heidegger's TV appearance in *Still Life in Real Time* (Durham: Duke Univ. Press, 1994), 124–27.

5. De Man, *Allegories of Reading*, 6.

6. Karl Marx, "Preface to the First Edition," *Capital: A Critique of Political Economy*, vol. 1, trans. Ben Fowkes (New York: Vintage, 1977), 104; "Vorwort zur ersten Auflage," *Das Kapital: Kritik der politischen Ökonomie* 1, in Marx and Engels, *Werke*, vol. 23 (Berlin: Dietz, 1984 [based on the Hamburg 1890 edition]), 31. I will also refer to the French translation, extensively revised by Marx: *Le Capital*, vol. 1, trans. Joseph Roy (Paris: Editions du Progrès, 1982 [Paris, 1872–75]), 11. References are first to the English translation and then to the German original; when the French text is cited, those page numbers appear following the other two, or by themselves.

7. "Preface to the French Edition," *Capital*, 104; *Le Capital*, 11.

8. On "difficulty" in reading *Capital*, see Louis Althusser, "Preface to *Capital* Volume One," in *Lenin and Philosophy*, trans. Ben Brewster (New York: Monthly Review Press, 1971), 71–106; "Avertisement aux Lecteurs du Livre I du *Capital*," in Marx, *Le Capital*, book 1 (Paris: Flammarion, 1969), 5–30: What will it require for "petit-bourgeois 'intellectuals'" to be able to read *Capital*?—not a "mere education," but a "rupture"; (101/25–26). Maurice Blanchot's brief but powerful "Marx's Three Voices" (trans. T. Keenan, *New Political Science* 15 [summer 1986]: 17–20; "Les Trois Paroles de Marx," *L'Amitié* [Paris: Gallimard, 1971], 115–17) emphasizes that reading Marx requires an encounter with a "plurality of languages, which always collide and disarticulate themselves." Blanchot's three pages, first published under the title "Lire Marx" in the same year as Althusser and Balibar's abridged *Lire le Capital*, insist that these "voices" resist being translated into one another, and that "the

divergence or gap, the distance that decenters them, renders them non-contemporaneous." This "effect of irreducible distortion" is the one Blanchot attempts to read, with perhaps more respect than Althusser, who remains committed to a number of the very philosophemes that Blanchot sees as undermined by Marx's text.

9. The prevailing English translation of *ungeheuere* as "immense" turns the opening sentence into a virtual transposition of Wordsworth's Immortality Ode: "Thou, whose exterior semblance doth belie / Thy Soul's immensity" (lines 108–9).

10. Gerhard Wahrig, *Wahrig Deutsches Wörterbuch* (Munich: Mosaik, 1987), 1330.

11. Karl Marx, *A Contribution to the Critique of Political Economy*, trans. S. W. Ryazanskaya, ed. Maurice Dobb (New York: International Publishers, 1970), 27; *Zur Kritik der Politischen Ökonomie*, in Marx and Engels, *Werke*, vol. 13 (Berlin: Dietz, 1961), 15.

12. Of course, Marx insists, some *thing* is used, or rather, some "body." Although a thing can be used and hence be a use-value, its status as a *value* does not make it nothing or leave it "suspended in mid-air"—on the contrary, "limited by the properties of the commodity-body [*Warenkörper*], it [use-value] does not exist without it." How this limitation works, though, remains unclear throughout the chapter. In any event, this body will return, and I will return to it.

13. Althusser quotes a note by Marx from 1883: "for me use-value plays a far more important role than it has in economics hitherto," in *Reading Capital*, trans. Ben Brewster (London: Verso, 1979), 79; *Lire le Capital*, vol. 1 (Paris: Maspero, 1968), 96. In my argument, which pursues some hints in the text about this unprecedented category, the encounter with its troubling difficulty requires going against much of the grain not only of Marx interpretation, but of *Capital* itself.

14. The *Critique of Political Economy* is more blunt: "a use-value has value only in use. . . . One and the same use-value can be used in various ways" (27/7). The same? Or does the iteration alter?

15. See Jacques Derrida, "Signature Event Context": "This is the possibility on which I want to insist: the possibility of disengagement and citational grafting which belongs to the structure of every mark, spoken or written. . . . Every sign, linguistic or nonlinguistic, . . . as a small or large unit, can be *cited*, put between quotation marks; thereby it can break with every given context, engendering new contexts infinitely, in an absolutely nonsaturable fashion. This does not imply that the mark is

valid outside of a context, but on the contrary that there are only contexts without any center or absolute anchoring. . . . What would a mark be that could not be cited? Or one whose origins would not get lost along the way?" (in *Limited Inc*, trans. Samuel Weber [Evanston: Northwestern Univ. Press, 1988], 12; "Signature Evénement Context," in *Limited Inc* [Paris: Galilée, 1990], 35–36). On use, the proper, and the question of value (Marx with Nietzsche and Saussure), see also Derrida's "White Mythology," in *Margins—of Philosophy*, trans. Alan Bass (Chicago: Univ. of Chicago Press, 1982), 214–19; "La mythologie blanche," in *Marges—de la philosophie* (Paris: Minuit, 1972), 254–60; as well as Jean-Joseph Goux, *Symbolic Economies: After Marx and Freud*, trans. Jennifer Curtiss Gage (Ithaca: Cornell Univ. Press, 1990), 9–63; *Economie et symbolique* (Paris: Seuil, 1973), esp. 53–113.

16. See Gayatri Chakravorty Spivak, "Speculations on Reading Marx: After Reading Derrida," in Derek Attridge et al., eds., *Post-structuralism and the Question of History* (Cambridge: Cambridge Univ. Press, 1987), 30–62, esp. 40 and n. 13; and her "Scattered Speculations on the Question of Value," *In Other Worlds* (New York: Routledge, 1988), 154–75. "In my reading . . . it is use-value that puts the entire textual chain of value into question and thus allows us a glimpse of the possibility that even textualization . . . may be no more than a way of holding randomness at bay. For use-value . . . cannot be measured by the labor theory of value . . . [while exchange-value] is also a superfluity or a parasite of use-value. . . . The part-whole relation is turned inside-out" ("Scattered Speculations," 162). In "Some Concept Metaphors of Political Economy in Derrida's Texts" (*Leftwright/Intervention* 20 [1986]: 88–97; "Il faut s'y prendre en se prenant à elles," in Philippe Lacoue-Labarthe and Jean-Luc Nancy, eds., *Les Fins de l'homme* [Paris: Galilée, 1981],505–16), Spivak argues that "Use-value is not a transcendental principle because it changes on each occasion or heterogeneous case . . . ; [it is] non-transcendental, material, and therefore incommensurable for the logic of binary exchange" (93/509). The illogic of use voids use-value of phenomenality, quality, and particularity (except in the odd sense of contextual particularity). Andrew Parker makes a similar argument in "Futures for Marxism: An Appreciation of Althusser," *Diacritics* 15, no. 4 (winter 1985): 57–72, although he reads *Capital*'s initial treatment of use-value, a " 'natural' property of the thing" ["exchange . . . knows only impropriety"], as "undercut [by its] rhetorical performance." It turns out that the text "divides nature from itself, . . . precluding the possibility of a natural

world conceived as a single, indivisible origin" (65–69). Jean Baudrillard (*For a Critique of the Political Economy of the Sign*, trans. Charles Levin [St. Louis: Telos Press, 1981], esp. "Beyond Use Value," 130–42; *Pour une critique de l'économie politique du signe* [Paris: Gallimard, 1972]) argues that in this respect Marx is an idealist: "utility . . . represents an objective, final relation of *destination propre*." The critique, though, reveals that "use value is an abstraction" (130–31). See also his "Critique of Use Value and Labor Power" in *The Mirror of Production*, trans. Mark Poster (St. Louis: Telos Press, 1975), 22–25; *Le Miroir de la production* (Paris: Galilée, 1985), 19–22.

17. Recall that a commodity, as opposed to a mere thing, is a thing "produced for others" and then "transferred [*übertragen*]"—at least this is how Engels understands it, in his inserted parenthesis (131/55). But "commodity" is more accurately a historical (or political) term, rather than a transcendental one, not simply because of the problems of intention inherent in the "produced for" construction but more crucially since (1) exchange is *always* a possibility and thus cannot simply be avoided as an accident and (2) the multiplicity and contingency of use already imply a divergence indistinguishable from exchange at the putative origin.

18. Throughout this chapter the translation of all words containing *gleich* hesitates between "similar," "(a)like," and "equal." As the fable of the raven and its likeness should illustrate, there is not much of a line separating similarity from equality or identity. As soon as comparison has been entered into, the slippage to equation is hard to resist: that is the aberrancy and the economy of the trope. If things were the same, there would be no need to compare or exchange them, but in order to be related, they must have something of the same available for the crossing . . . thus, *Gleichheit*, alikeness, as the mediation of identity and difference.

19. The text is free with analogies and examples here, for example, "a simple geometrical example will illustrate this. In order to determine and compare the areas of all rectilinear figures we split them up into triangles. Then the triangle itself is reduced. . . . In the same way [*Ebenso*] exchange values must be reduced" (127/51). "In the same way," it says—and thus the whole question of exchangeability or substitutability posed in the example of the triangles is posed *by* it as well. "In the same way" presumes that the analogy, any analogy, can be drawn between economics and geometry, that the two can be reduced to something common to both, exchanged by being reduced to something *eben*. This is what is at stake in

the analysis, and in the example language already plays with them, beside the "argument," taking everything for granted.

20. Karl Marx, *Capital* 1, ed. Frederick Engels, trans. Samuel Moore and Edward Aveling (New York: International Publishers, 1967 [London, 1887]), 37.

21. Otherwise, the whole question would be begged and the critical power of the analysis foregone. The common generality of human labor, as of use-value, is what the analysis refuses to take for granted. When the French translation risks "il ne reste donc plus que le caractère commun de ces travaux" (46), it cedes to the temptation otherwise resisted: if this commonality or generality could be found, and given things or labors could be seen as particular species of things or labors, then exchange would not be a problem. But precisely the status of this "common" term is in question in the analysis. Thus Marx, later in *Capital*, can raise the "possibility of crises" stemming from the asymmetry in "the antithetical phases of the metamorphosis of the commodity," namely "the personification of things and the reification of persons" (209/128).

22. Marx, *Critique of Political Economy*, 27n/15n.

23. Compare Hayden White's extended reading of Marx's "tropological analysis" of value (from metaphor to metonymy to synecdoche to irony) in "Marx: The Philosophical Defense of History in the Metonymical Mode," in *Metahistory* (Baltimore: Johns Hopkins Univ. Press, 1973), 281–330, esp. "The Basic Model of Analysis," on *Capital*, 287–302. Although White concludes that "the labor theory of value serves as the base line from which all erroneous conceptions [provided by the tropological reductions] of value can be transcended," because he thinks that for Marx things are "isolated individualities, particulars which appear to bear no essential relationship to one another," the reading of the figurative structure of the exchanges involved is powerful nevertheless (296, 293).

24. Paul de Man, "The Epistemology of Metaphor," *Critical Inquiry* 5, no. 1 (autumn 1978): 13–30. De Man is quoting the section in Condillac's *Essai sur l'origine des connaissances humaines* (1746) called "Des Abstractions." See Condillac's *Essai*, preceded by Jacques Derrida, "L'Archéologie de frivole" (Paris: Galilée, 1973), 174. As Derrida points out, Marx himself took a certain interest in Condillac in *Capital*, in "the confusion between use-value and exchange value" (*The Archeology of the Frivolous*, trans. John P. Leavey, Jr. [Pittsburgh: Duquesne Univ. Press, 1980], 103–4; "L'Archéologie," 70–71).

25. Pierre Fontanier, *Les Figures du discours*, ed. Gérard Genette (Paris: Flammarion, 1977 [1821–30]), 87.

26. Since this chapter was written and published in Emily Apter and William Pietz, eds., *Fetishism as Cultural Discourse* (Ithaca: Cornell Univ. Press, 1993), 152–85, Jacques Derrida has written *Specters of Marx*, trans. Peggy Kamuf (New York: Routledge, 1994); *Spectres de Marx* (Paris: Galilée, 1994). Derrida offers a systematic and nuanced reading of the tensions and movements of spectrality in Marx, including this *gespenstige Gegenständlichkeit* (167/264). There is no space here to take full, or even partial, account of Derrida's interpretation, other than to mark my fundamental accord with what he says (especially the reading of *Capital* in Chapter 5). For an early appreciation of *Specters*, see Fredric Jameson, "Marx's Purloined Letter," *New Left Review* 209 (January/February 1995): 75–109, which argues that "spectrality is here the form of the most radical politicization and . . . is energetically future-oriented and active" (104); see also Gayatri Spivak's "Ghostwriting," *Diacritics* 25, no. 2 (Summer 1995): 65–84, and in the same issue, Ernesto Laclau, " 'The Time Is Out of Joint,' " 86–96. And compare Derrida's earlier remarks on the economy of Marx's phantoms and ghosts in *The Post Card*, trans. Alan Bass, (Chicago: Univ. of Chicago Press, 1987), 268; *La Carte postale* (Paris: Aubier-Flammarion, 1980), 286.

27. On the question of the possibility of exchange in *Capital*, see Michel Henry's important chapter "The Transcendental Genesis of the Economy," in *Marx, A Philosophy of Human Reality*, trans. Kathleen McLaughlin (Bloomington: Indiana Univ. Press, 1983), 190–223; *Marx 1. Une Philosophie de la réalité* and *2. Une Philosophie de l'économie* (Paris: Gallimard, 1976), 2: 138–207. Henry's reading articulates the economic question of commodity exchange with the ethico-political question of equality in rights, and he produces a series of original interpretations of the crucial questions of *Capital*. But he does so in an ultimately insufficient manner, namely, by attributing to Marx "a philosophy of monadic subjectivity, [which] recognizes the irreducibility of each individual and as a result each of the modalities of his praxis, [which] excludes at the same time, along with any unit of objective measurement, the possibility of making apparent between different individuals and their different kinds of labor some sort of 'equality' and consequently, the very possibility of exchange" (194/2:145). Given this investment in praxis as *living* individual subjectivity, the question of *Capital* for Henry is simply "How is exchange possible starting from its own impossibility?" (199/2: 152). The

answer is clear: "real labor [organic subjectivity, the individuality of real praxis, essential particularity] produces the real object, the commodity in its materiality and as a use-value. Abstract [irreal] labor, which is the pure representation of this real labor, is in its turn represented in the commodity as its exchange-value" (208/2:168). Reading *Capital* next to the *Critique of the Gotha Programme*, he pursues "the insurmountable aporia of the possibility of any sort of equality [that might allow exchange or economy] between individuals, that is to say, between their different kinds [and experiences] of work . . . [which] find their actuality, precisely, in the irreducible, unrepresentable, and undefinable subjectivity of the absolute monad. This aporia of equality is at the same time that of right, for there is no right other than an 'equal right' " (194/2: 145). But if the questions are to the point, the solutions evade their rigor. Henry determines subjectivity quite traditionally as self-presence, which allows him to think abstraction simply as representation and not as figure. The "réalité fantomatique" of the ghost is allowed to escape, as it is quickly assimilated to "irréalité" (201/155) and set in opposition to the reality of "life." Thus the radicality of *Capital*'s gesture, and the difficulty of its challenge, is evaded: how to think the aporia of exchange and of right without confusing the singularity or the materiality of the individual or the thing with something present or phenomenal.

28. See Aristotle, *Nicomachean Ethics*, trans. H. Rackham (Cambridge: Harvard Univ. Press, 1975), 5.5.14 (p. 287).

29. Ibid., 5.5.11 (p. 285).

30. Louis Althusser, "Marxism and Humanism," in *For Marx*, trans. Ben Brewster (London: Verso, 1979), 229; "Marxisme et humanisme," in *Pour Marx* (Paris: Maspero, 1967), 236. Althusser's reading bases itself on the "absolute precondition that the philosophical (theoretical) myth of man is reduced to ashes." The essay's epigraph, from Marx, begins: "My analytical method does not start from man."

31. Marx is thus speaking strictly when he writes in a footnote: "In a certain sense, man is like the commodity. As he neither enters into the world in possession of a mirror, nor as a Fichtean philosopher who can say 'Ich bin Ich,' a man first sees or recognizes himself in another man. The man Peter only relates to himself as a man through his relation to the man Paul as his likeness" (144 n. 19/67 n. 18).

32. Spivak, "Some Concept Metaphors," 96; cf. her "Speculations," 50.

33. Spivak quotes the final sentence here in "Some Concept Metaphors," 94; see also Henry, *Marx*, 194/2: 145.

34. As Althusser points out in *Reading Capital*, Marx wrote quite directly in the *Critique of the Gotha Programme*: "Labor is not the source of all wealth" (quoted 171/2: 40). "In *Capital*," writes Althusser, "Marx breaks with the idealism of labor . . . 'as the essence of man'" (172/2: 41).

35. See Althusser's amusing and pointed discussion of the encounter with the sign that says "cross the frontier and go on in the direction of society and you will find the real," in "Marxism and Humanism," 244/255.

36. Walter Benjamin, "The Paris of the Second Empire in Baudelaire," in *Charles Baudelaire*, trans. Harry Zohn (London: Verso, 1983), 55–56 n. 41; "Das Paris des Second Empire bei Baudelaire," in *Charles Baudelaire*, ed. Rolf Tiedemann (Frankfurt am Main: Suhrkamp, 1980), 54n. Paul de Man calls attention to Jauss's discussion of this phrase in his Introduction to Hans Robert Jauss, *Toward an Aesthetic of Reception*, trans. Timothy Bahti (Minneapolis: Univ. of Minnesota Press, 1982), xxiii; Jauss, 178–79. De Man comments, "the commodity is anorganic because it exists as a mere piece of paper, as an inscription or a notation on a certificate." See de Man's reading of *Augenschein* in Kant, in his "Phenomenality and Materiality in Kant," in Gary Shapiro and Alan Sica, eds., *Hermeneutics: Questions and Prospects* (Amherst: Univ. of Massachusetts Press, 1984), 121–44.

37. Luce Irigaray, "Women on the Market," in *This Sex Which Is Not One*, trans. Catherine Porter with Carolyn Burke (Ithaca: Cornell Univ. Press, 1985), 177; "Le Marché des femmes," in *Ce sexe qui n'en est pas un* (Paris: Minuit, 1977), 173. See also her discussions of the ghost, abstraction, and the question of analogy between the exchange of commodities and of women, but also within *Capital* itself (174–75/170–71).

38. Paul de Man, "Aesthetic Formalization: Kleist's *Über das Marionettentheater*," in *The Rhetoric of Romanticism* (New York: Columbia Univ. Press, 1984), 265.

39. Georg Lukács, *History and Class Consciousness*, trans. Rodney Livingstone (Cambridge: MIT Press, 1971), 83.

40. See the series of articles by William Pietz, "The Problem of the Fetish," in *Res* 9 (spring 1985): 5–17; 13 (spring 1987): 23–45; and 16 (autumn 1988): 105–23.

41. George Puttenham, *The Arte of English Poesie* (Kent, Ohio: Kent State Univ. Press, 1970 [1589]), 190–91.

42. De Man, "The Epistemology of Metaphor," 21.

43. Deborah Esch, "'Think of a Kitchen Table': Hume, Woolf, and

the Translation of Example," in Donald G. Marshall, ed., *Literature as Philosophy, Philosophy as Literature* (Iowa City: Univ. of Iowa Press, 1987), 262–76.

44. Is a table ever simply a table? Here is a story "from de Man's seminar," recounted by Werner Hamacher: "the seminar was trying to clarify what a referent is, and the question seemed easily answered— someone said, this table here, for example, is a referent. No, countered de Man, this is not a referent, this—and here he knocked on it—is a table. In the story, at least, the table is no longer a table" ("Journals, Politics," in Werner Hamacher, Neil Hertz, and Thomas Keenan, eds., *Responses: On Paul de Man's Wartime Journalism* [Lincoln: Univ. of Nebraska Press, 1989], 460).

45. See Octave Mannoni, "Je sais bien, mais quand même . . . ," in *Clefs pour l'imaginaire* (Paris: Seuil, 1969), 9–33. Slavoj Žižek devotes the powerful first chapter of *The Sublime Object of Ideology* (London: Verso, 1989), "How Did Marx Invent the Symptom?," to complicating this "formula of fetishistic disavowal" (18). Although his book came to my attention only after this chapter was completed, Žižek's analysis of "real abstraction" (20), fetishism "in practice, not in theory" (31), the ideological fantasy (33), "belief [as] an affair of obedience to the dead uncomprehending letter" (43), and the leftover or residue of senselessness in ideological interpellation (43), is basically congruent with my argument here. (The same cannot be said for his interpretation, such as it is, of post-structuralism as "universalized aestheticization" [153] or of "the Derridean deconstruction" in chap. 2 of *For They Know Not What They Do* [London: Verso, 1990], 70–95, to which Rodolphe Gasché has responded in a long footnote to his "Yes Absolutely," in Ernesto Laclau, ed., *The Making of Political Identities* [London: Verso, 1994], 100 n. 17. I pursue some of these differences in the Conclusion.) I have also learned from Sarah Kofman's *Camera obscura—de l'idéologie* (Paris: Galilée, 1973), which offers an early and powerful deconstruction of the concepts of ideology and fetishism in Marx, and from the work of Etienne Balibar (in his two essays "The Vacillation of Ideology," in *Masses, Classes, Ideas*, trans. James Swenson [New York: Routledge, 1994], 87–124, 151–74, and esp. "Idéologie et fétichisme," in *La Philosophie de Marx* [Paris: La Découverte, 1993], 42–77).

46. Spivak, in "Some Concept Metaphors," cites a different passage, from the *Grundrisse*, to the same effect: "'madness . . . as a moment of economy'" (93/509).

Chapter 5

1. Alain Renault, "Le Combat du maître et du sujet," *L'Express* 1839 (October 3–9, 1986): 150–51.

2. Renault, 151. Let me here endorse and second the energetic footnote recently devoted by Derrida to contesting another version of this "revisionism" canard, in *Specters of Marx*, trans. Peggy Kamuf (New York: Routledge, 1994), 185 n. 5; *Spectres de Marx* (Paris: Galilée, 1994), 172 n. 1.

3. Renault, "Le Combat," p. 151.

4. Hence it demands the criticism leveled at it, obliquely, by Derrida in "The Ends of Man," in *Margins—of Philosophy*, trans. Alan Bass (Chicago: Univ. of Chicago Press, 1982), 109–36; "Les Fins de l'homme," in *Marges—de la Philosophie* (Paris: Minuit, 1972), 129–64. See Michel Foucault, *The Order of Things* (New York: Pantheon Books, 1970), 387; *Les Mots et les choses* (Paris: Gallimard, 1966), 398.

5. The citation is from the earlier announcement of this necessity in Luc Ferry and Alain Renault, *French Philosophy of the Sixties*, trans. Mary H. S. Cattani (Amherst: Univ. of Massachusetts Press, 1990), 211; *La Pensée 68* (Paris: Gallimard, 1985), 267. Didier Eribon devotes an excellent chapter of his second book on Foucault, *Michel Foucault et ses contemporains* (Paris: Fayard, 1994), 69–102, to demonstrating just how ridiculous the would-be "arguments" of Ferry and Renault really are.

6. Michel Foucault, "Politics and the Study of Discourse," trans. Colin Gordon, *Ideology and Consciousness* 3 (1978): 7–26; "Réponse à une question," *Esprit* 371 (May 1968): 850–74. The French text has recently been reprinted in the four-volume collection of Foucault's otherwise uncollected writing, *Dits et écrits* (Paris: Gallimard, 1994), 1: 673–95. I have tried to note when the texts I cite have been reprinted in these volumes.

7. Maurice Blanchot, "Michel Foucault as I Imagine Him," trans. Brian Massumi, in *Foucault/Blanchot* (New York: Zone Books, 1987), 76–77; *Michel Foucault tel que je l'imagine* (Montpellier: Fata Morgana, 1986), 29.

8. This is the responsibility to respond *without* consciousness or subject: "The question that I pose is not that of codes but of events: the law of the existence of utterances, of what makes them possible—them and none other in their place. . . . I try to respond to this question without referring to the consciousness, obscure or explicit, of speaking subjects" ("Politics and the Study of Discourse," 14/859).

9. Ibid., 26/873. See Eduardo Cadava, Peter Connor, and Jean-Luc Nancy, eds., *Who Comes After the Subject?* (New York: Routledge, 1991); originally Nancy's special issue of *Confrontations* 20 (winter 1989), "Après le sujet qui vient?"

10. "Politics and the Study of Discourse," 26/873–74.

11. "Milestones," *Newsweek*, July 9, 1984, 73. From paradox to irony: the obituary names the cause of death as "cancer."

12. Jürgen Habermas, "The Genealogical Writing of History: On Some Aporias in Foucault's Theory of Power," trans. Gregory Ostrander, *Canadian Journal of Social and Political Theory* 10, no. 1–2 (1986): 7; "Genealogische Geschichtsschreibung: Über einige Aporien im macht-theoretischen Denken Foucaults," *Merkur* 429 (October 1984): 751.

13. Habermas, "Genealogical Writing," 8. He echoes here the very early objection that Derrida had made to Foucault's *Madness and Civilization*—in "Cogito and the History of Madness," *Writing and Difference*, trans. Alan Bass (Chicago: Univ. of Chicago Press, 1978), 31–63; "Cogito et histoire de la folie," *L'écriture et la différence* (Paris: Seuil, 1967), 51–97—and that Foucault subsequently endorsed, in "Die Folter, das ist die Vernunft," interview with Knut Boeser, *Literaturmagazin* 8 (1977): 60–68 (now available, in French translation by Jacques Chavy, as "La Torture, c'est la raison," *Dits et écrits*, 3: 390–98).

14. Nancy Fraser, *Unruly Practices* (Minneapolis: Univ. of Minnesota Press, 1989), 17.

15. Charles Taylor, "Foucault on Freedom and Truth," *Political Theory* 12, no. 2 (May 1984): 174, 152. See also the exchange between William Connolly, "Taylor, Foucault, and Otherness," and Taylor, "Connolly, Foucault, and Truth," in *Political Theory* 13, no. 3 (August 1985): 365–76 and 377–85.

16. Foucault's critics return again and again to the word "paradox" in this context; see, e.g., Derek D. Nikolinakos, "Foucault's Ethical Quandary," *Telos* 83 (spring 1990): 123: "Many authors have located a paradox in Foucault's earlier work, specifically in his analysis of power and its ethical and political implications." The word "paradox" or "paradoxical" appears five times in the first three pages of this essay.

17. Much of what is problematic in Taylor's essays is captured in this phrase. A systematic drift takes Taylor from defining power as "domination" (the asymmetrical play of mobile and unequal force relations), as Foucault—at least in the texts Taylor considers—does, to power as "imposition," and then to "constraint," "prevention," "impediment," and

blockage. Taylor winds up understanding power as the imposition of constraint on desire (or its formulation)—precisely the negative and "juridico-discursive" view from which Foucault tried to disengage its analysis. Holding to the definitions Foucault is trying to displace, especially with a phrase like "otherwise the term loses all meaning" (176)—misses the point. The point is to put the existing "meanings" of the term in question, to grasp the inadequacy and the political effects of the "semantic field."

18. Michel Foucault, *The History of Sexuality, Volume I: An Introduction*, trans. Robert Hurley (New York: Vintage, 1978), 92; *La Volonté de savoir*, Histoire de la sexualité 1 (Paris: Gallimard, 1976), 121.

19. See Taylor on temporality, "Foucault," 177–80; or, more profitably, Paul de Man, "The Rhetoric of Temporality," in *Blindness and Insight*, 2d ed. (Minneapolis: Univ. of Minnesota Press, 1983), 187–228.

20. See de Man, *Allegories of Reading* (New Haven: Yale Univ. Press, 1979), and Shoshana Felman, *Writing and Madness*, trans. M. N. Evans, S. Felman, and B. Massumi (Ithaca: Cornell Univ. Press, 1985), 24–25. After Hayden White's early efforts (*Tropics of Discourse* [Baltimore: Johns Hopkins Univ. Press, 1978]), the only serious rhetorical analysis of Foucault with which I am familiar is that of Diane Rubenstein, "Food for Thought: Metonymy in the Late Foucault," in James Bernauer and David Rasmussen, eds., *The Final Foucault* (Cambridge: MIT Press, 1988), 83–101.

21. Michel Foucault, *Death and the Labyrinth*, trans. Charles Ruas (Garden City, N.Y.: Doubleday and Co., 1986), 15; *Raymond Roussel* (Paris: Gallimard, 1963), 23–24.

22. Pierre Fontanier, *Les Figures du Discours*, ed. Gerard Genette (Paris: Flammarion, 1977 [1821–30]), 137.

23. Richard Lanham, *A Handlist of Rhetorical Terms* (Berkeley: Univ. of California Press, 1968), 71.

24. Fontanier, *Figures*, 138, 140.

25. See, for an example of the considerable pseudo-dialectical totalizing power of aesthetic paradox, the work of Cleanth Brooks, especially "The Language of Paradox" and "The Heresy of Paraphrase," in *The Well-Wrought Urn* (New York: Harcourt, Brace, and Co., 1947), 3–21 and 192–214.

26. Fontanier, *Figures*, 140.

27. See the important series of articles by Richard Klein on paradox: "Under Pragmatic Paradoxes," *Yale French Studies* 66 (1984): 91–109;

"Nuclear Coincidence and the Korean Airline Disaster," *Diacritics* 16, no. 1 (spring 1986): 2–21 (with William B. Warner); and "The Future of Nuclear Criticism," *Yale French Studies* 77 (1990): 76–100.

28. Michel Foucault, "Critical Theory / Intellectual History," trans. Jeremy Harding, in Michel Foucault, *Politics, Philosophy, Culture*, ed. Lawrence D. Kritzman (New York: Routledge, 1988), 43; "Structuralisme et poststructuralisme," interview with Gérard Raulet, in *Dits et écrits*, 4: 454.

29. Compare, though, the excellent and under-recognized early book by Mark Cousins and Athar Hussain, *Michel Foucault* (New York: St. Martin's Press, 1984), 201, 227, 250: "There is one area to which Foucault and his commentators have given a central prominence but we do not, the power-knowledge relationship" (227).

30. On another rhetorical dash, also located somewhat tensely between knowledge and power, see Deborah Esch, "Toward a Midwifery of Thought: Reading Kleist's *Marquise von O . . .* ," in Mary Ann Caws, ed., *Textual Analysis: Some Readers Reading* (New York: The Modern Language Association of America, 1986), 144–55.

31. Garth Gillan and Charles Lemert, *Michel Foucault: Social Theory as Transgression* (New York: Columbia Univ. Press, 1982), x, 56, 60, 73, 75, 84, 86; emphasis added. This ill-advised book gets the treatment it deserves from Robert D'Amico in *International Studies in Philosophy* 18, no. 1 (1986): 91–93.

32. Michel Foucault, "The Concern for Truth," trans. Alan Sheridan, in *Politics, Philosophy, Culture*, 264. "Le Souci de la vérité," interview with François Ewald, *Magazine Littéraire* 207 (May 1984): 22 (reprinted in *Dits et écrits*, 4: 676).

33. Michel Foucault, "Histoire des systèmes de pensée: Théories et institutions pénales," *Annuaire du Collège de France* 1972 (Paris: Collège de France, 1972), 283 (reprinted in *Dits et écrits* 2: 389–90).

34. Michel Foucault, *Discipline and Punish*, trans. Alan Sheridan, (New York: Pantheon Books, 1977), 23; *Surveiller et punir* (Paris: Gallimard, 1975), 27.

35. Michel Foucault, *The Archeology of Knowledge*, trans. A. M. Sheridan Smith (New York: Pantheon, 1972), 209, 49; *L'Archéologie du savoir* (Paris: Gallimard, 1969), 272, 67. See also Foucault's brief, untitled text in Gérard Mordillat and Nicolas Philibert, *Ces Patrons éclairés qui craignent la lumière* (Paris: Albatros, 1979), 135–36 (reprinted as "Le Discours ne doit pas être pris comme . . . ," in *Dits et écrits*, 3: 123–24): "Discourse—

the simple fact of speaking, of using words, utilizing the words of others (free to return them), words that others understand and accept (and, eventually, return from their side)—this fact is in itself a force. Discourse is not only a surface of inscription for the relation of forces, but an operator."

36. Foucault, *History of Sexuality, Vol. I*, 68–69/92.

37. Foucault, "Critical Theory / Intellectual History," 39/451.

38. Foucault, *History of Sexuality, Vol. I*, 64, 61, 86, 82.

39. See also Michel Foucault, "Discourse and Truth: The Problematiz-ation of *Parrhesia*," transcripts of Fall 1983 lectures at the University of California at Berkeley, edited by Joseph Pearson. In these lectures Fou-cault analyzed the problem of telling the truth about oneself under the rhetorical figure *parrhesia*. Foucault characterized *parrhesia* as a complex act in which the subject of the utterance, the subject who speaks, and the "subject of the enunciandum" are all made to coincide, in an utterance of the form "I am the one who thinks this and that." Foucault argued that this triple superimposition is not just a performative utterance (Austin) or a speech act (Searle), but a "speech activity," given its unusual version of the "commitment between someone and what he or she says" (2). So *parrhesia* is not rhetorical by virtue of some dissimulation or twisting of the truth, but rather a paradoxical figure "without any figure, since it is completely natural. *Parrhesia* is the zero degree of those rhetorical figures which intensify the emotions of the audience" (9). The important refer-ence here is the discussion in *The Archeology of Knowledge*, 79–117/105–54, which attempts to divorce the consideration of the *énoncé* from questions of meaning and the subject. See also the May 1979 letter from Foucault quoted in Hubert Dreyfus and Paul Rabinow, *Michel Foucault: Beyond Structuralism and Hermeneutics* (Chicago: Univ. of Chicago Press, 1982), 46 n.1; and the reading of the phrase "I am mad" as the "reverse of the performative speech act," in "Sexuality and Solitude," *London Review of Books*, 21 May–3 June 1981, 3, 5–6.

40. Foucault, *The History of Sexuality, Volume I*, 100–1/133.

41. Michel Foucault, "The History of Sexuality," trans. Leo Marshall, in *Power/Knowledge*, ed. Colin Gordon (New York: Pantheon, 1980), 190; "'Les Rapports de pouvoir passent à l'intérieur des corps,'" interview with Lucette Finas, *La Quinzaine Littéraire* 247 (January 1–15, 1977): 6 (reprinted in *Dits et écrits*, 3: 234).

42. "Annexe," in Jean-Luc Nancy and Philippe Lacoue-Labarthe, eds., *Le Retrait du politique*, Travaux du centre de recherches philosophiques

sur le politique (Paris: Galilée, 1983), 203–4 n.1. Foucault and other French intellectuals signed a petition protesting Derrida's imprisonment in Prague: see Didier Eribon, "Tcheque-Connection: Trois Jours en Prison," *Libération* 198 (January 2–3, 1982): 12; "Prague: Jacques Derrida libéré," *Le Matin* 1511 (January 2–3, 1982): 24; and Peter Dews, "Derrida in Prison," *Radical Philosophy* 31 (September 1982): 42. Derrida's difficulties with the available political philosophemes are exemplified in his remarks on the inefficacy of the United Nations' 1973 declaration that "apartheid is a crime against humanity" (in "Racism's Last Word," trans. Peggy Kamuf, *Critical Inquiry* 12, no. 1 [autumn 1985]: 290–99; "Le Dernier Mot du racisme," in *Psyché* [Paris: Galilée, 1987], 353–62): "If this verdict continues to have no effect, it is because the customary discourse on man, humanism, and human rights has encountered its effective and as yet unthought [imit, the limit of the whole system in which it takes on meaning. . . . Beyond the juridico-political or theologico-political discourse, . . . it was, it will have to be, it is necessary to appeal unconditionally to the future of another right and another force lying outside [*par-delà*] the totality of this present" (298/361).

43. Felman, *Writing and Madness*, 21. Gayatri Spivak (in "More on Power / Knowledge," *Outside in the Teaching Machine* (New York: Routledge, 1994) has offered a strong account of Foucault and Derrida together, in terms of "an ethics inaccessible to humanism" (37). She argues that "the real usefulness of these two is in the lesson of their refusal to be taken in by victories measured out in rational abstractions, in the dying fall of their urge persistently to critique those dogmas for the few (in the name of the many) that we cannot not want to inhabit" (45). See also Roy Boyne, *Foucault and Derrida* (New York: Routledge, 1994 for a helpful account of the dispute between the two over reason and madness, albeit one that is a little over-eager in detecting a common "guiding spirit of their work" (4).

44. Among Foucault's other, more extended considerations of rights and human rights are: "Va-t-on extrader Klaus Croissant," *Le Nouvel Observateur* 679 (November 14, 1977): 62–63 (reprinted in *Dits et écrits*, 3: 361–65), about the extradition of the Baader-Meinhof group's lawyer to Germany after he had sought asylum in France and the "rights of the governed"; "L'Éthique de souci de soi comme pratique de liberté," interview, *Concordia* 6 (1984): 113–16 (*Dits et écrits*, 4: 726–28), trans. as "The Ethic of the Care of the Self as a Practice of Freedom" by J. D. Gauthier, S.J., *Philosophy and Social Criticism* 12, no. 2–3 [summer 1987]:

130–31; and, most interestingly, some of his comments around the 1982 Polish government crackdown on Solidarity, in particular " 'L'Expérience morale et sociale des Polonais ne peut plus être effacée," interview with Gilles Anquetil, *Les Nouvelles littéraires* 2857 (October 14–20, 1982): 8–9 (*Dits et écrits*, 4: 343–50): "human rights are above all what one opposes to governments. They are the limits that one poses to all possible governments. . . . Under the pretext of presenting a theory or a politics of human rights, we must guard against reintroducing a dominant thought. After all, even Leninism presented itself as a politics of human rights."

45. Michel Foucault, "Face aux gouvernements, les droits de l'Homme," *Libération*, 30 June–1 July 1984, 22; republished in *Foucault hors les murs*, *Actes* 54 (summer 1986): 22. My information about this initiative comes from the *Libération* editor's headnote, as well as contemporary newspaper accounts: Isabelle Vichniac, "Un Comité international contre la piraterie va affrêter un bateau pour venir au secours des 'boat people' vietnamiens," *Le Monde*, June 21–22, 1981, 2; Ariel Herbez, "Des Bateaux pour proteger les 'boat people' des pirates," *Le Matin* 1343 (June 20–21, 1981): 10; P. Sabatier, "Un Bateau contre les pirates," *Libération*, June 20–21, 1981, 15; and Bernard Kouchner, "Un Vrai Samourai," in *Michel Foucault: Une Histoire de la vérité* (Paris: Editions Syros, 1985), 85–89. In the posthumous collection of Foucault's occasional writings, the text is reprinted with this headnote: "M. Foucault had read this text, a few minutes after having written it, on the occasion of the press conference in Geneva anouncing the creation of the International Committee Against Piracy, in June 1981. Following that, it was a question of organizing the greatest possible response to this text, in the hope of yielding something that could be a new Declaration of Human Rights" (*Dits et écrits*, 4: 707–8). Foucault's declaration has been widely quoted of late, generally taken either as a merely tactical intervention or as a sure sign of his steadfast commitment to an "honorable tradition" of quasi-liberal values. The first position is that of James Miller (in *The Passion of Michel Foucault* [New York: Simon and Schuster, 1993], 315–16 and 452 n. 107), who uses a remark Foucault made in conversation at Berkeley, to the effect that rights discourse was simply "tactical," in order to write off the rich complexity of these aporias. The second is exemplified by David Macey (in his biography *The Lives of Michel Foucault* [New York: Pantheon, 1993], 437–38, and in "Michel Foucault: *J'accuse*," *New Formations* 25 [summer 1995]: 13), who wants to inscribe Foucault's political activism in the tradition of Zola and the protest against the state in the name of republican values. (Macey describes the scene, apparently thanks

to an interview with Bernard Kouchner, as follows: "Foucault addressed the conference without any advance publicity. His brief intervention was drafted on a piece of paper and then read without any revision or hesitation" [437].) More judiciously, as always, Didier Eribon (in *Michel Foucault*, trans. Betsy Wing [Cambridge: Harvard Univ. Press, 1991; orig. Paris: Flammarion, 1989]) calls the declaration "a sort of human rights charter [une sorte de charte des droits de l'homme]" (279/296). See as well the insightful deployments of the text by Jon Simons, *Foucault and the Political* (London: Routledge, 1995), 10, and William Connolly, "Beyond Good and Evil," *Political Theory* 21, no. 3 (August 1993): 380.

46. There is a slippage in Foucault's text between *droit* and *devoir*, which is not justified in that text. No doubt it could be, but until then it is worthwhile to keep in mind Blanchot's useful cautions about their difference, in a discussion of what might be considered the most important precursor to Foucault's declaration, the 1960 "Declaration Concerning the Right of Insubordination in the Algerian War," *Evergreen Review* 4, no. 15 (Nov.–Dec. 1960): 1–4; "Déclaration sur le droit à l'insoumission dans la guerre d'Algérie," in François Maspero, ed., *Le Droit à l'insoumission ("le dossier des 121")* (Paris: Maspero, 1961), 90–91.

47. Foucault's text has sometimes (Macey, *Lives*, 471 and in an editor's footnote in *Dits et écrits*, 4: 707) been credited with providing an early theoretical elaboration of the so-called *droit d'ingérence*, the right of "humanitarian intervention" (disregard for national sovereignty in the name of human rights) popularized by Bernard Kouchner (Kouchner and Mario Bettati, *Le Devoir d'ingérence* [Paris: Denoël, 1987]; Kouchner, *Le Malheur des autres* [Paris: Odile Jacob, 1991]), now the watchword of many international humanitarian relief organizations. One of the most interesting early cases of such an intervention was the intellectual commando raid Foucault organized (along with Claude Mauriac, Régis Debray, Yves Montand, Costa-Gavras, and others) to Madrid in September 1975, on behalf of eleven militants condemned to death in fascist Spain; see "Aller à Madrid," *Libération* 358 (September 24, 1975): 7 (reprinted in *Dits et écrits*, 2: 760–62): "Franquist power has, in its modes of action, surpassed the stage that calls for a simple protest. Petitions no longer have any meaning today, which is why we thought we had to reach it physically by going to the heart of Madrid to read this declaration." The protesters were expelled immediately by the Spanish police (see the photograph in Kouchner, *Michel Foucault: Une Histoire de la vérité*, 71), and the militants later executed.

48. This "difficulty with what is happening" echoes, in a way that

would bear some reflection, the rhetoric of "the intolerable" which the militants of the Prison Information Group, including Foucault, had employed earlier. "Intolérable" was the name of the book series published by the group; see Foucault's "Préface" to *Enquête dans vingt prisons* (Paris: Champ libre, 1971), 3–5 (reprinted in *Dits et écrits*, 2: 195–97). For one among many instances of his theorization of this concept, see "Sur les prisons," *J'accuse* 3 (March 15, 1971): 26 (reprinted in *Dits et écrits*, 2: 175–76): "The hunger strike last January compelled the press to speak. Let us take advantage of the opening: so that the intolerable, imposed by force and silence, stops being accepted. Our inquiry is not undertaken in order to accumulate knowledge, but to amplify our intolerance and make of it an active intolerance."

49. Derrida, "Declarations of Independence," trans. Thomas Keenan and Thomas Pepper, *New Political Science* 15 (summer 1986): 11; "Déclarations d'Indépendance," in *Otobiographies* (Paris: Galilée, 1984), 23.

50. Michel Foucault, "Truth and Power," interview with Allesandro Fontana and Pasquale Pasquino, *Power/Knowledge*, 121, emphasis added. "Entretien avec Michel Foucault," in *Dits et écrits* 3: 140–60, is a translation of the published Italian version.

51. Michel Foucault, "Two Lectures: Lecture Two: 14 January 1976," trans. Kate Soper, *Power/Knowledge*, 96; "Cours du 14 janvier 1976," *Dits et écrits*, 3: 178. These lectures ("Cours du 7 janvier 1976" [3: 160–74] and "Cours du 14 janvier 1976" [3: 175–89]) were first published in Italian, translated from a transcribed tape recording, as "Corso del 7 gennaio 1976" and "Corso del 14 gennaio 1976," in Michel Foucault, *Microfisica del Potere: Interventi politici*, ed. Allesandro Fontana and Pasquale Pasquino (Turin: Giulio Einaudi, 1977), 163–77 and 179–94. The English version is apparently translated from the Italian; the French transcripts were only published in 1994. Many of these arguments can be found in *History of Sexuality, Volume I*, 81–91/107–20.

52. Foucault, "Two Lectures," 88/169.

53. Foucault, *History of Sexuality, Volume I*, 88/116.

54. Foucault, "Two Lectures," 95–96/178.

55. Ibid., 96/178.

56. Foucault, *History of Sexuality, Volume I*, 89/118–19.

57. Foucault, "Two Lectures," 105–7/187–88.

58. I owe the phrase "double blind alley" to J. Hillis Miller, "The Mirror's Secret," *Victorian Poetry* 29, no. 4 (winter 1991): 345.

59. Habermas, "Genealogical Writing," 1/745. Habermas was fond of

the word "aporia" in reading Foucault; see his newspaper eulogy for Foucault, "Taking Aim at the Heart of the Present," trans. Sigrid Brauner and Robert Brown, with David Levin, in David Hoy, ed., *Foucault: A Critical Reader* (Oxford: Basil Blackwell, 1986), 106; "Mit dem Pfeil ins Herz der Gegenwart gezielt: Zu Foucaults Vorlesung über Kants 'Was ist Aufklärung?,' " *taz* (Berlin), July 7, 1984, 13.

60. Foucault, *History of Sexuality, Vol. I*, 90/119.

61. Immanuel Kant, "Introduction to the Doctrine of Right," *The Metaphysics of Morals*, trans. Mary Gregor (Cambridge: Cambridge Univ. Press, 1991), 58; "Einleitung in die Rechtslehre," *Metaphysik der Sitten, Immanuel Kants Werke*, vol. 7, ed. Ernst Cassirer (Berlin: B. Cassirer, 1922), 34; "Das Rechte (*rectum*) wird als das Gerade teils dem Krummen, teils dem Schiefen entgegen gesetzt." I owe this citation to Jacques Derrida's contribution to the entry "Droit" in *Les Immatériaux*, Epreuves d'écriture (Paris: Centre Georges Pompidou, 1985), 53, responding to François Chatelet's remarks on the opposition between *droit* and *courbe*.

62. Here, in another sense, we return to the phrase Claude Lefort borrows from Hannah Arendt, "the right to have rights," already broached in Chapter 1.

63. Foucault, "Critical Theory / Intellectual History," 37/450.

64. Michel Foucault, "Sex, Power, and the Politics of Identity," interview with Bob Gallagher and Alex Wilson, *The Advocate* 400 (August 7, 1984): 27.

65. Michel Foucault, "Il faut tout repenser, la loi et le prison," *Libération*, July 6, 1981, 2; reprinted in *Dits et écrits*, 4: 202–4.

66. See Michel Foucault, "Questions of Method," interview with historians, trans. Colin Gordon, *Ideology & Consciousness* 8 (spring 1981): 12–13; "On the Genealogy of Ethics," interview with P. Rabinow and H. Dreyfus, in *The Foucault Reader*, ed. Paul Rabinow (New York: Pantheon Books, 1984), 343; and "Polemics, Politics, and Problemizations," interview with P. Rabinow and T. Zummer, trans. Lydia Davis, in *Foucault Reader*, 385.

67. Michel Foucault, "Is it really important to think?," trans. Thomas Keenan, *Philosophy and Social Criticism* 9, no. 1 (spring 1982): 29–40; "Est-il donc important de penser?," interview with Didier Eribon, *Libération*, May 30–31, 1981, 21 (reprinted in *Dits et écrits*, 4: 178–82).

68. Foucault, "Critical Theory / Intellectual History," 36/448–49.

69. Michel Foucault, "Revolutionary Action: 'Until Now,' " trans. Donald Bouchard and Sherry Simon, in *Language, Counter-Memory,*

Practice (Ithaca: Cornell Univ. Press, 1977), 230; "Par dela le bien et le mal," interview with *lycée* students, *Actuel* 14 (November 1971): 46 (reprinted in *Dits et écrits* 2: 233–34.

70. We merely skim the extraordinary reading of Nietzsche's caesura in "Theatrum Philosophicum," *Language, Counter-Memory, Practice,* 194; *Critique* 282 (November 1970): 906 (reprinted in *Dits et écrits,* 2: 97): "On both sides of the wound, we always find that it [the caesura] has already happened (and that it had already happened, and that it has already happened that it had already happened) and that it will happen again (and that it will happen again that it happen again)." Guiding our reading here are Andrzej Warminski's pages on the caesura in Hölderlin, in *Readings in Interpretation* (Minneapolis: Univ. of Minnesota Press, 1987), 17–22 and 199–201: "rather than allowing the human subject to recognize himself in his own other, the caesura rips him out of his own sphere of life, out of the center of his own inner life, and carries him off into an other world and tears him into the eccentric world of the dead" (17).

71. Foucault, "Theatrum Philosophicum," 194/906.

72. Millicent Dillon, "Conversation with Michel Foucault," *The Threepenny Review* 1, no. 1 (Winter/Spring 1980): 5.

73. Claude Lefort, "Politics and Human Rights," in *The Political Forms of Modern Society,* trans. Alan Sheridan, ed. John B. Thompson (Cambridge: MIT Press, 1986), 243–44; "Droits de l'homme et politique," in *L'invention démocratique* (Paris: Fayard, 1981), 51; and "Human Rights and the Welfare State," in *Democracy and Political Theory,* trans. David Macey (Minneapolis: Univ. of Minnesota Press, 1988), 39; "Les Droits de l'homme et l'Etat-providence," in *Essais sur le politique* (Paris: Seuil, 1986), 54.

74. Lefort, "Human Rights and the Welfare State," 37/51.

75. Stephen White, "Foucault's Challenge to Critical Theory," *American Political Science Review* 80, no. 2 (June 1986): 430.

76. Claude Lefort, "The Question of Democracy," in *Democracy and Political Theory,* 15; "La question de la démocratie," in *Essais,* 24.

77. Lefort, "Human Rights and the Welfare State," 34/47.

78. Michel Foucault, "Space, Knowledge, and Power," interview with Paul Rabinow, trans. Christian Hubert, in *The Foucault Reader,* 247.

79. Joan Copjec, in *Read My Desire* (New York: Verso, 1994), has offered a powerful critique of the historicism, old and new, that has dominated the reception of Foucault in this country. I fully subscribe to

this challenge to "the return of history," but her effort to distinguish Lefort and Foucault on the question of power seems to me less successful. She concentrates on *Discipline and Punish*, in particular on the notion that "no one" occupies the position of power in the Panopticon's central tower, and compares it to Lefort's argument that power becomes democratic "when it proves to belong to no one." Tracing a seductive, but resistable, "quiver of paradox" in Foucault's theory of power (power is wielded by no one, but everyone is subjected to it), she pries him away from Lefort by arguing that when Foucault says "no one" he really means "no one in particular," which is to say, anyone, and hence she can conclude that "since the modern form of power—or law—has no external guarantees, it may be seen to guarantee itself." This means, she argues, that for Foucault "power . . . still seems inescapable," and that "the discourses of power seem to embrace everyone in their address." Thus, it seems, that in challenging the symmetrical opposition between totalitarianism and democracy Foucault has missed the democratic point: Lefort's " 'no one' is attached not to the fact that the law guarantees itself but to the fact that there are no guarantees. . . . The discourse of power—the law—that gives birth to the modern subject can guarantee neither its own nor the subject's legitimacy. There where the subject looks for justification, for approval, it finds no one who can certify it" (159–60). This is precisely how I understand *Foucault*'s claim, and I fear that an interpretation which treats his reading of the Panopticon as something like Max Weber's iron cage argument will not help in assessing what we can learn about politics, especially democracy, from him. Power is indeed inescapable, precisely because it has undergone what Lefort calls a "symbolic mutation"—it is no longer Power, the King's power to say no, but a productive and relational power, productive to the exact extent that it becomes relational. So if knowledge loses its oppositional exteriority and becomes linked to power in the strangeness of the dash, this does not mean, as Foucault emphasized again and again, that knowledge is no longer science but merely ideology, or that some contamination of an essential purity occurs in the relation. Because power is linked, tenuously, to knowledge, politics has a chance. Likewise, power addresses everyone, but without guarantees of success: these letters too can always not reach their destination. The context never fully saturates the utterances it embraces. While Copjec acknowledges that for Foucault "the social field cannot be totalized," she attributes this to the presence of "different and even competing discourses" (154). (She seems to accept the idea that

Foucault "substitutes a battle-based model of analysis for a language-based one" [7].) But Foucault locates the play of power not in the encounter between contradictory discourses or "different subject positions" but within discourse itself, within "the subject itself." Resistance and the play of forces, unguaranteed by anything, including themselves, are premised on the hyphen. The instability of this link is the condition of our politics. Foucault could not disagree with her summary: "It is to the fact that power is *disjoined* from knowledge, that the force which produces the subject is blind, that the subject owes its precious singularity" (160).

80. "Slalom" is the word Foucault used to describe his maneuvers between philosophy and the abandonment of seriousness, according to Dreyfus and Rabinow, *Michel Foucault*, 205.

81. The topography is complex: because we are always already elsewhere in politics (dispersed across a "plurality of positions" and a "discontinuity of functions" [Blanchot]), any appeal to *a* position, to a temporary or final solution, cannot but function as an alibi (elsewhere). But just as there is no outside "here," no external standpoint or last instance, there is likewise no securely bounded inside, within which the subject might organize itself into the unity which decision demands. Either all "positions" are elsewhere (alibis), or there are nothing but elsewheres.

82. Foucault never tired of repeating—it was his own cliché about himself—that his philosophico-political engagement could no longer be subsumed under the model of what he called the " 'universal' intellectual." He thought his practice as that of a " 'specific' intellectual," not as "the bearer of universal values" (*Power/Knowledge*, 126–33), and the respect for the singularity of those interventions demanded doing without rules and morals. "We no longer ask political theory to tell us what is to be done, we no longer need guardians" ("Une mobilisation culturelle," *Le Nouvel Observateur* 670 (September 12–18, 1977): 49; *Dits et écrits*, 3: 330). Jon Simons, in *Foucault and the Political* (124–25) offers an admirable paraphrase of this "position": "Foucault's passion is for a politics that embraces what cannot be finalized and what cannot be solved. . . . Foucault provides no prescription for what is to be done, but he does offer theoretical guidelines . . . : foreswear the dream of a perfect world in which all has been done and all is safe, but cherish the agonism of open strategic games in which everything remains to be done." And Didier Eribon, in *Michel Foucault et ses contemporains*, properly reminds us that

"Foucault always rejected the idea that he did research inspired by politics. On the contrary, his work consisted in posing questions to politics, which is to say, in interrogating its established categories and in enlarging the definition of politics" (87 n. 1).

83. Blanchot's extraordinarily precise formulation occurs in between these two sentences: "Did he not confide to Lucette Finas: 'I am fully aware that I have never written anything but fictions?' . . . But Foucault would not be Foucault if he did not emend or nuance this at once: 'But I believe it is possible to make fictions function within truth'," ("Michel Foucault," 94/46–47).

Conclusion

1. Jacques Derrida, "Eating Well," interview with Jean-Luc Nancy, trans. Peter Connor and Avital Ronell, in Eduardo Cadava, Peter Connor, and Jean-Luc Nancy, eds., *Who Comes After the Subject?* (New York: Routledge, 1991); "Il faut bien manger," *Confrontations* 20 (Winter 1989): "I repeat: responsibility is excessive or it is not a responsibility. A limited, measured, calculable, rationally distributable responsibility is already the becoming-right of morality; it is at times also, in the best hypothesis, the dream of every good conscience, in the worst hypothesis, of the small or grand inquisitors" (118/113).

2. Giorgio Agamben, *Moyens sans fins*, trans. Danièle Valin (Paris: Bibliothèque Rivages, 1995), 8. On politics as pure means, see also Etienne Balibar, "Violence et politique," in Marie-Louise Mallet, ed., *Le Passage des frontières* (Paris: Galilée, 1994), 210.

3. I have dealt with some of these questions in "No Ends in Sight," in *Els Límits del Museu* [*The Ends of the Museum*], exhibition catalogue (Barcelona: Fondació Antoni Tàpies, 1995), 17–29.

4. Claude Lefort, "Human Rights and the Welfare State," in *Democracy and Political Theory*, trans. David Macey (Minneapolis: Univ. of Minnesota Press, 1988), 33; "Les Droits de l'homme et l'Etat-providence," in *Essais sur le politique* (Paris: Seuil, 1986), 45.

5. From the first chapter of *Capital*, as I tried to show in Chapter 4, to the opening lines of the *Manifesto*, through the good and bad spirits of the *Eighteenth Brumaire* and the *German Ideology*, ghosts are everywhere in Marx's texts.

6. Žižek's most important text, the one on which I will concentrate, is *The Sublime Object of Ideology* (London: Verso, 1990). Similar arguments

are advanced in the numerous books Žižek has published since then as well: *Looking Awry* (Cambridge: MIT Press, 1991); *For They Know Not What They Do* (London: Verso, 1991); *Enjoy Your Symptom!* (New York: Routledge, 1992); *Tarrying with the Negative* (Durham: Duke Univ. Press, 1993); *The Metastases of Enjoyment* (London: Verso, 1994). After this chapter was written, I encountered Žižek's introduction to his edited collection of key texts on ideology, called (of all things) "The Spectre of Ideology," in *Mapping Ideology* (London: Verso, 1994), 1–33. Needless to say, we have very different ideas about these ghosts, beginning with the question of how many of them there are.

7. The ethics is one "of separation," something like the distance established by the quotation marks that proliferate in Žižek's analysis (around "illusion," "reality," "behind," "nothing," and so on). The separation and the marks correspond to the traces of the ideological operation, which tries to "efface its own traces" (102). Žižek outlines, in his introduction, "four different ethical positions, and at the same time four different notions of the subject" (2): they belong to the conceptual pairs Habermas-Foucault and Althusser-Lacan. Žižek aims to account for the repression of the second by the first, but what seems most striking, given the amount of energy expended later in the book on criticizing Derrida, is Žižek's omission of his name altogether.

8. I could not agree more with Žižek's powerful assertion that "the aspiration to abolish [antagonism] is precisely the source of totalitarian temptation: the greatest mass murders and holocausts have always been perpetrated in the name of man as harmonious being, of a New Man without antagonistic tension" (5).

9. See Ernesto Laclau and Chantal Mouffe, *Hegemony and Socialist Strategy*, trans. Winston Moore and Paul Cammack (London: Verso, 1985). Žižek's critique is presented in his appendix, "Beyond Discourse-Analysis," to Laclau's *New Reflections on the Revolution of Our Time* (London: Verso, 1990), 249–60.

10. Werner Hamacher, "Afformative, Strike," trans. Dana Hollander, *Cardozo Law Review* 13, no. 4 (December 1991): 1133.

11. Joan Copjec and Michael Sorkin, "Shrooms: East New York," *Assemblage* 24 (August 1994): 97: "we define privacy as that which no one has, no one possesses." On trauma, see Cathy Caruth, "Unclaimed Experience," *Yale French Studies* 79 (1991): 181–92, and Caruth, ed., *Trauma: Explorations in Memory* (Baltimore: Johns Hopkins Univ. Press, 1995). In her introduction to the latter volume, Caruth insists that the

traumatic memory or flashback is what we cannot possess, what no one possesses, because it possesses us: "the event is not assimilated or experienced fully at the time, only belatedly, in its repeated possession of the one who experiences it. To be traumatized is precisely to be possessed by an image or event" (4–5).

12. Jean-François Lyotard, "The General Line," in *Political Writings*, trans. Bill Readings and Kevin Paul Geiman (Minneapolis: Univ. of Minnesota Press, 1993), 111; "Ligne générale," in *Moralités postmodernes* (Paris: Galilée, 1993), 110.

Index

MERIDIAN

Crossing Aesthetics

Library of Congress Cataloging-in-Publication Data

Keenan, Thomas, 1959–
  Fables of responsibility : aberrations and predicaments in ethics and
politics / Thomas Keenan.
      p. cm. — (Meridian : crossing aesthetics)
   Includes bibliographical references and index.
   ISBN 0-8047-2826-7 (cloth : alk. paper). — ISBN 0-8047-2827-5
(paper : alk. paper)
   1. Political ethics. 2. Democracy. 3. Responsibility. 4. Politics and
literature. 5. Deconstruction. I. Title. II. Series: Meridian (Stanford,
Calif.)
JA79.K44   1997
172—dc20   96-41625
                                                                      CIP

⊛ This book is printed on acid-free, recycled paper.

Original printing 1997

Last figure below indicates year of this printing:
06 05 04 03 02 01 00 99 98 97